Also by Craig Unger

The Fall of the House of Bush:
The Untold Story of How a Band of True Believers
Seized the Executive Branch, Started the Iraq War,
and Still Imperils America Today

House of Bush, House of Saud:
The Secret Relationship Between the World's
Two Most Powerful Dynasties

BOSS ROVE

INSIDE KARL ROVE'S
SECRET KINGDOM OF POWER

Craig Unger

SCRIBNER

New York   London   Toronto   Sydney   New Delhi

SCRIBNER
A Division of Simon & Schuster, Inc.
1230 Avenue of the Americas
New York, NY 10020

First Scribner hardcover edition September 2012

SCRIBNER and design are registered trademarks of The Gale Group, Inc.,
used under license by Simon & Schuster, Inc., the publisher of this work.

For information about special discounts for bulk purchases,
please contact Simon & Schuster Special Sales at
1-866-506-1949 or business@simonandschuster.com.

The Simon & Schuster Speakers Bureau can bring authors to your live event.
For more information or to book an event contact the Simon & Schuster Speakers Bureau
at 1-866-248-3049 or visit our website at www.simonspeakers.com.

DESIGNED BY ERICH HOBBING

Manufactured in the United States of America

1   3   5   7   9   10   8   6   4   2

ISBN 978-1-4516-9493-2
ISBN 978-1-4516-9660-8(ebook)

Portions of this book originally appeared in somewhat altered form in the
September 2012 issue of *Vanity Fair*.

To Phyllis

CONTENTS

BOSS ROVE

ONE

The Man Who Swallowed
the Republican Party

On Wednesday, April 21, 2010, about two dozen Republican power brokers gathered at Karl Rove's five-bedroom Federal-style townhouse on Weaver Terrace in Northwest Washington, D.C., to strategize about the upcoming midterm elections in the fall.

Rove, fifty-nine, had hosted this kind of event many times before. Six years earlier, he held weekly breakfasts for high-level GOP operatives to plan for the 2004 fall elections. Back then, as senior adviser and deputy chief of staff to President George W. Bush, a bureaucratic title that belied his extraordinary power, Rove oversaw Bush's reelection campaign. More important, he was attempting to implement a master plan to build a permanent majority through which Republicans would maintain a stranglehold on all three branches of government for the foreseeable future. The plan was not merely to win elections. It represented a far more grandiose vision: the forging of a historic realignment of the nation's political landscape, the transformation of America into effectively a one-party state.

But now Rove was no longer in the White House. He had been one of the most powerful unelected officials in the United States, but, to many Republicans, his greatest achievement—engineering the presidency of George W. Bush—had become an ugly stain on the party's reputation. "Karl Rove will be a name that'll be used for a long, long time as an example of how not to do it, as opposed to an example of how to do it," says GOP consultant Ed Rollins, who served as President Reagan's political director.

A prime suspect in the two biggest political scandals of the decade, the Valerie Plame Wilson affair and the U.S. attorneys scandal, Rove had left the White House in 2007 under a cloud of suspicion, barely escaping indictment. His longtime patron had left the White House with the lowest approval rating in the history of the presidency: 22 percent. And in 2008 the Democrats vaporized Rove's dreams by winning the ultimate political trifecta: the House, the Senate, and the White House. Finally, on the right, there was the insurgent Tea Party, to which he personified the free-spending Bush era and the Republican Party's establishment past, not its future.

Rove's personal life and finances had also fared poorly. His 2009 divorce from Darby, his wife of twenty-four years, meant the loss of more than half of his assets. And there were enormous legal bills resulting from the scandals. "I had to worry about retirement," he told *New York* magazine. "I had to worry about getting back to Texas."

But Rove was not without resources. Thanks to his columns in *Newsweek* and the *Wall Street Journal,* and a lucrative contract with Fox News, he had straightened out his personal finances and, in just two years, created a lofty bully pulpit from which to bestow upon the public the Rovian narrative about American politics.

During his seven years in the White House, Rove had been able to dispense the perks that are so vital to building political capital with the powers that be. "Having control of the White House is very heady stuff," says Roger Stone, a GOP operative who has known Rove for forty years. "Inviting them to the White House mess, state dinners, and so on. He has a big Rolodex of Texas millionaires."

Another arrow in Rove's quiver came courtesy of Michael Steele, then the hapless chairman of the Republican National Committee. An unfailing source of fodder for late-night comics, Steele had just outdone himself when the RNC squandered nearly $2,000 at a lesbians-in-bondage-themed strip club in Hollywood—precisely the kind of thing the party of family values and evangelicalism didn't need when its coffers were bare. Whether he was discussing abortion, Afghanistan, or even asserting, preposterously, that the Republican Party needed "a hip-hop makeover," Steele had been so out of step with the party that conservative donors were desperately seeking an alternative.

Finally, Rove had one other enormously powerful ally. It could be fairly said that no other political strategist in history was so deeply indebted to the U.S. Supreme Court. In December 2010, in *Bush v. Gore,* one of the most notorious decisions in its history, by a 5–4 vote, the Court effectively resolved the 2000 United States presidential election in favor of Rove's most famous client, George W. Bush. Then, on January 21, 2010, three months before his luncheon, the Supreme Court once again provided the answer to Karl Rove's prayers, this time, in the form of *Citizens United v. Federal Election Commission,* another landmark decision, ruling that the First Amendment prohibits the government from limiting spending for political purposes by corporations and unions. This last decision was also made by a 5–4 majority, and this time, two of the justices voting with the majority, Samuel Alito and John Roberts, in part owed their lifetime appointments to Rove and to support from political action committees (PACs) such as Progress for America, which was tied to Rove. The first decision legitimized Rove's power during the two administrations of George W. Bush. The second allowed Rove to reestablish his power and resurrected his efforts to create a permanent Republican majority.

The implications of the *Citizens United* decision were staggering. In the 2008 election cycle, organizations of all types—whether they were for-profit corporations, nonprofit organizations, or unions—had been prohibited from airing broadcast, cable, or satellite communications that mentioned a candidate within sixty days of a general election or thirty days of a primary. To be sure, there were many ways for wealthy individuals or corporations to funnel money to political action committees. But the 2002 Bipartisan Campaign Reform Act, better known as the McCain-Feingold Act, specifically prohibited corporations from engaging in "electioneering communications" intended to influence the outcome of an election. As a case in point, Citizens United, a conservative nonprofit group known for its right-wing documentaries, produced *Hillary: The Movie,* a film critical of then senator Hillary Clinton, but had been prevented by the courts from promoting it on television or airing it during the 2008 election season. The organization appealed all the way to the U.S. Supreme Court—and won.

The gist of the decision could be boiled down to two words: anything goes. Corporations were people now, too, ruled the court. And just as John Q. Public could say anything he liked about politics, thanks to an extraordinarily broad interpretation of the meaning of "freedom of speech," come election time, so, too, could Wall Street, big oil, pharmaceutical companies, the tobacco industry, and billionaire cranks flood the airwaves with millions of dollars' worth of political commercials.

To Democrats, the ruling was devastating. In his January 27, 2010, State of the Union Address, President Barack Obama asserted that "the Supreme Court reversed a century of law to open the floodgates for special interests—including foreign corporations—to spend without limit in our elections. Well, I don't think American elections should be bankrolled by America's most powerful interests, or worse, by foreign entities."

"The money spent in the airtime purchase by deep-pocketed interests will dwarf the voice of average Americans . . ." predicted Senator Chuck Schumer (D-N.Y.). "It's probably one of the three or four decisions in the history of the Supreme Court that most undermines democracy."

In the immediate aftermath of the ruling, thousands of articles were written about *Citizens United* as a truly historic development in the American electoral process, but one voice was conspicuous by its absence. Karl Rove did not mention the subject in his *Wall Street Journal* columns. Karl Rove did not mention it during his appearances on Fox News. In fact, not a word from Karl Rove on the subject was to be found in *any* medium. This, despite the fact that he was indisputably a leading expert on the subject, that three out of the five conservative justices voting in the majority—Clarence Thomas, John Roberts, and Sam Alito—had been given lifetime appointments by his patrons, George H.W. and George W. Bush, and, most important, despite the fact that he would become arguably the single greatest beneficiary of the ruling.

Karl Rove was the dog that didn't bark.

Rove, of course, was not the only one who would be able to take advantage of the *Citizens United* ruling. On the Democratic side of the aisle, unions and wealthy liberals such as George Soros would benefit. And there were other Republicans, notably David and Charles Koch, the billionaire brothers backing the Tea Party, and casino mogul Sheldon Adelson, a Newt Gingrich man, who often were at odds with Rove.

But with his keen eye for strategy and his ties to disaffected millionaires in the GOP establishment, Rove was the first to seize the initiative. He immediately met with Ed Gillespie, the former RNC chair who had served in the Bush administration with Rove. The two men were a potent duo. "Ed's got the better rap and Karl's got the better Rolodex," a Republican lobbyist told the *National Journal*.

Within two weeks of the Supreme Court decision, American Crossroads, Rove and Gillespie's new 527 advocacy group, had its website up. There was no mention whatsoever of Rove. His exact relationship to the group was informal and was described in Politico as providing "a laying on of hands" to encourage wealthy Republican donors. He and Gillespie took off for Texas to meet with some of the men who funded the money machine that had served Rove for more than twenty-five years, and came away with a major pledge from Dallas billionaire Harold Simmons, a longtime donor to Rove's causes. Crossroads GPS, a sister group, was in the works under almost identical leadership. Thanks to its nonprofit status, it would not have to disclose the identity of its contributors.

And so, as a result of *Citizens United*, the SuperPAC was born. A new kind of political action committee, officially known as "independent expenditure–only committees," SuperPACs were allowed to raise unlimited sums from individuals, corporations, unions, and other groups, provided they operated correctly and did not coordinate their expenditures with the needs of any given candidate.*

Soon there would be SuperPACs of every stripe imaginable. As Al Kamen reported in his column in the *Washington Post*, there would be Your America Inc., not to be confused with My America Inc. There would be Americans for a Better Tomorrow, Tomorrow and

---

* This last provision, of course, was a point of contention—and amusement—to observers, such as TV satirists Jon Stewart and Stephen Colbert, who pointed out that the needs of various electoral candidates were abundantly clear to anyone following the news, and SuperPACs could follow the news just like anyone else.

Americans for a Better Tomorrow Today. There would be the Faith Family Freedom Fund and the Family Faith Future Fund. For geometry lovers, there was even Americans for More Rhombus.

On March 8, 2010, Gillespie was off to New York, where he pitched other Republican millionaires. Meanwhile, Rove's list included Carl H. Lindner Jr., a Cincinnati businessman who owned the American Financial Group, a holding company whose primary business is insurance; and Robert B. Rowling, whose TRT Holdings owns Omni Hotels and Gold's Gym. In just one month, American Crossroads had obtained commitments of more than $30 million—about four times what the RNC had in its coffers. "Karl has always said: People call us a vast right-wing conspiracy, but we're really a half-assed right-wing conspiracy," explained one Republican fund-raiser. "Now, he wants to get more serious."

Finally, in April, Gillespie sent out an invitation that was a model of understatement, asking his colleagues to Rove's home for "an informal discussion of the 2010 political landscape." It was implicit that the 2010 midterms were merely a dress rehearsal for the larger political goal of the 2012 presidential elections, in which these same men would try to topple President Barack Obama. And so, over chicken pot pie, they gathered in Rove's town house, its wood-floored living room lined with built-in bookshelves.

With few exceptions—Mary Cheney, the daughter of the former vice president; former senator Norm Coleman (R-Minn.); and GOP fund-raiser Fred Malek, the CEO and chairman of the fledgling American Action Network and a former aide to both Richard Nixon and George H.W. Bush—those attending were operatives and fund-raisers whose names were of interest only to political insiders. "They were a number of like-minded people who were alarmed by the direction the country was taking and trying to counter that," says one operative who was there.

"As we saw it," says another, "this was a license to raise big money and participate in a new paradigm."

In addition to Gillespie, Rove enlisted another former RNC chair, Mike Duncan, as chairman of Crossroads. Jo Ann Davidson, a former co-chair of the RNC, was made director. Haley Barbour, the former governor of Mississippi, was an ally as well and yet another former RNC chair. That made a total of four former RNC chairs affiliated with Crossroads.

Rove also brought on Steven J. Law, former general counsel of the U.S. Chamber of Commerce, as president of American Crossroads. In selecting Law as its president, Crossroads had effectively formed an extraordinarily powerful alliance with the Chamber. Once the epitome of Babbitt-like conformity and small-town boosterism, the Chamber of Commerce, under the aegis of its persuasive president, Tom Donohue, had been transformed into the biggest and most powerful lobbyist in the United States. From Goldman Sachs to British Petroleum, Microsoft to Wal-Mart, PepsiCo to General Motors, it represented oil companies, pharmaceutical giants, insurance companies, Wall Street investment banks, automakers, and more. In 2009 alone, the Chamber spent $120 million lobbying—five times what Exxon Mobil, the number-two lobbyist, spent.

Meanwhile, Rove and Gillespie put Crossroads in a network with four other groups—the American Action Network, the American Action Forum, Resurgent Republic, and the Republican State Leadership Committee—as part of an immense fund-raising and advertising machine, separate from the Republican National Committee, to win back both Congress and the White House. Greg Casey's Business Industry Political Action Committee, also present, planned to spend $6 million to turn out the pro-business vote for the midterm elections. Norm Coleman's American Action Network expected to spend $25 million. And the Chamber of Commerce was to announce a record election budget of $75 million—double what it had spent in 2008, a presidential election year—most of which would be targeted on nine or ten key Senate races and about three dozen House contests.

Altogether, according to the *National Journal,* the groups at Rove's luncheon planned to spend $300 million to help scores of GOP congressional candidates, especially in battleground states such as Florida, Colorado, Nevada, Ohio, and Pennsylvania. That was enough money to produce anti-Democratic attack ads that could run tens of thousands of times, that could produce tens of millions of pieces of negative mail, as well as tens of millions of automated phone calls. Under the new laws, all of this could take place with virtually no oversight.

7

Rove and Gillespie pitched American Crossroads as the answer to outside groups such as George Soros's Democracy Alliance or labor unions that had historically supported Democrats. "Where they have a chess piece on the board, we need a chess piece on the board," said Gillespie, who is involved in all five groups in roles ranging from chairman to informal adviser.

But in fact it was much more than that. American Crossroads was an alternative to the RNC, which had crumbled under Michael Steele. "Karl set up a parallel organization," says Roger Stone. "The center of energy will always be where the money is. Karl is playing for control of the party. That's where the power and the money is."

ABC Radio talk-show host John Batchelor, a Republican, put it in perspective. "America is a two-party state," he says. "There are the Democrats. Then there's Karl Rove."

To anyone who *really* follows him, Rove's seminal but low-profile role in American Crossroads was no surprise. Ubiquitous though he is as a public figure, when it comes to being a political operative, when it comes to how he actually operates, Rove's hallmark is his absence. No fingerprints. That's how he's always worked. And precisely because Rove is so visible, because he is the most famous political operative in America, it's difficult to believe that you are seeing only the tip of the iceberg.

Reporters have long sought to determine why, from an early age, Rove took such a different course from most of his peers. In the early sixties, as a young boy, while his peers worshipped sports heroes like Mickey Mantle and Johnny Unitas, Rove read Milton Friedman, subscribed to the *National Review,* and collected Barry Goldwater paraphernalia. The self-described nerd from Salt Lake City, Utah—briefcase, pocket protector, Hush Puppies, and all—was, by the time he graduated from high school in 1969, on the road to becoming America's most celebrated political operative by dint of an encyclopedic mind capable of assimilating vast amounts of data, finely honed political instincts, and message-centric iron discipline.

Some have speculated that the answer may lie in Rove's troubled family life. "My mother [thought about] what it was that she wanted in life, and not necessarily what was good or right for her family,"

Rove told the reporter Thomas Edsall in an unusually candid interview in 1997, before he was well known. "And that was just her way. She never grew up."

The family's difficulties came to the surface in 1969, during Rove's freshman year at the University of Utah, when his father left his mother on Christmas Day, which happened to be Karl's nineteenth birthday. Subsequently, she deserted the family, occasionally borrowing money from Karl and sending him packages with magazines from his childhood, broken toys, and the like. "It was like she was trying desperately to sort of keep this connection," he recalled.

But keeping that connection alive was difficult in a family with as much turmoil as Rove's. Soon, Karl learned that Louis C. Rove, the man he thought was his father, was really his adoptive father. Eventually, Rove discovered that one reason his parents' marriage did not work may have been that Louis Rove was gay. All of which played itself out in 1981, when his mother "drove out to the desert north of Reno and filled the car with carbon monoxide, and then left all of her children a letter saying, don't blame yourselves for this."

It was, Rove said, "the classic fuck-you gesture."

In any case, Rove took refuge in politics. He particularly admired Mark Hanna, the legendary industrialist and political kingmaker who put William McKinley in the White House more than a century ago, and who is famous for saying, "There are two things that are important in politics. The first thing is money, and I can't remember what the second one is."

And while Hanna may be an obscure figure to most Americans, to Rove he was iconic, a Republican senator from Ohio who was more significant as a power broker of the Gilded Age, the first famous "handler" of a politician, the political mastermind behind the presidency of William McKinley and the most expensive political campaign ever seen at the time.

Like Hanna, from the beginning Rove was not about lofty statecraft. He was about winning. Even while attending the University of Utah during the Nixon era, Rove had an affinity for dirty tricks that he learned as a member of College Republicans, a no-holds-barred band of ambitious young pols. He was a protégé of Watergate trickster Donald Segretti, who was sentenced to prison for forging phony Democratic campaign literature.

Democrats were not the only ones to bear the brunt of his attacks. "The ruthlessness he learned in those days is exactly consistent with the way he acts as an adult," says a prominent Republican consultant who has known Rove since the seventies. "The wars we had in college never resolved themselves in his mind. He carries grudges and never lets go. Thirty years. You can't be just ninety-five percent on his side. That's not enough."

Like any great intelligence operative, Rove was a master of deniability. "Karl Rove would be able to teach the CIA a thing or two," said Larry Johnson, a former CIA operative who, as a friend of Valerie Plame Wilson's, regards Rove's role in the Plame affair as "despicable." "I would have loved to see him frog-marched from the White House [during his years in the Bush administration]. But on some level I admire him. When it comes to covert actions, he has real skills. You don't want to reveal all the bells and whistles. You want to set up front groups so that it appears there are independent operations even though they are beholden to you. When you bring all that together, it can be very powerful."

So what about the unseen Karl Rove? How far do the tentacles of his power *really* reach? "I'm a myth," Rove told the op-ed pages of the *Wall Street Journal* in a 2007 interview when he was leaving the White House. "There's the Mark of Rove. I read about some of the things I'm supposed to have done, and I have to try not to laugh."

Rove's impulse to laugh stands in stark contrast to a substantial list of questions about his long tenure in the White House. Was it Rove who orchestrated the various whispering campaigns smearing opponents as pedophiles, lesbians, and crooks? When he was in the Bush White House during the U.S. attorneys scandal, did Rove use the judiciary as a political weapon, to such an extent that, for many Democrats, running for high office carried with it the risk of a trip to the penitentiary? Did Rove direct the U.S. attorneys and the Justice Department to go after Alabama governor Don Siegelman, who was jailed on highly questionable bribery charges, and other rising stars in the Democratic Party?

And what about the charges in a civil rights lawsuit brought in 2006 against Rove lieutenant Kenneth Blackwell, then the Ohio secretary of state? Did Rove play a part in the conspiracy claimed in this action through which the vote totals for Ohio were allegedly rigged in favor of Bush rather than John Kerry, thereby altering the outcome of the 2004 presidential election? How on earth did SmarTech, a Chattanooga-based tech firm servicing a who's who of the Republican Party, end up providing highly sensitive technology for the Ohio votes in the 2004 presidential election? What was Rove's role, if any? Had he pulled off the dirtiest trick of all—the theft of a presidential election—and gotten away with it? And what about the destruction of countless government documents on SmarTech's servers, including Rove's emails, which were later sought by federal investigators? Was it possible that cyber warfare, Karl Rove style, had already come to American politics . . . and we didn't even know it?

Finally, in the wake of the *Citizens United* decision, expenditures for political advertising in the 2012 election season were projected to be an astronomical $7 billion. On the Republican side, to what extent would Rove control the purse strings? Given his penchant for dirty tricks, what has been Rove's real sub-rosa role in the bloody Republican primaries? What did he have in the works for the November 6, 2012, general election? Ultimately, how much damage has Rove's grandiose vision done to American democracy?

These are important questions, and the reader has a right to know who is asking them and why. The answer is that this writer, who is roughly the same age as Rove, grew up in Dallas, and even as a youth acquired more than a passing familiarity with the political terrain that Rove encountered in Texas. As a young boy, I attended Camp Longhorn in the Texas Hill Country with an older camper named George W. Bush. My childhood friends and classmates included heirs to great Texas oil fortunes, including those of Clint Murchison and H. L. Hunt. In Dallas, we celebrated the Christmas holidays each year at the home of family friend Bob Strauss, the chairman of the National Democratic Party, who was an immensely charming and legendary wheeler-dealer and a confidant of such icons as Lyndon Johnson and John Connally.

In October 1963, my eighth-grade teacher took me to hear Adlai Stevenson, then the U.S. ambassador to the United Nations, give a speech on United Nations Day, only to have banners unfurled that read "UN Red Front," as he was spat upon and struck by placards wielded by an ultraconservative mob. It was my first contact with the radical right.

A few weeks later, on November 22, my parents were seated at a luncheon in the Dallas Trade Mart, waiting for John F. Kennedy. What happened next, of course, was one of the great tragic moments in history. My father, a doctor, rushed to Parkland Hospital. The president was dead. Jackie Kennedy stood there in her blood-spattered dress. Dallas, my hometown, became known as "the city of hate."

Perhaps as an antidote, in my high school and college years I devoured the populism of Molly Ivins and Ronnie Dugger in the liberal *Texas Observer*. I smiled benignly when a friend started the No Use for Bruce Committee, protesting our local Republican congressman, Bruce Alger, a darling of the right. And many years later, I wrote two books on the Bushes, *House of Bush, House of Saud*, about George W. Bush's ties to the Saudis and the events leading up to 9/11, and *The Fall of the House of Bush*, about how the same president, working with neoconservatives and evangelicals, started the Iraq War under false and faulty premises. All of which made for a solid background from which to ferret out the truth about many of the unanswered questions regarding Rove.

But I also realized that to understand his methodology, to appreciate Rove's power and how he wields it, would require much more. One would have to interview little-known operatives who have worked with him and done his bidding, though not necessarily while on his payroll. One would have to understand how Rove was able to dispense favors, often very lucrative ones, to functionaries through third parties. One would have to find operatives who have worked for Rove's rivals and nursed decades-long grudges against him. One would have to interview prominent Democrats who did battle with Rove and his operatives.

One would have to interview his foes in Washington and the people who investigated him. One would have to find sources not just in Texas, where he started out, and in Washington, where he came to power, but in Alabama, where Rove had a little-known base of operations that effectively took over the state judiciary and transformed it from Democratic to Republican. One would have to study his methodology, and understand how he incorporated essential elements of intelligence tradecraft such as compartmentalization and need-to-know deniability.

One would have to put aside the notion that the most serious charges against Rove were merely the paranoid delusions of "tin foil"-hatted conspiracy nuts, and genuinely investigate Republican tech operations by interviewing their employees in Tennessee and Ohio, as well as the technology apparatus in the Secretary of State's Office in Ohio. One would also have to understand the mechanics of voting in Ohio. And then, with an eye to the 2012 election, one would have to examine what happened to the candidacies of Texas governor Rick Perry, Sarah Palin, Herman Cain, and Newt Gingrich, and other candidates for whom Rove displays such disdain.

Even after all that, one would still not get all the answers. But one could nonetheless compile a narrative showing that for three decades Rove has been putting together a systematic attempt to game the American electoral system by whatever means necessary. It would show Rove fabricating a campaign to restrict the rights of citizens to sue major corporations for damages—as a means of creating a cash machine for the Texas Republican Party. It would show him playing a leading role in drumming up a campaign against voter fraud by immigrants—a phenomenon that is negligible at best—in order to institute Jim Crow–like laws requiring government-issued photo IDs in more than thirty states, thereby disenfranchising millions of minorities, immigrants, and college students, the vast majority of whom are Democrats. It would show Rove's candidates taking over the judiciary in Texas, Alabama, and even in the United States itself over the last twenty years, and, while in the White House, politicizing the Justice Department as never before, in a way that would have extraordinary and enduring consequences.

It would also show dazzlingly clever ways of manipulating election results. It would show that on November 2, 2004, computer servers belonging to SmarTech, a Chattanooga, Tennessee–based computer company, did in fact link up with servers for Ohio's election results at approximately 11:14 p.m., after which highly irregular returns began to favor George W. Bush over John Kerry, in the process giving Ohio's twenty electoral votes—and the presidency—to Bush.

It would show that Karl Rove, while not directly tied to SmarTech, benefited from it repeatedly, and that SmarTech had provided technology services to Republicans and right-wing groups for more than a decade. Similarly, it would show the destruction of countless electronic government documents later sought by investigators examining Rove's role in the Valerie Plame Wilson scandal and the U.S. attorneys scandal.

As substantial as these issues were, they became all the more relevant as the November 2012 election neared. Rove was not only making his comeback but playing the political poker match of his life. After all, he had become the party boss of the Republicans at a time of chaos, in which rump elements were in ascent, in which the unruly right-wing populist Tea Party ran roughshod over what was left of the Republican establishment. In the prelude to Mitt Romney's nomination as the Republican candidate, the party of Abraham Lincoln had suddenly jumped the shark and was transformed into a circuslike reality show starring an ensemble of cartoonish clowns and buffoons, including, at one time or another, the sexy, big-game hunting, right-wing MILF from Alaska, Sarah Palin; billionaire real estate huckster-cum-reality host Donald Trump, with his acrobatic hairstyle that was simultaneously combed forward, blown dry, and folded back in the shape of a ship's prow; pizza king Herman Cain displaying his foreign policy prowess about "Uz-beki-beki-beki-stan-stan"; Michelle Bachmann asserting that the Founding Fathers, in writing the Constitution, outlawed slavery; Rick Perry, with his dubious debating skills; Newt Gingrich, with his endless stream of ethics scandals and titillating marital history highlighted by allegations from an ex that he sought an "open" marriage; and Rick Santorum, clad in his sweater vest, ranting against contraception, public schooling, and the like.

Through the last half of 2011 and the first five months of 2012, Rove patiently watched and waited, content to sit back and quietly undermine the aforementioned candidates, all the while halfheartedly backing presumptive nominee Mitt Romney, knowing that Romney would ultimately have to come to terms with him.

As the November 6, 2012, elections neared, Karl Rove had completed a remarkable transformation. His political apparatus was fully funded and operational. His relationships with Fox News and the *Wall Street Journal* gave him a bully pulpit that allowed him to put forth his own Rovian narrative, while at the same time he manipulated events behind the scenes. A number of his former operatives had taken key positions working for Mitt Romney, who was not the perfect candidate for Rove by any means, but potentially viable. Romney's major political opponent, Barack Obama, was burdened by a sputtering economy and the disappointment of many who had voted for him in 2008.

Even the most astute observers of Rove, with few exceptions, had made a crucial miscalculation. Given Rove's close relationship with Bush, they had assumed that his mission had to be accomplished during the two George W. Bush administrations. But Rove had always played the long game. He was not merely a creature of the Bushes. He was a political force in his own right. Now America would find out if Karl Christian Rove could create a permanent Republican majority on his own.

TWO

A Nixonian Education

I t's six o'clock on a warm September evening in Cedarville, Ohio, population 3,962. There's still an hour before showtime, but the Cedarville University auditorium is already beginning to fill with patrons anxious to get good seats. Karl Rove is in town.

Rove would be hard-pressed to find a friendlier crowd anywhere. After all, Cedarville University is a "Christ-centered" institution whose stated mission is to "glorify God" by promoting the tenets of creationism and biblical inerrancy, and Rove, though hardly a religious man himself, made his mark by marshaling the Christian Right into a force powerful enough to propel George W. Bush into the White House.

By seven p.m., with Christian rock playing in the background, the 3,400-seat auditorium—big enough to seat almost everyone in Cedarville—is nearly full. Then Mark Smith, director of Cedarville's Center for Political Studies, introduces "the greatest political mind of his generation." Greeted by a standing ovation, Karl Rove takes center stage.

With the impeccable timing of a seasoned performer, Rove plays the folksy, good ole boy from Texas and the self-deprecating "recovering bureaucrat." He mixes tales of patriotism and heroism with the Horatio Alger–like account of how his unschooled grandfather became a successful purveyor of butcher supplies, even though "all he had was a dream and drive and a willingness to work hard and that's what this country is based on." Rove tells the crowd that Obama's plan to tax the rich will breed "resentment and class warfare," and destroy the "doers and dreamers" who made this country great. The hardworking people of Cedarville—per capita income $9,499—love it and enthusiastically applaud low taxes for the rich.

But two middle-aged men in the audience are less than enthralled. Cliff Arnebeck and Bob Fitrakis are the two attorneys from Columbus, Ohio, who brought a 2006 lawsuit against Ohio Secretary of State Ken Blackwell and who are convinced that Karl Rove stood at the heart of an ongoing conspiracy to deprive Ohio voters of their rights.

How one responds to such grave accusations is a reflection of one's political biases. If you revile Karl Rove and the Bush presidency he brought to power, you may see the lawsuit, *King Lincoln Bronzeville v. Blackwell,** as evidence that Rove is capable of the ultimate treachery, one that betrays the very foundation of democracy: stealing a presidential election. On the other hand, if you're a die-hard Republican, or just someone who finds the charges outlandishly paranoid, these tales come across as the hallucinations of connect-the-dot conspiracy nuts lost in a world of political intrigue and cyberwarfare.

For the most part, conventional wisdom has sided with the latter camp. The suit languished in the courts for more than five years before being dismissed on jurisdictional grounds. Now Arnebeck says he plans to file a racketeering complaint against Rove. Likewise, the few reporters and bloggers who have dared to pursue the allegations have been marginalized and demonized as part of the "tin-foil hat" brigade. But no matter whom you side with, the charges raise provocative questions about the state of American democracy.

After his speech, Rove retires to a side room in the auditorium to meet with admirers and sign copies of his book, *Courage and Consequence,* with its peculiarly Jane Austenesque title, which prompted Stephen Colbert to call it "just like *Pride and Prejudice,* but even more prejudiced."

Political junkie that he is, Rove has never been the most impressive physical specimen on the planet. GOP operative Roger Stone, a buff libertine who is no friend of Rove's, likens him to "a wax pear that's been sitting on the radiator too long."

---

* King Lincoln Bronzeville is a largely African-American neighborhood in Columbus, Ohio.

On this occasion, however, that last assessment may be going too far. The absence of six-pack abs notwithstanding, Rove is energized by a legion of enthusiastic fans and at the peak of his powers. He has blue eyes and thinning hair, but most of all he is affable, jocular, and extroverted, and one gets the clear impression that he truly enjoys what he is doing.

But what Rove is actually doing is far more than he appears to be doing. Truly great political operatives are masters of indirection, sleight of hand, hiding how they actually operate. Unlikely as it is that he will reveal his secrets, I ask a question about SmarTech that no reporter has ever raised with him.

Rove doesn't miss a beat. "I have no idea who SmarTech is," he says.

The answer is somewhat surprising, given that Rove has been subpoenaed in the *King Lincoln* lawsuit and identified "as the principal perpetrator in an Ohio racketeering conspiracy" involving SmarTech, so I repeat the question.

"Is that the firm that supposedly did some work for us in 2004?" Rove asks.

"Yes."

"I am so many layers removed from that I wouldn't even know who those guys were."

Has he ever been to their offices?

"No," he says.

Then Karl Rove pauses for a split second and utters a phrase that is familiar to anyone who has seen him testify before a grand jury: "Not that I recall."

Allegations that the 2004 presidential election was stolen are nothing new. In 2005, an investigation by the House Judiciary Committee concluded that Ohio, the most crucial swing state of all in the Electoral College, conducted its election in a way that had so many "massive and unprecedented" irregularities that it raised "grave doubts" about the legality of the outcome of the entire presidential election.

Beyond that investigation, however, the forces pursuing the case against Rove were not exactly titans who would put the fear of God in the greatest political operative of our time. Articles by Bobby Kennedy Jr. and by Mark Crispin Miller have been published in

Rolling Stone and *Harper's,* respectively, but have failed to sway the mainstream. Most media outlets pursuing the story were little-known blogs such as ePluribus Media, Raw Story, The Brad Blog, Freepress.org, Legal Schnauzer, and the like.

Nor are the two Ohio attorneys who filed the suit household names. Bob Fitrakis is an author and a political science professor at Columbus State Community College who also serves as the editor of a liberal blog called the Free Press. Lead attorney Cliff Arnebeck is a Harvard Law School graduate who served as counsel to Bob Dole's 1988 presidential bid and was a Republican until Newt Gingrich drove the party rightward in the nineties. Since then, he has become a professional legal watchdog, serving as national co-chair and attorney for the Alliance for Democracy and as head of legal affairs for Common Cause Ohio. For the most part, this quixotic assortment of bloggers, journalists, lawyers, and academics has been ignored or scorned—often by presumably friendly left-of-center critics, including Salon, *Mother Jones,* and even, at times, the Democratic Party itself.

To anyone familiar with Rove's history, however, such allegations, no matter how momentous, are par for the course. Indeed, dirty tricks were part of Karl Rove's life before he even got out of college. There, as a member of College Republicans at the University of Utah, Rove worked for Senator Ralph Smith of Illinois in an unsuccessful special election bid in 1970 against Democrat Adlai E. Stevenson during which, Rove later admitted, he stole stationery from the offices of a Democratic candidate and used it to fabricate phony invitations to a party at Democratic headquarters with "free beer, free food, girls and a good time for nothing."

Just twenty years old, Rove caught the eye of national figures in the party, and won a position as executive director of College Republicans in Washington. Adept at assembling direct-mail programs and brochures, Rove became a master of distilling complicated messages into simple, forceful, highly targeted talking points. He traveled widely, giving weekend seminars for college conservatives all over the country.

It was as if he were fully formed by the time he got to college. "I think he is exactly the same person," says Joe Abate, a GOP political consultant in Arizona who has known Rove since the two men were in College Republicans together in 1970. "He was creative. Talented. He could put together these great brochures for direct-mail campaigns that did very, very well. He was far above anyone at his age."

Back then, College Republicans was a hotbed of right-wing radicals who rebelled against everything that had anything to do with the leftish sixties counterculture. Among them were no-holds-barred operatives Lee Atwater, Roger Stone, Terry Dolan, and Donald Segretti.

Nixon was president, and College Republicans perfected the "ratfucking" techniques of the Watergate era, as Donald Segretti famously called them. There were false press releases or "leaked documents" bearing the names of Democratic rivals, jammed phone lines, spying on opponents, purloined speeches, hired "rioters" and activists planted in enemy camps, and push polls in which volunteer pollsters hunkered down in phone banks for hour after hour, disseminating disinformation and smears about opponents.

In 1973, Rove, then twenty-two, ran for the national chairmanship of College Republicans, with South Carolinian Lee Atwater, a year younger but already on his way to becoming the legendary bad boy of the Republican Party, serving as his campaign manager in the South. A man of dubious culinary tastes (cornflakes for breakfast, doused with Tabasco sauce), Atwater drove Rove around for six days, rounding up support in Florida, Georgia, Alabama, and Mississippi, showing him the region as only a true son of the South could.

The battle between Rove and his opponent, Robert Edgeworth, was so ferocious that participants have held bitter grudges ever since. "There's nothing more vicious than a young Republican fight, nothing, nothing," said Roger Stone, who was part of the anti-Rove faction—and remains so nearly forty years later. Arguments nearly became fistfights. Credentials were challenged. There were allegations that Rove's side stole votes. In the end, both sides declared victory, which meant that Republican National Committee chairman George Herbert Walker Bush had to make the final decision.

Before Bush reached a decision, however, one of Rove's foes leaked a story to the *Washington Post*, which was then in the midst of breaking the Watergate scandal, that Rove's seminars consisted of teaching "dirty tricks" classes to the young Republicans. Rove was even investigated by the FBI.

The future president was horrified—but not by the dirty tricks. No, what shocked Bush was that any Republican would be so disloyal as to air the party's dirty linen. As a result, he not only awarded the election to Rove but also wrote Edgeworth "the angriest letter I have ever received in my life. I had leaked to the *Washington Post,* and now I was out of the Party forever." To add insult to injury, Bush then hired Rove as a special assistant.*

Bush's reaction taught Rove an important lesson, said author and journalist Joe Conason: "You could play the hardest of hardball and get away with it."

And for Rove it was the start of a journey in which he began to acquire the tools he needed: a mastery of the tradecraft necessary to be a successful political operative; an enduring money machine to which he, and he alone, would have access; and, ultimately, a candidate who would be the perfect match for him.

In some ways, Atwater was everything Rove wasn't. Irresistible and hyperkinetic, Lee Atwater was the roguish gunslinger, the outlaw, the badass guitar-picking Southern frat boy. A uniquely adept spinmeister who was brilliant at seducing the media, Atwater would arrive at a breakfast interview, blues guitar in hand, a gentle reminder that he played with rhythm-and-blues legends Carla Thomas, Isaac Hayes, Sam Moore, Chuck Jackson, and B.B. King.

Reporters ate it up. Who among them had so effortlessly crossed America's bitter racial divide? Atwater traded licks with B.B. King! Yet this was the same man who had no compunction about orchestrating an overtly racist campaign for the White House.

When it came to dealing with colleagues, Atwater was far better liked than Rove. "With Lee, you could have a battle with him and work with him afterward," said Tom Pauken, a former chairman of the Texas Republican Party who worked with both Atwater and Rove. "Karl just

*Edgeworth says he was falsely accused and that a colleague was the real source for the *Post.*

wanted you to salute. Unless you were with him one hundred percent, you were his enemy." Ninety-nine and a half wouldn't do.

Over time, Rove learned the fine points of political hardball at the feet of the master. But in fact Atwater was not particularly keen on Rove, a doughy bookworm. "Atwater put up with Rove because he was there," said Roger Stone. "But he never really liked him. Most of the time, we just rolled our eyes at Karl."

So while Atwater made national headlines, Rove planted his flag in Texas, at the time an unlikely place for a Republican with grand ambitions. To be sure, in the sixties the Republican Party's bold Southern Strategy had already begun to win millions of conservative Democrats over to the GOP throughout the South. But Texas was different. The Democratic Party there still had popular conservative candidates, such as Governor John Connally and future senator Lloyd Bentsen, who were so pro-business that high-rolling executives saw no reason to fund the Republican Party.

As a result, Texas was effectively a one-party state—Democratic—and Rove's ascent was glacial. In 1978, he had a junior position in George W. Bush's first congressional bid—a loss. In 1984, he managed to run Phil Gramm's successful campaign for the U.S. Senate, and handled direct mail for the Reagan-Bush campaign. For the most part, however, he was largely mired in races for the state Agriculture Commission, the Texas judiciary, and the like. As late as 1990, two years after Atwater engineered George H.W. Bush's memorable scorched-earth campaign to win the White House, Rove was still a minor regional figure.

Rove, however, had a vision. Other top consultants were strategists or pollsters or media people creating ads, but Rove developed expertise in a vital but unsexy specialty: direct mail. "He came into the business in an odd way," said Wayne Slater, a reporter with the *Dallas Morning News*, who, with James Moore, co-wrote *Bush's Brain* and *The Architect*, the two essential books on Rove. "But knowing direct mail meant that he had a hands-on understanding of the money people."

Rove went so far as to install his own photocopying machine in the Secretary of State's Office in Austin, Texas, so he could assemble lists of campaign donors. The advent of computerized databases meant he could instantly access the lists for use in future campaigns. He had created something that became the Holy Grail for political consultants. "He controlled the mechanism of developing fund-raising," said Slater.

In the late eighties and early nineties, Rove's time was consumed by judicial races in Texas and Alabama, a mission that seemed beneath someone harboring such extravagant dreams. But taking over state judiciaries was an elemental part of Rove's vision. "Given that the Republican business guys are not making donations to the Party, how do you get them to give money?" asked Slater. "You push the button that affects them most. It ain't the social issues like abortion. It's the issues that affect their pocket book."

Rove's genius was to take an uninspiring, sleep-inducing issue that no one cared about and change it into a sizzling hot-button topic that could amp up a new Republican money machine that would be all but wholly controlled by Karl Christian Rove. The issue in question was a real snoozer—product liability, or, as Rove and his PACs referred to it, "tort reform."

Tort reform? The phrase was basically unknown to the general public, but, in legal terms, a tort is essentially a civil wrong—that is, an act that causes harm or loss to someone else. Whether it was applied to tobacco companies selling cancer-causing cigarettes or to pharmaceutical companies selling drugs, like thalidomide, that caused horrifying birth defects, tort law gave the Average Joe a fighting chance against huge corporations.

The tricky thing about tort reform as formulated by Rove, however, was that "reform" was intended to *curtail* rather than enhance the ability of consumers to sue cigarette companies, pharmaceutical companies, and the like. To dramatize that such verdicts could be bad for the business community, Rove zeroed in on a case in which an Alabama doctor was awarded $4 million from BMW because his new car had been damaged by acid rain and repainted, thereby diminishing its value. "It was the poster-child case of outrageous verdicts," Bill Smith, a political consultant who worked with Rove, told *The Atlantic*. "Karl figured out the vocabulary on the BMW case and others like it that point out not just liberal behavior but outrageous decisions that make you mad as hell."

Of course, corporations *were* victimized by extravagantly generous verdicts from jurors on occasion. But those were the exceptions, not the rule, and more often it was the other way around. "You had insurance companies not paying life insurance after the customer had paid a lifetime of premiums—egregious stuff, real rip-offs," said Doug Jones, a former U.S. attorney in Alabama. And Rove's mission was to get the little guy to give up one of the few means he had of redressing grievances against corporate America.

The reason he selected this issue was simple. "Rove was smart enough to understand that tort reform was a cash cow, and a rising divisive issue between Republicans and Democrats," said Craig McDonald of Texans for Public Justice. "So he put a wedge between the trial lawyers and the business community."

Taking over the judiciary was vital to his strategy. In the eighties, the Democrat-dominated Texas Supreme Court had become known as a plaintiff's court, siding with the little guy almost all the time against the big corporations. But Rove was determined to change that. "Raising money from the high-rolling business community had not been done by Republicans," said Craig McDonald. "It had all been conservative Democrats. But the South had been going through a paradigmatic change since the Civil Rights Act and Rove convinced big business to invest in an infrastructure for Texas Republicans. He made a point of looking for donors who would benefit from such legislation." So he assured donors that if they invested in the campaigns of Republican officials they could save billions down the road in exorbitant judgments.

Having found his angels, Rove set out to demonize Democratic judicial candidates as tools of "wealthy personal-injury trial lawyers" who were greedily looking for spectacular punitive damages. TV commercials ridiculing rich trial lawyers flooded the airwaves. The term *trial lawyer* became an epithet. Suddenly, tort reform was the hot issue of the moment. Late-night comics joked about extravagant verdicts. There was even a tort reform episode on *Seinfeld*. To the uninitiated who saw the countless ads, there appeared to be a massive spontaneous uprising against "jackpot justice."*

---

*As shown in the documentary *Hot Coffee,* by Susan Saladoff, the case of Stella Liebeck, an Albuquerque woman who was awarded nearly $3 million after spilling hot coffee on herself at McDonald's, became a poster child for the issue, and was considered funny enough that it provided material for a *Seinfeld* episode. As the docu-

But in fact these "citizens" committees were all part of a carefully orchestrated campaign organized by Rove. The ads were actually paid for by "astroturf" citizens groups—that is, phony grassroots committees that were really funded by huge corporations. There was Texans for Lawsuit Reform, Citizens Against Lawsuit Abuse, and Texas Civil Justice League. According to "Tort Dodgers: Business Money Tips the Scale of Justice," a report by Texans for Public Justice, by 1997 there were no fewer than twenty-two PACs in Texas spending more than $3 million in the 1996 election cycle, an astounding amount at the time, in an effort "to get the Texas Legislature to relieve businesses of their responsibility for seriously injuring employees, customers and neighbors."

It took years, but, by and large, Rove succeeded in using tort reform to build a semipermanent Texas money machine.

In addition to a longtime backer, homebuilder Bob Perry, Rove had found new contributors, including billionaire Dallas industrialist Harold Simmons; San Antonio communications executive Houston H. Harte; Houston beer distributor John Nau; and Julia Matthews and her son, Kade, who were ranching and energy investors based in Abilene.

Just as Rove had hoped, the money rolled in—from the health care industry, the petrochemical and energy industry, land development executives, corporate defense lawyers, tobacco interests, and others. Likewise, as he did on a national level with American Crossroads many years later, Rove made sure donations went to his political action committees rather than to the Republican Party itself, which did not make him popular with party regulars. "When Karl didn't feel that the party chairman was a sufficient ally, then on his own he just discouraged people from giving to the party," said Slater.

---

mentary points out, crucial facts were omitted from the version that became widely accepted—namely, that the seventy-nine-year-old woman suffered grotesque third-degree burns, that she was not driving a car at the time as was widely reported, that she sought only $10,500 in medical expenses from McDonald's, and that the vast majority of the award came after jurors decided punitive damages were necessary because McDonald's kept the temperature of its coffee at 190 degrees Fahrenheit as a matter of policy even though there were more than seven hundred similar cases filed against the burger chain.

By cutting off donations to the Texas Republican Party and redirecting them to his PACs, Rove effectively supplanted the state party apparatus. "He did exactly what he's doing now with the Super-PACS," said Tom Pauken, a Dallas attorney and former chairman of the Texas Republican Party. "But ultimately I don't think it works, because it is fundamentally inauthentic. Karl has done a lot of damage to conservatives."

Nevertheless, Rove's donors remained loyal to him, because they got enormous bang for their buck. In the eighties, the Texas Supreme Court was a pro-plaintiff court with nine Democratic judges and no Republicans, but over time Rove completely remade it and turned it into a pro-business court consisting of nine Republican judges and no Democrats. In addition, there were no fewer than forty-four tort bills before the Texas legislature that reduced the ability of victims to hold wrongdoers responsible for crippling or fatal workplace injuries, medical malpractice, unsafe products, unfair insurance practices, and consumer fraud.

On a personal level, no one gained more than Rove himself. For many years, Rove was on the payroll of Philip Morris, which stood to lose billions in class-action suits, with a mandate to keep the Texas attorney general from joining with other states in suing the tobacco companies. Much of the PAC money went to aid the campaign of Rove's chief client, Governor George W. Bush. "When you look at Rove's donor base," said McDonald, "the same donors for Texans for Lawsuit Reform absolutely supported Bush when he ran for governor in 1994. They were the biggest independent PACs when they were created and they remain the biggest to this day."*

While Rove labored away in Texas, Lee Atwater had been making a name for himself on the national stage, becoming chairman of the Republican National Committee after running the victorious 1988

---

* Bob Perry and Harold Simmons were among those who also later contributed to George W. Bush's gubernatorial and presidential campaigns, to various judicial races, to Swift Boat Veterans for Truth in the 2004 presidential race, and other PACs. And in 2011 the donors Rove rounded up for that campaign were responsible for over half of the initial donations to American Crossroads. Simmons and Perry led the pack in 2011, with $7 million and $2.5 million in contributions, respectively.

presidential campaign of George H.W. Bush. The courtly visage of the genteel vice president notwithstanding, Atwater ran a campaign that was so breathtakingly vicious that even his Republican colleagues were astounded. In his 1996 book *Bare Knuckles and Back Rooms,* Ed Rollins, who, as Ronald Reagan's political director hired Atwater, describes his acolyte as "ruthless," "Ollie North in civilian clothes," and someone who "just had to drive in one more stake."

A dyed-in-the-wool South Carolinian, Atwater was a son of the South whose DNA was embedded with bitter memories of Dixie's defeat at the hands of the North. As a result, he knew exactly which buttons to push, racial and otherwise, in the service of the party's Southern Strategy. The 1988 presidential campaign was right up his alley, pitting Democrat Michael Dukakis, a passionless liberal technocrat, against George H.W. Bush, a tall, lanky Texan—albeit one who was really a blue-blooded Eastern establishment transplant from the cosseted suburbs of Greenwich, Connecticut.

At times, Atwater could be extraordinarily candid about how coded racial language and imagery could be used to woo Southern white voters. "You start out in 1954 by saying, 'Nigger, nigger, nigger,'" Atwater said. "By 1968 you can't say 'nigger'—that hurts you. Backfires. So you say stuff like forced busing, states' rights and all that stuff . . . [talk] about cutting taxes. . . . and a by-product of them is [that] blacks get hurt worse than whites. . . . Obviously, sitting around saying, 'We want to cut this' is . . . a hell of a lot more abstract than 'Nigger, nigger.'"

One didn't have to be a world-class cryptologist to decipher the new codes. In the 1988 presidential election, the dominant issue in Bush's campaign against Dukakis was concocted deliberately to win Southern support by raising the specter of America's greatest stain: racism. It began before the Democratic National Convention in Atlanta that year, when Atwater, Bush's campaign manager, told a group of fellow Republicans about "a fellow named Willie Horton." A convicted felon serving a life sentence for murder, William R. Horton (he used "William"; the Bush campaign popularized "Willie") was the beneficiary of a Massachusetts prison-reform program who did not return from his weekend furlough, and committed assault, armed robbery, and rape.

Of course, prison reform in Massachusetts was hardly an issue of global concern, but that didn't matter. The Horton ad did far more than just criticize Dukakis for being soft on crime. It evoked an atavistic racial fear. It reawakened a deep-seated cultural resentment about a pointy-headed Harvard liberal elite who had contempt for the South. The ad,* which was created by media consultant Larry McCarthy, was epochal in the annals of negative campaigning, one of the most provocative in the history of American politics. Its key image, a mug shot of Horton, a black man with an unkempt Afro, was so menacing that McCarthy's first reaction was "God, this guy's ugly. This is every suburban mother's greatest fear." According to the PBS documentary *Boogie Man,* Atwater vowed to "strip the bark off the little bastard [Dukakis] and make Willie Horton his running mate."

Before the ad aired, Atwater invited Roger Stone over to see it, but even Stone, a protégé of the merciless fixer Roy Cohn and no shrinking violet when it came to hardball politics, told him not to air it because it was too racist.

Atwater was not convinced. "Y'all a pussy," he replied.

To make sure that his candidate had deniability, Atwater saw to it that the Willie Horton ad was paid for not by the Bush campaign itself, but by a third party, the National Security Political Action Committee (NSPAC). When the votes were counted, of course, Bush beat Dukakis in a landslide—having swept virtually the entire South.†

Similarly, Rove began to master the tricks of the trade. One of his first breakthroughs came even before the Willie Horton episode, in 1986, when he was working for Bill Clements, former Republican governor of Texas, who was then running against Democratic governor Mark White, the man who had knocked him out of office. It took place on Sunday, October 5, 1986, just before the one and only televised debate, a crucial event that was expected to be a decisive factor—and an inauspicious one, given that Clements was a notoriously weak

---

*http://www.livingroomcandidate.org/commercials/1988/willie-horton.
†To be precise, Bush won every single state in the South except West Virginia, a border state that is not always considered part of the South.

debater. Perhaps because of that, the Clements campaign brought in a private security firm to sweep its offices and found an electronic eavesdropping device behind a picture frame in Karl Rove's office, close enough to have transmitted all of Rove's phone conversations.

And so, as recounted in *Bush's Brain,* while the debate was being set up, Rove briefed reporters not on what Clements might say but on wireless microphones, secret miniature transmitters, and political espionage. "I do not know who did this," Rove said, "but there is no doubt in my mind that the only ones who could have benefited from this detailed sensitive information would have been the political opposition."

As it happened, the true beneficiaries were Clements and Rove, not the opposition. It wasn't long before both reporters and investigators suspected that Rove planted the device himself (its battery life was so short, it would have been all but useless)—which he denied, of course. More to the point, coverage of the well-timed bugging story overwhelmed the debate, and Clements won.

About a year later, a woman named Patricia Tierney Alofsin happened to be invited to a small dinner party with some of Texas's top political consultants, including Rove. "Karl all but came out and said, 'I did it,'" she told Wayne Slater and James Moore. "He was proud of it. . . . I don't remember the exact words, I remember being shocked. It was like those cases where people murder people and then they leave clues because they do this fabulous murder, and they want the police to know they did it. . . . He was so proud of it. . . . It came across 'Wasn't I a clever boy?' That's the way it came across. He left the impression, 'Wasn't I clever, and didn't it work and let me rub your nose in it.'"

In 1991, Atwater, still very much a renowned and feared campaigner at the height of his powers, died of a brain tumor at the age of forty. That meant there was room at the top of the Republican Party for Rove, even though his ascent had been slow. "He'd spent his career toiling in Texas and he needed to find a horse to ride," says one high-level Republican political consultant.

Enter George W. Bush. Back in 1973, when he had been the assistant to George H.W. Bush, Rove met George W. for the first time, and came away suitably impressed. "I can literally remember what he was wearing," he told *The New Yorker.* "An Air National Guard flight jacket, cowboy boots, bluejeans. . . . He was exuding more charisma than any one individual should be allowed to have." For their part, the Bushes regarded Rove patronizingly, not as family but as a necessary evil. Hence, George W. called him "turd blossom," and Laura Bush referred to him as "Pigeon."

Dubya, as he was known in Texas, had inherited much of his father's legacy—Andover, Yale, Skull and Bones, Texas, and the oil business. But, unlike his father, he had nothing but antipathy for the Ivy League ethos he encountered at Yale and Harvard Business School. A genuine born-again Christian who read the Bible and prayed daily, Dubya eschewed the trappings of a rich family heritage that was deeply embedded in the Eastern Establishment.

All of which added up to a big political advantage over his father. Bush senior personified the Eastern aristocracy to such an extent that when Ann Richards, who later became governor of Texas, delivered a sound bite about him at the Democratic National Convention in 1988, it reverberated throughout the United States. "Poor George," she said, "he can't help it. He was born with a silver foot in his mouth."

By contrast, Dubya identified far more with the rural Texas archetypes forged on the ranch, in the oil fields, and in the locker room. He cast a figure that could be reminiscent of the cowboys who once strode Texas's wide-open spaces.

It was an image Rove thought would be enormously attractive to Texas voters. In 1990, while the elder Bush was still president, Rove tried to persuade the son to run for governor. But Dubya begged off, in part because his thin résumé was dominated by his failures as an oilman—and a losing race for Congress.

So it was not until 1994 that Bush, by then the popular owner of the Texas Rangers, decided to run, and Rove undertook the daunting task of running a political neophyte against the sassy, smart, funny, popular incumbent, Richards, who had been hailed on the cover of the *Texas Monthly* astride a white-and-chrome Harley-Davidson as a "White Hot Mama."

But soon, thanks to Rove, the unschooled candidate became quite well schooled indeed. Thanks to Rove, Bush's bookshelves were filled with the latest in evangelical and neoconservative thought—Myron Magnet's *The Dream and the Nightmare,* Marvin Olasky's *The Tragedy of American Compassion,* James Q. Wilson's *The Moral Sense* and *On Character,* and Gertrude Himmelfarb's *The Demoralization of Society.* Thus, the ruthless operator and autodidact schooled the Ivy League scion of a former president in what became packaged as "compassionate conservatism." Thanks to Rove, Bush attended rigorous tutorials on crime, welfare reform, the state education system, and, of course, the tort reform that was so dear to Rove's heart. And thanks to Rove, the unassailable good ole girl, Governor Ann Richards, soon became quite assailable indeed.

Whatever his relationship with Atwater, Rove had no compunction about picking up tricks from the former about defining one's opponent through constant attacks. "If there's any single thing that defines a Rove campaign, it's smash-mouth politics," said Wayne Slater. "He goes after you hammer and tong. . . . Attack, attack, attack is sort of the model that he used."

In spite of, or perhaps because of, his unusual upbringing, Rove knew few boundaries. His adoptive father, Louis Rove, was not just openly gay, he was such an icon in the tattoo and piercing subculture that, thanks to his thirty-seven piercings, most of which were in his genitals, he was featured as the cover story in *Piercing Fans International Quarterly.**

Rove has said he does not know how or why his parents' marriage ended and, in *Courage and Consequence,* adds that his father "refused to say why or how their marriage had dissolved." But a source who knows Rove says he was quite aware that his father came out of the closet, and that Louis Rove's sexual orientation did not seem to bother him or interfere with a close father-son relationship right up until the father's death in 2004.

Perhaps as a result, Rove was, in private, quite open-minded about homosexuality and alternative lifestyles, especially for someone whose major constituency was the overtly antigay Christian Right.

---

*In the article, the elder Rove confesses that his piercings provoked considerable anxiety the first time he went through airport security screening. However, he subsequently discovered that because the piercings were gold, they were invisible to the scanning device.

"Karl is very liberal-minded on this stuff," says someone who knows him. "But I think after his father came out, he became acutely aware of the power of knowing people's sexual behavior."

In most cases, these attacks took place via surrogates, so that the candidate—in this case, George W. Bush—could maintain the pretense that he was conducting a "positive" campaign. One favorite technique, of which Atwater was a pioneer, was the push poll, in which fake pollsters were hired to ask questions—at least one of which was certain to stir up a furor. "The first few questions are routine," recalled former ABC newsman Sam Donaldson. "The next question is "Well, if you came to believe that Governor X was a pedophile, would that change your opinion?' Now, the poller hasn't said that Governor X is a pedophile, simply planted the idea."

Because deniability was built into the process, nothing was out of bounds—race, anti-Semitism, lesbianism, pedophilia, you name it. Famously, in a South Carolina congressional race Atwater destroyed the political ambitions of candidate Max Heller, thanks to push polls asking voters what they thought about a Jew who did not worship Jesus Christ.

In his memoir, Rove himself decries the use of push polls, asserting that "the practice is inexpensive and underhanded, and like most cheap and sleazy tactics, it tends to blow back on its sponsor." Nevertheless, he and his candidates benefited from it repeatedly. Such was the case in Texas in 1994, with push polls asking whether people would be "more or less likely to vote for Governor Richards if [they] knew her staff is dominated by lesbians."

Rove has denied having anything to do with the push polls, and candidate Bush, who scrupulously avoided making direct personal attacks on Richards, repeatedly asserted, "This is not an issue in this campaign."

But, to many, those denials were merely window dressing. One reason was that Bush surrogates, such as Republican state senator Bill Ratliff, the East Texas chairman for the Bush campaign, criticized Governor Ann Richards for appointing "avowed homosexual activists" to state jobs, saying that "[homosexuality] is not something we encourage, reward, or acknowledge as an acceptable situation."

Flyers featuring gay men, stripped to the waist, kissing, appeared on car windshields at churches all over Texas, with the legend reading, "This Is What Ann Richards Wants to Teach Your Children in Public Schools."

Especially in East Texas, word was out that Ann Richards was a lesbian. "I thought it was a joke," Richards said. "I never took that seriously. I have dealt with that in every race I've ever run. When I ran for county commissioner, I told [ex-husband] David, you know that before this is over, they're going to have me sleeping with every man in this county. Little did I realize it was going to be every woman."

"There was clearly an organized Republican movement to keep out there a couple of issues, gays and guns, in the forefront," said Chuck McDonald, a spokesman for Ann Richards's press secretary. "And I don't think it's any secret that the person who really set the Republican agenda was Karl Rove."

In any case, the tactic was enormously effective. When the race started, the charismatic, wisecracking Richards had a 67 percent approval rating and was being touted as having the potential to become the first woman president. An iconic Texas good ole girl, she was going up against an opponent who had never won a race. Yet Bush won, by nearly eight percentage points, and as governor of Texas would have the platform for even higher office—the presidency, of course.

Similarly, throughout Rove's career his candidates would have the good fortune to face opponents who were said to be pedophiles, lesbians, or crooks, or to have fathered illegitimate, mixed-race babies. In each case, Rove could claim that neither he nor his candidate was responsible for such slurs because, as Slater and Moore write in *Bush's Brain,* he "puts a layer of operatives between himself and the actual implementation of any plan of attack. All of the investigative roads can be expected to lead back to Rove, but . . . they will wash out from a deluge of deception before they get to their destination."

To elect George W. Bush president, however, required much more than push polls, dirty tricks, and tort reform. But Rove had other weapons at his disposal. One of them was technology.

THREE

Chattanooga Choo Choo

With a population of just 167,000, Chattanooga, Tennessee, is not the first place one would look to uncover a secretive high-tech political operation serving the interests of the grandmaster of the political dark arts. For one thing, when it comes to power and money even the wealthiest Chattanoogans can't compete with the Beltway power brokers in Washington, the captains of industry on Wall Street, or the oil barons of Dallas and Houston. For another, the Colorado-born, Utah-bred Karl Rove has largely based his operations in Texas and Washington, and, aside from one pit stop at a Chattanooga barbecue in 2007, has had little presence in the city.

But there's more to Chattanooga than meets the eye. A rare boomtown in recession-racked America, Chattanooga's revitalized Tennessee River waterfront embodies the New South, with a huge new aquarium, museums, and public parks. Nearby Lookout Mountain on the Tennessee-Georgia border serves as the icon of the South's Old Money, and in Chattanooga that means the handful of families whose billions are rooted in the fortune created by the Coca-Cola Bottling Company. The Tennessee Valley Authority, the Atomic Energy Commission's Oak Ridge National Laboratory, and NASA's nearby facility in Huntsville, Alabama, provide ample technological resources and brainpower.

The story of what became widely known as SmarTech began in the late nineties, when Michael Cunnyngham, a brilliant Chattanooga technologist, launched NextLec, also known as st3, having developed pioneering techniques to stream massive amounts of video data. As *eWeek* magazine, a weekly trade publication, put it, he had created one of "the first top-tier networks with the purpose of delivering video at very high quality."

Enter Mercer Reynolds and Bill DeWitt, founders of the Cincinnati-based investment firm Reynolds, DeWitt & Company, who invested a total of $9.5 million in the company. This was the era of the first dot-com bubble, and the two men were not immune to its allure. "Bill and Mercer were in it because it was hot," Cunnyngham said. "They had no grand thoughts for the Republican Party."

Nevertheless, Reynolds and DeWitt were both stalwart Republicans, and, more to the point, George W. Bush loyalists. The two men had first met Bush in Midland, Texas, in the early eighties, when he was a struggling oilman in West Texas and, through their own oil company, Spectrum 7 Energy, eventually came to the rescue when Bush's company was in trouble.*

Over time, Reynolds and DeWitt entered into an even deeper relationship with Bush. Mercer Reynolds, in particular, became close friends with the future president. He partied with Bush, worked out with him, and witnessed firsthand Bush's transformation from a hard-drinking, aging frat boy to a devout evangelical.

As for Bill DeWitt, a scion of baseball royalty whose father had owned both the St. Louis Browns and the Cincinnati Reds, he heard that the Texas Rangers baseball franchise was for sale. Even though the oil venture with Bush had been disastrous, DeWitt brought Bush in on the deal—and Bush ultimately walked away with $15 million on an initial investment of just $606,000. Later on, the DeWitts were thrilled to be so close to someone who might occupy the White House. "It's crazy," said Bill DeWitt's wife, Kathy. "It's like having a cousin [running for president]. Let's put it this way: Their phone number in Midland is in my book right here."

Meanwhile, Michael Cunnyngham had begun building a private nationwide fiber network capable of delivering data and streaming media across the country. Thanks to its past as a vital railroad

---

* For an extended account of the unusual financial dealings between Bush's operations and Spectrum 7 Energy, see the author's *House of Bush, House of Saud: The Secret Relationship Between the World's Two Most Powerful Dynasties* (New York: Scribner, 2004), pp. 113–27.

hub—celebrated in the swing era hit "Chattanooga Choo Choo"—vast quantities of fiber-optic cable had been laid parallel to countless miles of railroad tracks, providing Chattanooga with a broadband capacity that was unparalleled in the United States. It was the perfect site.

Cunnyngham's company was hailed for its revolutionary technology. Long before YouTube, which was launched in 2005, it developed a network of 24,000 fiber circuit miles capable of streaming as many as 200,000 simultaneous broadcast-quality video streams, and then joined forces with other companies to stream films and other video content over the Internet. In 1999, NextLec/st3 handled video streaming for Woodstock '99, a celebration of the famed rock festival's thirtieth anniversary. In 2001, the company acquired rights to stream the pilot of a new sitcom set in Chattanooga called *Mystic Java Café*. Then it partnered with Apple's Quicktime to stream Twangfest, a bluegrass, rock, and honky-tonk music festival.

According to Cunnyngham, other investors put a total of $38 million in the company. But pioneering the field of streaming video meant moving into uncharted territory in a capital-intensive industry. Costs mounted. Capital ran low. Soon, the company would make a radical change in a completely different direction.

By 1999, Karl Rove had already engineered two successful gubernatorial campaigns for Bush, and had positioned the Texas governor as a strong contender for the Republican presidential nomination. He had devised a step-by-step blueprint—The Plan, it was called—for Bush to win the presidency.

From the beginning of the campaign, Rove paid special attention to Ohio, which was both a crucial battleground state and the home turf of Rove's heroes, President William McKinley and Mark Hanna. As the election drew nearer, political writers increasingly made comparisons between Bush's Brain, as Rove was becoming known, and Hanna, the brains behind McKinley.* "Everything you know about

---

* As Jacob Weisberg put it on Slate, "McKinley was an affable, none-too-bright former congressman when Hanna helped elect him governor of Ohio. In 1896, Hanna raised an unprecedented amount of money and ran a sophisticated, hardball campaign that got McKinley to the White House. One could go on with the analogy:

William McKinley and Mark Hanna is wrong," Rove told *The New Yorker*'s Nicholas Lemann in early 2000. "The country was in a period of change. McKinley's the guy who figured it out. Politics were changing. The economy was changing. We're at the same point now: weak allegiances to parties, a rising new economy."

Rove and Hanna, a wealthy Cleveland industrialist who advised President McKinley not as a political operative but as a U.S. senator, are so different that comparisons of the two men are fraught with problems. But the larger point is that Rove, like Hanna, had come to the conclusion that the electorate in 2000, as in 1896, was ready for a historic realignment—that is, the permanent majority. One might argue that the conditions at the time—peace and prosperity—did *not* militate for such a realignment, but Rove was determined to use various powers at his disposal toward that end.

In that regard, the importance of Ohio in the Electoral College jibed perfectly with the Republicans' newfound technological weapons. Even though the company was located in Chattanooga, lead investor Mercer Reynolds, an Ohioan, was appointed finance chairman for the Bush campaign in Ohio and hosted Bush for a private fund-raiser at his Cincinnati home. Reynolds's relationship with Bush and Rove put him in a position to bring in both Bush and the Republican National Committee as clients for his new tech company. Mercer Reynolds was described as "the Gray Fox, the schmoozer," in the company, with DeWitt being the more discreet, low-profile brain behind it.

Soon, the company started by Mike Cunnyngham was transformed from a tech start-up into a full-fledged political operation. One of Cunnyngham's most important early decisions was to hire Jeff Averbeck and acquire one of Averbeck's companies, SmarTech. "The Republican clients originally came through Bill, Mercer, or Bill's son-in-law Jay Kern [a managing director at Reynolds DeWitt]," said Cunnyngham, "and Averbeck handled them." That meant that on a day-to-day basis, Averbeck took care of political operations, but when it came to important issues, Cunnyngham said, Jay Kern often

McKinley governed negligently in the interests of big business and went to war on flimsy evidence that Spain had blown up the USS Maine."

acted as an intermediary with the RNC. As Averbeck puts it, finally "that dot-com bubble crap went away."

Initially, the RNC didn't have a clue about the Internet. In Smar-Tech, it now had a huge technological tool kit that enabled it to raise funds and manage telecommunications. "We told the RNC they should be using the Internet to collect money," said Cunnyngham, "for voice communications so they could be more flexible, to maintain organizational rosters to send newsletters and stay in better contact with their base, and gather the kind of intelligence they needed." The vast majority of these innovations, he said, came from Averbeck.

SmarTech put together what Cunnyngham called "the best piece of spamming software on the planet," capable of driving millions of emails per hour past spam filters. And perhaps most striking of all, SmarTech hosted Voter Vault, an enormously powerful data-mining database for Republicans that now bills itself as "the single greatest advancement in political technology since the personal computer," a development that is "even more important than email and the Internet" because its "enhanced voter files" tell candidates just about everything they need to know about every single voter in the country, thanks to records that cross-reference public and consumer information such as phone numbers, driver's licenses, hunting and fishing licenses, veterans records, property records, census results, and more.

All in all, the data in Voter Vault, which was said to put the FBI and the NSA to shame, provided the last word in microtargeting and enabled GOP candidates to use various means of communication—direct mail, phone calls, home visits, television, radio, web ads, email, text messaging—to craft targeted messages specifically tailored to various subgroups in the electorate to build support and eventually to get voters to the polls on election day.

"When they hooked up with us and started getting ideas about how to use the Internet to do their fund-raising, organize their base, and manage their telecommunications, that was a fundamental change for Republicans," said Cunnyngham. "That gave them a tool they never had before. It was big." Ultimately, they would be able to communicate with all 110 million households in America in a single afternoon.

* * *

One of SmarTech's most important new clients was New Media Communications, a small Ohio-based firm that designed websites and database systems for a Republican clientele, and hosted their sites on SmarTech's servers. The person behind New Media was a handsome, six-foot-one-inch-tall man with blue-green eyes and thick dark hair named Mike Connell. "He was extremely intelligent, very passionate, very caring and loving," his wife, Heather, told me. "He had a lot of integrity, and he loved our political system."

Raised as an Irish Catholic Kennedy Democrat in Peoria, Illinois, Connell first became politicized in 1984, when, as a student at the University of Iowa, he worked briefly for the presidential campaign of Democrat Gary Hart. But when Hart became embroiled in the *Monkey Business* sex scandal, Connell, a devout Catholic who prayed before meals and went to Mass daily, switched to the Republicans. He never looked back. "His politics really changed," said Cecilia Ham Meisner, a classmate. "He had been a JFK liberal, but suddenly he became very, very conservative. He sort of made a big shift and kind of disappeared from our lives."

In part, the transformation grew out of Connell's Catholic upbringing. "We were brought up picketing abortion clinics," said his sister, Shannon Walton, who is considerably more liberal than her brother. "I'm not proud of that, but we were in the right-to-life movement after *Roe v. Wade*. Once he flipped to the Republican Party I was really disappointed, but he was committed to it with his whole heart.

"He believed in the cause. He equated the right with right-to-life. It was my mom's big issue. If we could get *Roe v. Wade* overturned, that was something my mom always wanted. He believed in that."

But Connell's shift may also have grown out of his friendship with his college roommate, Barry Jackson. More than just roommates at the University of Iowa, the two were fraternity brothers, and later, when Connell married Heather, Barry Jackson served as Mike's best man. Both were active members of College Republicans, the same aggressive no-holds-barred outfit that Karl Rove himself once ran. But it was Jackson, not Connell, who led the nascent conservative movement on campus. "Barry was trying to start up Republicanism at the college level, to shake things up," recalled one classmate. "There was not a lot of Republicanism until Barry tried to get students involved."

"To liberals, Barry was sort of the boogeyman," said another. "He was one of those people who always knew where he wanted to go. He was looking to go places politically, not as a candidate but as an operative."

Over the next fifteen years, both Connell and Jackson won key positions in Republican politics. In 1988, they both worked for George H.W. Bush's presidential campaign in the Iowa caucuses, after which Connell was promoted to Bush's Washington headquarters and tasked with developing a database to track delegates attending the Republican National Convention. When the elder Bush became president in January 1989, Connell, only twenty-five, won a presidential appointment to the Department of Energy.

Meanwhile, in 1991 Barry Jackson became chief of staff to a newly elected congressman named John Boehner (R-Ohio). In 1994, while still working for Boehner, Jackson became director of Newt Gingrich's Contract for America. He is said to have played a powerful role behind the scenes as architect of the Contract for America, and in helping the Republicans win back control of the House in 1994.*

In 1994, Connell formed New Media Communications, a small tech shop he and Heather operated out of the basement of their home in Richfield, Ohio, midway between Cleveland and Akron. It was the dawn of the Internet, and Connell knew technology could play a key role. "He was a very self-motivated guy," said Mark Brabant, a graphic designer for New Media. "I had no idea how connected he was politically."

The Connells' home proudly displayed a photo of Connell with the Bushes at the 1989 inaugural of George H.W. Bush. "He was scrambling, trying to get into the big time," said Len Peralta, a freelancer for New Media.

He wasn't just building websites. Connell put together voter lists and targeting models to project voter turnout down to the precinct level. He developed databases and web services for David Horowitz's

---

*More recently, as chief of staff to Speaker of the House Boehner, Jackson played a key role in steering the bitterly contentious 2011 debt deal through the House of Representatives.

frontpagemag.com, John Kasich's (R-Ohio) Pioneer PAC, Dick Armey's (R-Tex.) Majority Leader's Fund, and the Freedom Project PAC, a political action committee run by Boehner. "Mike was the concept man," explained Heather. "He said, 'This is where the Internet is going; this is what your website needs to do.' In terms of technology, it was as if he could see into the future."

By 1997, Connell was designing Jeb Bush's website for the '98 Florida gubernatorial race. At a time when most sites merely posted text and photos online, Connell created a truly interactive site that was hailed by an Ohio business magazine as "the first real statewide site that truly tied together the technology of the Internet and the mechanics of getting elected."

In 1998, Jeb Bush won in Florida, and another New Media client, Bob Taft, was elected governor of Ohio. Connell was on a roll. Immediately after Jeb's victory, Connell won IT contracts in Florida for the executive office of the governor and for the Departments of Education and Community Affairs. The highly partisan Connell had penetrated the nonpartisan public-service sector for the first time.

New Media opened offices in Tallahassee, Florida, the state capital, and in Washington, D.C. Then, New Media joined forces with the DCI Group, a high-powered strategic public affairs consultancy and lobbying firm run by Thomas J. Synhorst, to form DCI/New Media LLC, based in Connell's home of Richfield, Ohio. By late 1998, New Media put together sites for GOP organs in Nebraska, Ohio, New Jersey, Iowa, Pennsylvania, and Florida. Soon, the Republican National Committee signed on.

"He was the best in the business," said Bert Coleman, a GOP consultant based in Arizona. "He understood not just web-based voter outreach, he also understood politics. Some Internet companies may understand all the bells and whistles, but they also have to understand messaging. Mike did."

By 2000, Connell's modest business had grown into a $3 million operation with thirty-eight employees. New Media won no fewer than eleven Pollie Awards, presented by the American Association of Political Consultants, for creating the best political websites. Corporate clients include AT&T and Microsoft. Whether they were senators or governors, lobbyists or think tanks, on the right anyone who was anyone became a client of New Media—the National Rifle Association, the Republican Jewish Coalition, Elizabeth Dole, Bob Taft, Lamar Alexander, John Thune, Haley Barbour, Griffith & Rogers, Mike Bloomberg, George W. Bush.

The client list also included a number of projects that were near and dear to Karl Rove's heart: Jeb Bush for governor; the Florida Executive Office of the Governor; the Florida Republican Party; and last, but not least, www.georgewbush.com. Even the Republican National Committee signed on. As the *Cleveland Plain Dealer* put it in an article on Connell, "a GOP geek star" had been born.

So by the time he took George W. Bush out on the presidential campaign trail in the 2000 election season, Karl Rove had access to a powerful technological weapon. But what was his connection to the new political-information companies? On the one hand, in a corporate and legal sense, Rove had absolutely nothing whatsoever to do with any of these companies. On the other, they were astoundingly effective tools that could serve his interests.

SmarTech was a case in point. Launched as Talon Communications, aka NextLec, the company also did business as st3, a name it acquired when it bought SmarTech and hired Jeff Averbeck. In late 2001, the original company filed for bankruptcy, but it was soon relaunched as Airnet, frequently using the SmarTech brand, with Averbeck as CEO, and continued to acquire more and more political clients.

Altogether, it was such a bewildering array of dot-coms that no one connected them to Rove. And it wasn't just SmarTech that had so many identities. Mike Connell's operations, which were hosted at SmarTech, included New Media and GovTech Solutions. And Tom Synhorst had at least ten companies in Arizona alone.*

Moreover, these companies served a wide range of Republicans—not just Rove. "Everybody uses SmarTech," explained one well-placed Republican operative, a Rove rival as the 2012 election approached. "It's not a Karl Rove creation." In addition to hosting George W. Bush's sites and Rove's emails, among the hundreds of other sites the company hosted were scores of sites for Newt Gin-

---

*TSE Enterprises, DCI Properties, DCI Group, DCIG Holdings, FLS DCI, FYI Messaging, Goodsijn, Autocall, and DCI Companies.

grich, Rick Santorum, the Koch brothers, and other political figures who were not terribly fond of Rove.

Finally, aside from a visit in 2007 to a Chattanooga barbecue joint, Rove's presence in the city was nil. SmarTech's principals said they had no contact with him. Employees never saw him or heard him call.

But because of the way Rove and his associates structured their relationships, that mattered little. Through Reynolds, DeWitt's investments in SmarTech's predecessor, the company was already firmly established as a political operation serving Rove and his associates. As a result, the company depended on conservative political clients for most of its revenues. "Jeff Averbeck was now running it and he knew how to get political clients through Reynolds," said one figure close to SmarTech, "and what he had to do to make them happy."

The source added that Rove was not a presence in the office, but that Averbeck regularly talked to Mike Connell, who, of course, was working for Rove's candidate.

"Rove and his people work through surrogates, so it is really hard to account for what they do," the source added. "Those guys run those operations almost like they are running black ops. That's the way it's going to work every time. Rove is careful enough that there's no way to hold him directly to account for anything. There's nothing more than a conversation he had with somebody. No emails. It was always a guy who knows a guy who is actually doing the work."

Which wasn't difficult, given that key figures such as Mike Connell, the chief architect of George W. Bush's website and the Bush-Cheney transition site, also swore fealty to the entire Bush family. "I wouldn't be where I am today without the Bush campaign and the Bush family," Connell told a reporter. "I'm loyal to my friends and I'm loyal to the Bush family, so there is only one place I can be in 2000."

Rove delighted in his new technological resources. "It's only natural that Karl would get into technology," said Roger Stone. "He was always technologically advanced. It used to be handbills or direct mail, and now it is emails. All that has changed is the method of delivery."

As George W. Bush's first presidential campaign got under way, operatives such as Mike Connell, Barry Jackson, and Tom Synhorst began to play key roles. On February 1, 2000, Bush, who had been touted as the inevitable Republican nominee, was routed by John McCain in the New Hampshire primary, losing by nearly twenty points. A Bush victory in the South Carolina primary on February 19 was essential. As had happened in other campaigns run by Rove, dirty tactics rose to the fore. Bush supporters distributed flyers calling McCain the "fag candidate," spread rumors that McCain's wife, Cindy, was a drug addict, that he had fathered an illegitimate child with a black prostitute, and that McCain's years as a North Vietnamese prisoner of war had rendered him mentally unstable, unfit for the presidency.

To make matters worse, the illegitimate child rumor played off the fact that the McCains had adopted a dark-skinned infant from a Mother Teresa orphanage in Bangladesh.

In Moore and Slater's *The Architect,* John Weaver, a former business partner of Rove's who ended up managing McCain's race for president against Bush, is cited pointing out the corruption of the electoral process. "It's gotten to where you have to actually destroy— not just defeat, but destroy—your opponent," he said. "And not just destroy them politically but destroy them personally, professionally; drive them not only from the political battlefield but from being able to be gainfully employed, try to get them indicted, attack their family. That's beyond winning and losing. That's about destruction. Some of that is evil, pure evil."

According to Bush forces, the man behind the whispering campaign about McCain was Tom Synhorst. A master at the art of push polls, Synhorst was widely suspected of conducting a similar operation for Bob Dole's presidential campaign in 1996, asking whether voters could support presidential candidate Steve Forbes given that he had a "promiscuously homosexual father."

Even though Rove had no official links to Tom Synhorst's companies, Synhorst had worked Bush's Texas gubernatorial campaigns and his presidential campaign, and got tens of millions of dollars in contracts after Rove endorsed his work. "I know these guys well," Rove said. "They become partners with the campaigns they work with. From designing the program to drafting scripts, from selecting targets to making the calls, in a professional, successful way they work as hard to win your races as you do."

Another company, DCI, which Synhorst owned with Mike Connell, was so closely tied to Rove that Democrats called it "Karl Rove Central." DCI was referred to as the "center to the Washington conservative dark arts" by the *Washington Monthly*, and DCI consultants were pioneers in "astroturfing" and the use of incendiary push polls. But these operatives were not on Rove's payroll, so what they did could not be blamed on him. No fingerprints.

Similarly, when it came to astroturfing, DCI took pride in eschewing mass media in favor of direct contact between constituents and elected officials. In addition to its push-poll phone banks, affiliates of DCI offered to generate for its clients hundreds of thousands of letters "on your behalf—all unique, but conveying your desired message. Each letter is personalized, individually signed, and often includes a handwritten postscript from the constituent." The campaigns got into trouble, the *Los Angeles Times* reported, only when it became clear some of the letters had been written by dead people and others were from nonexistent cities, such as Tucson, Utah. Nevertheless, thanks to his ties to Rove, says one rival Republican operative, Synhorst "became a very wealthy man. . . . He got fed a lot of Bush work. Monster contracts."

If these tactics seemed extreme, a key to them could be found in a 2000 pamphlet called "The Art of Political War," by David Horowitz, which Rove praised as "the perfect guide to winning on the political battlefield." In it, Horowitz wrote, "In political warfare you do not fight just to prevail in an argument, but to destroy the enemy's fighting ability. Republicans often seem to regard political combats as they would a debate with the Oxford Political Union, as though winning depended on rational arguments and carefully articulated principles. But the audience of politics is not made up of Oxford dons, and the rules are entirely different. . . . Politics is war. Don't forget it."

By April 2000, Bush's nomination was all but inevitable. Anticipating that their star client would soon occupy the White House, Connell and Synhorst launched GovTech Solutions, an offshoot of New Media that would handle government websites, just as Connell had begun to do in Florida. New Media had focused on earning a reputation as the "Bell Labs of the Republican Party," and had cultivated a highly partisan clientele, but GovTech was the opposite. It was touted as a "nonpartisan" and "woman-owned IT solutions firm." That meant Synhorst was an equal partner, but Connell's wife, Heather, was the president. In reality, Connell and Synhorst ran the show.

As the 2000 campaign wore on, New Media assumed a higher and higher profile. In June, it was hailed by Internet Campaign Solutions as having created two of the best political websites in the country, for Senator Rick Santorum and House Majority Leader Dick Armey. In July, New Media announced the redesign of georgewbush.com. On July 31, New Media began live webcasts from the Republican National Convention in Philadelphia.

Meanwhile, Connell's old friend Barry Jackson helped Rove orchestrate a twenty-five-state barnstorming tour of GOP governors for Bush two weeks before the election. Though still relatively low-profile, Jackson had become a real player, which was no surprise to those who knew him. "Barry has never been out in the forefront," said consultant Bert Coleman. "He's a behind-the-scenes guy. He understands politics, very intelligent."

On election day, of course, the entire outcome came down to whether George Bush or Al Gore had won Florida. According to *The New Republic*, in the midst of the bitterly contentious Florida election recount controversy Jackson worked with Republican strategist Ed Gillespie to orchestrate the campaign against the recount and the "spontaneous" GOP mini-riot on November 22, in which scores of Brooks Brothers–clad Republicans chanted, "Hey, hey, yo, yo, dimpled chads have got to go!" The chanting was so troublesome that ultimately they succeeded in disrupting the recount. According to *Newsweek*, the Miami-Dade canvassing board decided that it was impossible to recount by hand all the county's ballots by its Sunday deadline, and instead decided to count only those ballots which had been rejected by machines because of hanging "chads" or other imperfections. This, in turn, incensed the Republicans, who continued to turn on the political pressure.

On December 4, well before the contested election was resolved, Connell's New Media launched bushcheneytransition.com, and began handling the tech component behind Bush's Presidential Inaugural Committee. Once Bush took office, Connell was not the only one on Rove's tech team to benefit. Mercer Reynolds, who personally gave more than $456,000 to the GOP during the election cycle, was appointed ambassador to Switzerland. As for Bill DeWitt, he was appointed to the President's Foreign Intelligence Advisory Board, and his wife, Kathy, served on the National Council on the Arts.

As for Mike Connell, now that Bush was president, he had ties to Rove through Barry Jackson. Tasked with running the portentously named White House Office of Strategic Initiatives, Jackson had become deputy senior adviser to the president of the United States.

Even at this point, to the business world SmarTech was best known as another exciting new dot-com start-up that was staking its claim to the burgeoning new market of video streaming. Reports in publications such as the *Nashville Business Journal* did not even make note of any political connections.

But, in truth, most of SmarTech's revenue came from political organizations on the right. Of course, there was no reason political organizations—left, right, or center—should not use the latest technological tools. But now that Karl Rove was in the White House the calculus between SmarTech, New Media, and their clients was radically transformed. SmarTech's clients were no longer merely political partisans who were sources of revenue. They were the most powerful people in the world, and in a position to dispense favors that were enormously lucrative. Even more important, favors done for those clients by SmarTech could have extraordinary political implications.

The fact that the Republicans now controlled both the White House and Congress opened a whole new vista of possibilities. SmarTech and Connell's operation heretofore had served GOP-affiliated clients. But what if the highly partisan forces behind GovTech, which was owned by the Connells and Synhorst, hosted nonpartisan governmental bodies for which security was vital? What if the firewall that protected sensitive government documents was safeguarded by rabidly partisan Republicans—with no oversight whatsoever?

On paper, GovTech was run by Connell's wife, Heather. But in reality there was no difference between GovTech and Connell's New Media Communications. "There was no real company," said Stephen

Spoonamore, a cyber security expert who was friends with Connell. "There was just Mike. He was a political operative and the guys around him showed him how to set it up so the same company could do government contracts without even changing desks." As Connell described it to *Crain's Cleveland Business,* initially, at least, GovTech was simply a way for New Media to brand its government-related business. "When [GovTech Solutions] emerges as a separate entity remains to be seen," he said. "We'll figure it out in the next 12 to 18 months."

In early April 2001, GovTech had only a handful of government clients, most notably the executive office of the governor of Florida, then occupied by Jeb Bush. Then GovTech won contracts to build official congressional sites for various Republican representatives— among them Heather Wilson, Kay Granger, Mike Pence, Ed Schrock, and House Majority Whip Tom DeLay—many of whom used Connell's services at New Media for their campaigns.

But there were many more possibilities. Now that the GOP controlled the House of Representatives in the nation's capital, the House Administration Committee, chaired by Bob Ney (R-Ohio), awarded contracts to host sites for congressional committees and other House bodies. By mid-2002, GovTech's contracts included the House Financial Services Committee, the House Judiciary Committee, the House Ways and Means Committee, and the House Intelligence Committee. Each of these congressional committees dealt with sensitive information and, according to a source with firsthand knowledge of SmarTech, their data resided in the basement of the old Pioneer Bank Building in Chattanooga. "SmarTech and GovTech's data were all in the same facility," said this source. "It was all in SmarTech's basement."

Over time, GovTech and its successor, GSL Solutions, became a significant force in technology on Capitol Hill, having built databases and content management systems for thirty-seven members of Congress and more than a dozen congressional committees. And it wasn't just Congress. GovTech got contracts from the White House, the Department of Energy, and other government organs.

"There is a fundamental conflict of interest in having someone whose loyalty is not exclusively to the government," said Cliff Arnebeck, the Ohio attorney who has sued Blackwell and threatened to sue Rove. "It's essential that there be a Chinese wall that would completely bar potential conflicts of interest."

But now that firewall had been breached. GovTech and SmarTech, two extraordinarily partisan companies, were safeguarding highly sensitive information both in terms of partisan politics and relating to national security.

That meant political operatives at SmarTech had access to any information transmitted via these sites. "Anybody with an administrative access can see what's being developed," added Spoonamore. "Emails, committee reports, internal documentation, instant messaging, whatever they wanted. Drafts, chat, you can look at any of it."

And SmarTech provided another advantage to Rove. Now that he was in the White House, Rove's emails were subject to the Presidential Records Act mandating the preservation of all presidential records, including official emails of staffers. Rove used a SmarTech server for the vast majority of his emails so he and other White House staffers did not have to use normal White House servers and, theoretically at least, if investigated, would have the ability to evade scrutiny.

It is not clear how often, if ever, GOP partisans obtained such sensitive information. But the possibility was there. "The data is residing in their hands," said one techie in Chattanooga who was familiar with SmarTech. "They decide what they want to do with it, whether it is moral, ethical, or not."

At the time, in 2001, the era of the Internet and digital communication was very much in its infancy, and it is possible that such glaring security breaches were merely the product of innocence. But it is worth remembering that just seventeen years earlier, an American president had been forced to resign after being tied to a break-in that gave him access to just one file belonging to his Democratic rivals.

Now, for the first time, a highly partisan technology company was in the delicate position of safeguarding highly sensitive government documents and as a result had access to many thousands of files. Only time would tell what the implications of such powers might be when Bush sought reelection in 2004 or if his administration was beset by scandal.

FOUR

Sweet Home Alabama

Now that Rove was in the White House, his hands were on the levers of power as never before. After being mired in the petty minutiae of state politics for decades, he was at last firmly ensconced in the West Wing of the White House, widely seen as the brains behind the most powerful man in the world. Specifically, Rove oversaw the Office of Political Affairs, the Office of Public Liaison, and the aforementioned White House Office of Strategic Initiatives.

In short, he ran politics in the White House. And this was a White House in which politics continually trumped policy. Famously, John J. DiIulio, the University of Pennsylvania professor who ran Bush's Office of Faith-Based Initiative,* left the White House after only eight months because he came to feel his project's mission of helping the poor had been betrayed, and that it had been turned instead into a means of supporting evangelicals who were an essential part of Bush's political base.

An earnest academic who had been attracted by the rhetoric of "compassionate conservatism," DiIulio soon encountered evidence that other, less high-minded, forces were at play when he heard Karl Rove shouting about some poor anonymous soul: "We will fuck him. Do you hear me? We will fuck him. We will ruin him. Like no one has ever fucked him."

Even more appalling, DiIulio found that no one in the White House cared a whit about policy. "There is no precedent in any mod-

---

* Bush's faith-based initiative program was a project to support religious institutions that provided a safety net in economically deprived parts of the country.

ern White House for what is going on in this one: a complete lack of a policy apparatus," DiIulio told journalist Ron Suskind in his book *The Price of Loyalty*. "What you've got is everything—and I mean everything—being run by the political arm. It's the reign of the Mayberry Machiavellis."

Though he considered himself a passionate supporter of the president, DiIulio went on, in a seven-page memo, to be even more damning in his specificity: "I heard many, many staff discussions but not three meaningful, substantive policy discussions. There were no actual policy white papers on domestic issues. There were, truth be told, only a couple of people in the West Wing who worried at all about policy substance and analysis. . . . [T]he lack of even basic policy knowledge, and the only casual interest in knowing more, was somewhat breathtaking."*

In other words, White House policy—virtually all of it—was filtered through the prism of politics, which was Rove's bailiwick. Whether it was the economy, presidential appointments, national security, foreign policy, even war and peace, to a large extent the biggest concern in the White House was how such issues could help serve to build Rove's vision of a permanent majority.

As Rove pitched it to the press, his notion of realignment would be accomplished by winning over independents via the "compassionate conservatism" of George W. Bush and programs such as No Child Left Behind, the Faith-Based Initiative, Social Security reform, and the like.

But in fact Rove also benefited from highly questionable tactics that included the systematic suppression of voting among minorities, immigrants, and other groups that strongly favor Democrats and a constant drumbeat of attacks, by whatever means necessary, on Dem-

---

* After DiIulio's quotes caused a furor, White House spokesman Ari Fleischer informed the press corps that "any suggestion that the White House makes decisions that are not based on sound policy reasons is baseless and groundless." Just two hours later, the University of Pennsylvania press office issued a release using similar wording, saying, "John DiIulio agrees that his criticisms were groundless and baseless due to poorly chosen words and examples. He sincerely apologizes and is deeply remorseful." But the original quotes came from a three-thousand-word memo labeled "For/On the Record" and were given to the Pulitzer Prize–winning Ron Suskind after several months of conversations.

ocrats. "It is breathtaking," said Thomas Mann, an expert on politics at the Brookings Institution. "It's the most hard-nosed effort I've seen to use one's current majority [to try] to enlarge and maintain that majority."

It has long been common practice for incoming presidents to appoint members of their own parties as U.S. attorneys in each of ninety-three federal district courts, in which the appointee would serve as the senior federal prosecutor. And so, after taking office, one by one, as those openings occurred, the Bush administration began to fill those slots. Among the first, in the spring of 2001, just after Bush took office, were two highly prized openings for U.S. attorneys in Alabama.

Alabama, of course, has long had a curious relationship with justice. Home to both Jefferson Davis and Rosa Parks, it is not just where Davis was inaugurated as president of the Confederacy, but it is also, fittingly, where the civil rights movement was born when Martin Luther King Jr. launched the historic Montgomery Bus Boycott. In the thirties, Alabama was the site of the infamous Scottsboro Boys "nigger rape case," in which nine black youths were sentenced to death after being wrongfully convicted of rape. In the forties and fifties, Phenix City, Alabama, served as a capital of gambling and prostitution, and became notorious for violent crimes, political conspiracies, and assassinations. In 1963, it was the site of the 16th Street Baptist Church bombing by the Ku Klux Klan, which killed four young girls in Birmingham. In the seventies, it was where George W. Bush drank and partied during his controversial "lost years" in the National Guard.

It was also the locus of the untold story of Karl Rove's Alabama. Most observers saw Rove largely as a creature of Texas politics and the Bush family, but in fact he had also established a low-profile but nonetheless powerful base in Alabama. His roots there went back to 1994, when he was invited by the Business Council of Alabama to run a slate of Republican candidates for the Alabama Supreme Court. Rove seemed to feel there were no holds barred in Alabama and outdid himself in a judicial race in which Rove's candidate faced incumbent Democrat Mark Kennedy, who, as a juvenile and family-court judge, had spent years working with foundations devoted to aiding abused children. But, in the blink of an eye, Rove transformed Kennedy's strength—his campaign commercials even showed Kennedy holding hands with kids—into his weakness, thanks to a whispering campaign asserting that Kennedy was a pedophile. "We were trying to counter the positives from that ad," a former Rove staffer told *The Atlantic Monthly*'s Joshua Green. "It was our standard practice to use the University of Alabama Law School to disseminate whisper-campaign information. . . . The students at the law school are from all over the state, and that's one of the ways that Karl got the information out."

At the time, Rove was just another ambitious political consultant and was in the process of taking on the daunting task of running George W. Bush against the popular incumbent Texas governor, Ann Richards. "I didn't know who Rove was," said Don Siegelman, who was elected Alabama's lieutenant governor that year and served as governor from 1999 to 2003. "I wouldn't have recognized him if I'd seen him."

Overseeing a handful of judicial races in Alabama might appear to be too lowly a task for someone who harbored Rove's grandiose dreams. But taking over state judiciaries, as he had already started doing in Texas, was an elemental part of his vision of turning America into a one-party state. "If you control the court, you can do favors for clients like big oil and big tobacco or others," said Siegelman. A Republican judiciary meant that the money would be rolling in for both Rove's consultancy and his candidates' campaigns, so it would be easier to elect Republican governors, state legislators, and federal judges for years to come.

At the heart of Rove's Alabama operation was Bill Canary, a loyal Republican operative from Long Island who had served as an aide to President George H.W. Bush and as national field director for the Bush-Quayle campaign in 1992. Described by RNC chairman Rich Bond as an "expert political paratrooper" and "someone you dropped into a state where something needed fixing and it got fixed," Canary moved to Alabama and soon he and his wife, Republican attorney Leura Garrett Canary, were on their way to becoming the newly crowned Republican power couple in Montgomery.

"Canary had a lot of clout in the business community," said Doug

Jones, a former U.S. attorney in the state who represented Siegelman. "He's a very detailed political strategist, someone who has a constituency and whose goal has been to change the appellate judges throughout the state."

Together, throughout the nineties, with Canary's help Rove replicated his Texas "tort reform" campaign in Alabama, branding trial lawyers as villains who had created a tort hell for which the only solution was a Republican judiciary. He transformed the Alabama judiciary from Democratic to Republican, eventually crafting an 8–1 Republican majority on the state's high court.

But now that Rove was in the White House he had additional strings to pull. In the fall of 2001, former circuit court judge Alice Martin and Assistant U.S. Attorney Leura Garrett Canary were appointed U.S. attorney for Alabama's Northern District and Middle District, respectively. Because Martin was a client of Bill Canary's, and Leura Canary was his wife, that meant Rove potentially had a powerful new weapon. Come election time, he and Bill Canary could run Republicans for the highest offices in the state, while his friends in the U.S. Attorney's Office—Canary's wife, Leura, for example—could prosecute anyone they chose, including their Democratic opponents. "Rove had learned a couple of things from Watergate . . ." said Siegelman. "You don't have to create a plumbers unit inside the White House. If you take over the Department of Justice and have your people appointed, they can do a lot more and you can control elections that way."

It is not clear precisely when Rove trained his crosshairs on Don Siegelman, but it would have been more surprising if Siegelman had escaped Rove's notice. Starting out in the sixties as a protégé of Allard Lowenstein, the late antiwar activist and liberal New York congressman in the Vietnam War era, Siegelman had become the brightest star in the progressive, anti–George Wallace wing of the Alabama Democratic Party. Long after conservative Dixiecrats had fled the Democratic Party for the resurgent Alabama GOP, Siegelman somehow managed to win again and again. In the 1994 Alabama elections, Siegelman was elected lieutenant governor, as the lone Democrat among the major state officeholders in what was otherwise a GOP sweep.

Likewise, in 1998 Siegelman managed to be elected governor by a landslide, once again, the only Democrat who was victorious.

Then, in December 1998, just a few weeks after the election, at a meeting of the National Governors Association in Washington, Siegelman ran into George W. Bush, who had just been reelected governor of Texas and was now a strong contender for the White House. "We were in the lobby of the hotel and I spent about maybe ten minutes with him, talking to him, listening to him," said Siegelman, who couldn't get a word in edgewise. "I walk away and I think this guy is an arrogant airhead. I was so absolutely turned off."

Almost immediately, Siegelman called Vice President Al Gore. "I don't care who else runs," he said. "As far as I'm concerned, you're the strongest horse in the barn. We have got to beat this guy. He is bad for America. We cannot let this happen." So on March 30, 1999, just after being sworn in as governor of Alabama, Siegelman became the first governor to endorse Al Gore for the 2000 presidential race.

In other words, Siegelman was a dynamic, attractive Democrat who had been elected to each of the four statewide offices—secretary of state, attorney general, lieutenant governor, and governor—in one of the most conservative states in the Union. To Karl Rove, for whom the Solid South was vital, Siegelman was that rara avis that Republicans feared most—a Clintonesque Democrat who was perfectly positioned to break the Republican stranglehold on the South. Siegelman had just put a bull's-eye on his back.

That became even more apparent at about eight p.m. on a February evening in 2002, as Don Siegelman and his wife, Lori, took their seats at the annual National Governors Association dinner in the State Dining Room of the White House. The Siegelmans had attended the event regularly since Siegelman's election in 1998 as governor of Alabama, but now that the Republicans were riding high, for a Democrat this was the dreariest such occasion yet.

"It was awful," Siegelman recalled. "Clinton parties were *parties.* We had all kinds of entertainers, all sorts of camaraderie. Going from the Clinton era to the Bush era was like going from West Berlin to East Berlin during the Cold War."

The governors were being toasted that evening by George W. Bush, whom Siegelman had disliked from the start. Seated at Siegelman's table were a number of prominent Republicans of whom the governor was not particularly fond. To make things even more uncomfortable, Siegelman saw one other unnerving figure. In the unquestioning, jingoistic aftermath of 9/11, Karl Rove was riding high. He made his way over to the table where Siegelman sat. Finally, he tapped someone on the shoulder, pointed at Siegelman, and said, "I'd like to sit next to him."

Exactly what happened next was unclear. "I really don't remember what Rove said," said Siegelman. Besides, the words were unimportant. "It's so revealing," said a source close to the Siegelman affair. "Karl just couldn't resist seeing his prey up close and personal."

Meanwhile, GOP operatives in Alabama had begun strategizing against Siegelman, who was up for reelection in November 2002. One of the most important of those operatives was an Alabama attorney named Dana Jill Simpson. A lifelong Republican who has worked on campaigns for Ronald Reagan, George H.W. Bush, George W. Bush, and Alabama governor Bob Riley, Simpson had grown up in politics, with a father who was an active Democrat and a mother who was a dyed-in-the wool Republican.

After graduating from the University of Alabama Law School, Simpson built a legal practice in Rainsville, Alabama, and specialized in obtaining contracts from the Federal Emergency Management Agency (FEMA) for "storm gypsies"—itinerant workers who remove debris after hurricanes, tornadoes, ice storms, and other disasters. Since such contracts were both highly lucrative and depended on political contacts, Simpson made a point of cultivating her law school classmate Rob Riley; his father, Bob Riley, who later became governor of Alabama; and Rove, whose Alabama clients she had worked for.

Simpson was not on the payroll of Rove, the Republican Party, or any GOP official. Instead, according to her testimony before the House Judiciary Committee in September 2007, Rob Riley did favors for Simpson, such as helping her "storm gypsy" clients get paid for federal contracts, and, on occasion, enlisting powerful associates to help her, including Karl Rove. In return, Simpson said she provided Republicans with opposition research and discreetly followed Democratic candidates around in hopes of digging up some dirt.

* * *

In 2001, Simpson began working for the Republican gubernatorial campaign of then congressman Bob Riley against Siegelman, and regularly discussed strategy with Rob Riley, the candidate's son. "[Rob] would ask me to do little odds and ends for him, such as follow Don Siegelman," Simpson testified. "And then . . . if I needed somebody to write a letter to speed up a client getting a check or whatever, he would see if he could find somebody that would help me with that. And it was not uncommon for him to talk to Karl Rove and Stewart Hall [a partner at the Federalist Group lobbying firm] about that because he would make reference to it."

By this time, of course, Rove had become a legend in politics. In addition to putting Bush in the White House, he had almost single-handedly revitalized the Alabama Republican Party. His knowledge of state politics was encyclopedic. Getting him on board would be a great coup for Riley.

According to Simpson, at a meeting in 2001 Rove finally offered some advice to the Riley campaign in terms of how to bring down Siegelman. In an interview on CBS's *60 Minutes,* she said Rove asked her to try to take photos of Siegelman cheating on his wife.

"Karl Rove asked you to take pictures of Siegelman?" asked CBS's Scott Pelley.

"Yes," replied Simpson.

"In a compromising, sexual position with one of his aides?" said Pelley.

"Yes, if I could," Simpson said.

Simpson said she spied on Siegelman for several months, but found nothing.

In the past, Republican officials in Alabama had investigated Siegelman in an effort to link him to a campaign contributor suspected of bid rigging to get a contract from the state. They found nothing of substance against the governor. Nevertheless, within weeks of her appointment as U.S. attorney, Leura Canary reopened the case, so that by early 2002 state and federal prosecutors began reviewing Siegelman's personal financial records. As Siegelman began his reelection campaign that spring, the headlines blared, "Siegelman's

Finances Probed." Republican candidates vowed to restore integrity to the governor's office.

That these investigations took place in the wake of Kenneth Starr's witch hunt–like probes of the Clinton administration—Whitewater, Travelgate, and Monica Lewinsky—was not lost on Siegelman. "I absolutely saw parallels with Clinton," he says. But now that he was in the governor's mansion in Montgomery, Siegelman was "trying to prove that the people of Alabama had made the right decision."

To Siegelman attorney David Cromwell Johnson, there was another problem with the investigation. According to the Justice Department's code of ethics, officers of the court should be recused if there is an "appearance of impartiality." In this case, the conflict was clear. Leura Canary would benefit because her husband, Bill, would represent Bob Riley, the Republican candidate opposing Siegelman in the upcoming gubernatorial election, and because another of his clients, Attorney General William Pryor, had initiated the case. Asserting that it was "imperative that Mrs. Canary be removed from this matter," Johnson filed papers with the Department of Justice demanding that she be recused. Canary later announced that she was acceding to this request "out of an abundance of caution."

But it was not at all clear whether she was telling the truth. Normally, when a U.S. attorney is recused procedure dictates that a conflict of interest certification and a certificate of divestiture must be submitted. But, as reported in an article by Scott Horton in *Harper's,* no such formal papers were filed. Nor was the absence of such documents the only irregularity. Standard procedure also calls for a neighboring U.S. attorney to take over the case. But in this instance Louis Franklin, the head of Leura Canary's Criminal Department and, as such, someone whose career depended on her approval, was assigned to take over the Siegelman case. For all practical purposes, Leura Canary was still in charge.

When the 2002 gubernatorial race got under way that spring, the fact that Siegelman was under criminal investigation provided Republican gubernatorial hopeful Bob Riley with a ready-made campaign against the Democratic governor. Again and again, Riley railed about "the indictments, convictions, no-bid contracts, charges of corruption and pending state and federal investigations that have swirled around [Siegelman's] administration."

At the same time, Siegelman's major campaign contributors suddenly found themselves being investigated by the FBI. "An FBI agent was at their door and they were being questioned about their relationship with me," said Siegelman. "It was totally chilling. They didn't want to have anything more to do with politics after that."

Meanwhile, the stars of the Republican Party descended on Alabama to campaign for Bob Riley. House Majority Leader Dick Armey came to Auburn on July 2. Vice President Dick Cheney was in Montgomery on August 15. In October, even President Bush, who was enormously popular in Alabama, campaigned for Riley. Armed with leaks from Canary's investigation of Siegelman, Riley railed against the governor's "no-bid crony contracts and sweetheart deals" and called his administration "the most corrupt administration in my adult lifetime."

On election day, November 4, 2002, the Siegelman-Riley race was still neck and neck as returns came in late through the night. Finally, at 12:30 a.m., with 99 percent of the precincts reporting, Siegelman stood before his supporters in downtown Montgomery with his wife and children at his side. The Associated Press declared Siegelman the winner. He called on Riley to concede.

But at about the same time, Kelly McCullough, an aide to Rove who was also regional director of the Republican National Committee, called Riley and told him not to give in. The reason: There was a problem with the returns from Republican-dominated Baldwin County. Initial reports gave Siegelman 19,070 votes and Riley 31,052 in Baldwin. Even though Riley won the county, statewide, Siegelman still had enough to win the election by 3,139 votes. But after midnight officials revised the figures. The new numbers eliminated more than 6,000 Siegelman votes in Baldwin. That revision meant Riley had won.

Baldwin County probate judge Adrian Johns, the election overseer, blamed the discrepancy between the two tallies on a mysterious "programming glitch in the software." But Siegelman didn't buy it. "We knew something wasn't right," he said. "We didn't expect to win [Baldwin] county. But we knew that we could not have lost it by the margin that they claimed we did." Moreover, it was curious that the revised tally purging thousands of Siegelman votes took place late at night—immediately *after* all the Democratic observers at the polls had gone home. And it didn't make sense that a computer glitch would affect the gubernatorial race between Siegelman and Riley but not other races tabulated by the same machines using the same program. "It was as if the voters went Democrat on every ticket, but then got to the governor's race and inexplicably went Riley," Siegelman said. "Keep in mind that this anomaly only happened in this one area of this one county, the one with Republicans hanging around the voting machine in the middle of the night."

"When Baldwin County reported two sets of results, it was clear to me that someone had manipulated the results," said Auburn University political scientist James H. Gundlach in a report on the controversy, "A Statistical Analysis of Possible Electronic Ballot Box Stuffing." "There is simply no way that electronic vote counting can produce two sets of results without someone using computer programs in ways that were not intended." According to Gundlach, such electronic ballot stuffing could be accomplished by having access to the "tabulating computer at some time before the election to install [a special electronic] card and after the election to remove the card." Ultimately, he concluded, "The only way we will know for sure is if the paper ballots for Baldwin County are recounted."

Under Alabama law, each county's votes were to be sealed at noon on the Friday after the election. However, Attorney General Bill Pryor, a Republican foe of Siegelman's, decided that Baldwin County's votes had to be certified immediately, without a recount, and that anyone who broke the seal would be breaking the law. "[That's when] it really hit me," Siegelman said. "They took these ballots and treated them as a special case. They certified them . . . earlier than the law said, so that we would have to challenge the outcome."

Going to court was now Siegelman's only option. "But it was a waste of time to go to the Alabama Supreme Court, because Rove had already made it an 8 to 1 Republican majority," he said.

At just before eleven a.m. on November 18, 2002, thirteen days after balloting, with the outcome still officially in doubt, Dana Jill Simpson, known as Jill, called Rob Riley to discuss the status of the election. Riley put Simpson on the speakerphone and had Bill Canary and Terry Butts, a former justice on the Alabama Supreme Court who was now a lawyer on Riley's team, join the conversation. Even though Siegelman had effectively lost, and conceded that day, according to Simpson, Rob Riley still referred to Siegelman as "the biggest threat that we had."

"Rob, he had several names for [Siegelman], but one was 'the golden child.' Don Siegelman is kind of like a golden child for the Democratic party in our state . . . an incredible fund-raiser."

"Rob kept saying, 'I want Don Siegelman not to run' . . ." Simpson testified. "[W]e don't want to face Don running again in the future."

Then, according to Simpson, Bill Canary explained that he knew how to take care of Siegelman. "'Rob, don't worry,'" he said. "'My girls are getting him, will take care of him.'"

Simpson didn't understand exactly what Canary meant when he referred to "my girls." "I was not sure . . . I just said, 'Who's his girls?'"

Because various people appeared to be speaking on a speakerphone, Simpson was not always certain who was talking. But she is reasonably sure the man talking was Bill Canary: "I believe it was Bill Canary . . . saying, 'Leura's my wife, Jill. She works for the middle district of [Alabama as U.S. attorney]—and then Alice Martin [a former client of Canary's] works for the northern district.'"

In other words, Canary was assuring Rob Riley that his wife, Leura, and Alice Martin would use their powers as the highest federal law-enforcement officers in the state to neutralize Siegelman. "Bill Canary told him not to worry. He had already got it taken care of with Karl," Simpson said. "And that Karl had spoken to the Justice Department and the Justice Department was already pursuing Don Siegelman."

According to Simpson's testimony, that didn't satisfy Riley, however, so Canary continued: "Bill said, 'Look, I know pretty much all about this. The Justice Department's already pursuing [Siegelman].' . . . And I got the impression it had been going on for some time. . . . [W]hat I believed Mr. Canary to be saying was that he had had this ongoing conversation with Karl Rove about Don Siegelman, and that Don Siegelman was a thorn to them and . . . they were pursuing Don Siegelman as a result of Rove talking to the Justice Department at the request of Bill Canary."

At the time, Simpson found her conversations with Canary and the Rileys so extraordinary that she shared them with a friend. "She told me this stuff before the Siegelman stuff ever happened," said Mark Bollinger, a fellow Alabama attorney. "I never doubted her credibility, but it seemed far-fetched that our Department of Justice was plotting the overthrow of Don Siegelman. Who the hell would have believed her?" Exactly how reliable was Simpson's testimony?

Simpson's account has been disputed by Bill Canary, Rob Riley, and Governor Bob Riley, who asserted, "Dana Jill Simpson has no, zero, credibility. Anyone who has ever talked to her, anyone who has ever listened to her, understands that." Likewise, Karl Rove dismissed her as "a complete lunatic."

In his memoir, *Courage and Consequence,* Rove devotes no fewer than six pages in an attempt to destroy Simpson's credibility. "[B]ecause I never met the woman," he writes, "or had any of the dealings with her that she claims, I could only conclude that she must be a nut looking for a television camera and brief celebrityhood. That became clear after Simpson spoke to the House Judiciary Committee staff in September 2007."

But there are a number of reasons to take Simpson's stories about Siegelman seriously. She has survived vetting by both the House Judiciary Committee investigating the Siegelman matter and producers at CBS's *60 Minutes.* Colleagues on both sides of the political divide have corroborated key aspects of her story. Simpson has testified under oath before Congress about Siegelman. And she has produced phone records and other documents backing up her assertions that she had contacts with various key figures.

Thanks in part to her pronounced backwoods Alabama accent, Simpson, a self-styled "hillbilly from hell," has been "horribly underestimated," said her former attorney, Priscilla Duncan. "I sure wouldn't want her working against me . . ." said Tommy Gallion, another attorney in Montgomery who is close to the case. "She's brilliant. If you ask her what time it is, she'll tell you the inner workings of the clock."

In addition, in his attempt to discredit Simpson, Rove has resorted to certifiable lies. In an interview he gave in 2008 to Lisa DePaulo for *GQ* magazine, which was posted on ABC News's website, Rove tore into Simpson yet again. "She's a complete lunatic . . ." he said. "No one has read the 143-page deposition that she gave congressional investigators—143 pages. When she shows up to give her explanation of all this, do you know how many times my name appears? Zero times. Nobody checked!"

But in fact an electronic search of the document shows that Karl Rove's name appears at least fifty times in the deposition, and that Simpson offers up a number of long narratives regarding Rove's role in the Siegelman affair, which, as time would show, was by no means over.

FIVE

Unintended Consequences

In 2002, of course, few people knew or cared about Karl Rove's machinations in Alabama. The nation was still reeling from the 9/11 terrorist attacks that had taken place the previous year. Arab terrorists had destroyed the Twin Towers of the World Trade Center. Nearly three thousand innocent people had been killed. In the aftermath of the worst terrorist assault ever on American soil, President Bush's approval ratings soared to 92 percent, the highest of any president since polling began.

But for the Bush administration, going into Afghanistan in search of Osama bin Laden and al-Qaeda was not enough. For decades, neoconservative policy makers had advocated an American foreign policy in which, as Lawrence Kaplan and William Kristol wrote in *War Over Iraq,* America "must not only be the world's policeman or its sheriff, it must be its beacon and its guide."

Specifically, for neoconservatives, many of whom had found positions of power in the Bush administration, the time had finally come to implement a radical and grandiose vision of redrawing the map of the Middle East, first by overthrowing the brutal Iraqi dictator Saddam Hussein and then by "democratizing" the entire region. Neocon firebrand Michael Ledeen, a key figure in the Iran-Contra scandal, put it rather less delicately: "Every ten years or so, the United States needs to pick up some small crappy little country and throw it against the wall, just to show the world we mean business."

In the past, however, there had not been much enthusiasm in the United States for war with Iraq. But then came 9/11. Even though Osama bin Laden and al-Qaeda were to blame, not Saddam Hussein, the Bush administration established the White House Iraq Group, consisting of Chief of Staff Andrew Card, Cheney aide Mary Matalin, Deputy National Security Adviser Stephen Hadley, Cheney's chief of staff, Lewis "Scooter" Libby—and Karl Rove. Its mission was simple: to sell the nation on the idea of going to war with Iraq.*

Rove, of course, was no card-carrying neoconservative ideologue. "Karl is about power and money," said Roger Stone. "No one can say Karl Rove is a conservative or a neoconservative."

Nonetheless, to Rove, a war with Iraq was a good move politically. After all, he knew that tens of millions of evangelical Christians in Bush's constituency saw America as a Promised Land, a redemptive nation ordained to fight tyranny all over the world. The ideology of the neocons and the theology of the Christian Right meshed perfectly.

Speaking at the Republican National Committee's annual winter conference, on January 18, 2002, he argued that the war on terror was an issue that could help Republicans win the upcoming midterm elections. "We can go to the country on this issue [of terrorism]," he said, "because [Americans] trust the Republican Party to do a better job of protecting and strengthening America's military might and thereby protecting America."

Or, as he explained to *The New Yorker,* "[Voters] will see the battle for Iraq as a chapter in a longer, bigger struggle. As a part of the war on terrorism."

As a media event, this was Rove's war. From his command post in the West Wing of the White House, Rove gave talking points to press secretary Ari Fleischer, wooed the *Washington Post*'s David Broder or syndicated columnist Robert Novak, and kept the mainstream press in line at CNN, the *Wall Street Journal,* and Fox News.

---

* Test marketing for the campaign began in August, with Cheney and his surrogates asserting repeatedly that "many of us are convinced that Saddam will acquire nuclear weapons fairly soon." Making Cheney seem moderate by comparison, a piece by Michael Ledeen appeared in the *Wall Street Journal* on September 4, suggesting that, in addition to Iraq, the governments of Iran, Syria, and Saudi Arabia should be overthrown. But the real push was delayed until the second week of September. As Chief of Staff Andy Card famously put it, "From a marketing point of view, you don't introduce new products in August."

At the heart of Rove's plans was a full-fledged marketing campaign scheduled to start after Labor Day, 2002, featuring images of nuclear devastation and threats of biological and chemical weapons from a rogue Iraq with a brutal and insane dictator at the helm. The campaign even had a slogan: "We don't want the smoking gun to come in the form of a mushroom cloud." The catchphrase was such a hit that President Bush, Vice President Cheney, Secretary of Defense Donald Rumsfeld, and National Security Adviser Condoleezza Rice all used it at one time or another, sending it out repeatedly to billions of people all over the world. The problem, of course, was that the evidence that Saddam had a nuclear program was less than overwhelming—and even that turned out to be fraudulent.

Privately, Rove was quite candid about precisely what he was doing—most famously in a conversation he had with author Ron Suskind that, at the time, was not for attribution. According to Suskind, an anonymous White House source later identified as Rove "said that guys like me were 'in what we call the reality-based community,' which he defined as people who 'believe that solutions emerge from your judicious study of discernible reality.' . . . 'That's not the way the world really works anymore,' [Rove] continued. 'We're an empire now, and when we act, we create our own reality. And while you're studying that reality—judiciously, as you will—we'll act again, creating other new realities, which you can study too, and that's how things will sort out. We're history's actors . . . and you, all of you, will be left to just study what we do.'"

Creating that reality was a two-part exercise. On the one hand, it involved a campaign of manufactured spectacles and carefully selected leaks to the media that would give life to Rove's narrative casting Bush as a heroic figure defending America and the free world against savage Arab terrorists. On the other hand, it called for a damage-control campaign calibrated to destroy and discredit anyone who characterized the Iraq War as one built on lies, forgeries, and falsified intelligence, or who reported on the looting, chaos, and sectarian violence that swept Iraq, and on the failures of Bush's foreign policy.

The Valerie Plame affair has been reported at length in myriad newspapers and magazines, and in more than a dozen books, including the author's *The Fall of the House of Bush*. There has been a movie, *Fair Game,* starring Sean Penn and Naomi Watts, based on both Plame Wilson's book of the same title and her husband Joe Wilson's *The Politics of Truth.* And former White House press secretary Scott McClellan, in *What Happened: Inside the Bush White House and Washington's Culture of Deception,* offers a compelling insider account of how he was tricked into lying to the press by Bush officials intent on starting a war based on lies and forged documents.

Finally, Rove himself writes about these events in *Courage and Consequence,* putting forth an account unlike the others, one in which he is a martyred public servant hounded by prosecutors and vilified by the press for supporting a president who is bravely waging war against savage terrorists and a brutal dictator.

But in light of what we now know about Rove's modus operandi, it is worth reexamining Karl Rove's role in these historic events, which led to hundreds of thousands of deaths and reshuffled the geopolitical landscape of the Middle East.

The disinformation operation that helped launch the Iraq War began nine months before 9/11—before Bush even took office—when there was a break-in at the embassy of the Republic of Niger in Rome around New Year's Day, 2001. Not long afterward, Rocco Martino, a freelance intelligence operative, was approached by an agent of SISMI, the Italian spy agency for which Martino occasionally worked, with a proposition.* Subsequent to the embassy break-in, SISMI had assembled a file for Martino to disseminate to Western intelligence agencies and media outlets regarding Niger's relations with Iraq. The most explosive document in the file, dated July 27, 2000, was a two-page memo purportedly sent to the president of Niger concerning the sale of five hundred tons of pure uranium, or "yellowcake," per year by Niger to Iraq. This last document was particularly important because it appeared to back up later claims by the Bush administration that Iraqi dictator Saddam Hussein was developing nuclear weapons.

There was just one problem: It was fake.

---

* SISMI, Servizio per le Informazioni e la Sicurezza Militare (Military Intelligence and Security Service) was disbanded in 2007 and replaced by the Agenzia Informazioni e Sicurezza Esterna.

Exactly who, on the American side, was most responsible for making sure this information—or, rather, disinformation—became a key component of America's march to war is a mystery that has never been solved. But one name that has come up repeatedly is that of Michael Ledeen, who held the Freedom Chair at the American Enterprise Institute think tank and became chief rhetorician for the neoconservatives who wanted to remake the Middle East in the image of the West. "Creative destruction is our middle name, both within our own society and abroad," Ledeen wrote just nine days after the attacks. "We must destroy [our enemies] to advance our historic mission."

His incendiary rhetoric aside, Ledeen is also known for his participation in disinformation operations, sometimes done in conjunction with SISMI, that have served the neoconservative cause for more than two decades.* Because he had ties to both Italian intelligence and top

---

* According to an investigation in the *Wall Street Journal,* in 1980, Ledeen, who was then the Rome correspondent for *The New Republic,* teamed up with Francesco Pazienza, a charming and sophisticated operative in SISMI, the Italian intelligence agency, in a SISMI disinformation operation to tilt the 1980 American presidential election by writing articles critical of Jimmy Carter's brother Billy in the scandal that became known as Billygate. According to Pazienza, Ledeen even had a coded identity, Z-3, and received at least $120,000 from SISMI that was sent to him in a Bermuda bank account.

Not long afterward, according to *The Rise and Fall of the Bulgarian Connection* by Frank Brodhead, a series of articles by Ledeen about what was known as the Bulgarian Connection, falsely tied the 1981 attempted assassination of Pope John Paul II to the KGB.

Most famously, during the Iran-Contra scandal of the eighties, Ledeen won notoriety for introducing Oliver North to his friend the Iranian arms dealer and con man Manucher Ghorbanifar, who had been labeled "an intelligence fabricator" by the CIA. According to Larry C. Johnson, a former CIA officer who was deputy director of the State Department Office of Counterterrorism from 1989 to 1993, "The C.I.A. viewed Ledeen as a meddlesome troublemaker who usually got it wrong and was allied with people who were dangerous to the U.S., such as Ghorbanifar."

By the time Bush took office in 2001, Prime Minister Silvio Berlusconi had appointed two men known to Ledeen to powerful positions in the Italian national security apparatus. Minister of Defense Antonio Martino was a well-known figure in Washington neocon circles and had been close friends with Ledeen since the 1970s. Ledeen also occasionally played bridge with the head of SISMI under Berlusconi, Nicolò Pollari. "Michael Ledeen is connected to all the players," said Philip Giraldi, who was stationed in Italy with the CIA in the 1980s and has been a keen observer of Ledeen over the years.

officials in the Bush administration, including Rove, knowledgeable observers have suggested Ledeen may have participated in a disinformation operation that played a key role in triggering the Iraq War.

Ledeen has denied the charges.

In any case, as the Niger documents in various forms were disseminated to sundry media outlets and intelligence agencies, analysts at the CIA, the State Department, the Pentagon, and other Western agencies repeatedly assessed them as fraudulent. "The reports made no sense on the face of it," said Ray McGovern, a CIA analyst for twenty-seven years. "Most of us knew the Iraqis already *had* yellowcake. It is a sophisticated process to change it into a very refined state and they didn't have the technology."

"The whole idea of the Niger deal was absurd," added Colonel Lawrence Wilkerson, who served as chief of staff to Secretary of State Colin Powell at the time. "The idea that you could get that much yellowcake [five hundred tons] out of Niger without the French knowing that you have a train big enough to carry it, much less a ship, is absurd. The fact that people swallowed the story shows how woefully ignorant most people are."

Nevertheless, even though American analysts had already discredited the documents, in February 2002, Vice President Dick Cheney, in his zeal to launch an invasion against Iraq, gave the claims new life, and urged the CIA to check them out again. A few hours later, Valerie Plame Wilson, who worked in the Counterproliferation Division of the CIA, got a call from the vice president's office saying Cheney was "interested and wanted more information" about whether Iraq had been seeking yellowcake from Niger. In response, she wrote a memo to the division's deputy chief, saying, "My husband has good relations with both the PM [prime minister] and the former Minister of Mines (not to mention lots of French contacts), both of whom could possibly shed light on this sort of activity."

And so, on February 26, 2002, Plame Wilson's husband, who had been a trusted member of George W. Bush's diplomatic team in Iraq before the Gulf War and who later served as ambassador in two African nations, went to Niger to find out whether there was any truth to the claims.

When Wilson returned, he told CIA officials that he had found no evidence to support the uranium charges. But the White House wouldn't let go. Over the next year, the claims made in the Niger documents surfaced repeatedly in one form or another in Italy, England, and the United States and were batted down each and every time by French intelligence, by analysts at the CIA in Rome and Langley, the State Department, the ambassador to Niger, Joe Wilson, and others—on at least fourteen different occasions in all. Yet each time, neoconservative policy makers and operatives from Vice President Cheney's office brought them back into play.

"They were just relentless," said Lawrence Wilkerson. "You would take it out and they would stick it back in. That was their favorite bureaucratic technique—ruthless relentlessness. Stick that baby in there forty-seven times and on the forty-seventh time it will stay. I'm serious. It was interesting to watch them do this. At every level of the decision-making process you have to have your ax out, ready to chop their fingers off. Sooner or later you would miss one and it would get in there."*

Then, on January 28, 2003, in his State of the Union address, President Bush uttered the famous sixteen words that launched the Iraq War: "The British government has learned that Saddam Hussein recently sought significant quantities of uranium from Africa."

On March 7, five weeks later, in a report to the United Nations Security Council, the International Atomic Energy Agency director general Mohamed ElBaradei publicly exposed the Niger documents as forgeries. The *Washington Post* put the story on its front page: "A key piece of evidence linking Iraq to a nuclear weapons program appears to have been fabricated, the United Nations' chief nuclear inspector said yesterday in a report that called into question U.S. and British claims about Iraq's secret nuclear ambitions."

Likewise, on March 8, Wilson appeared on CNN and, without discussing his own trip to Niger, debunked charges that Niger sold

* Last-minute negotiations between the White House and the CIA led to a decision to attribute reports about the Niger uranium deal to British intelligence rather than to classified American intelligence. The British repeatedly claimed to have other sources but refused to identify them.

uranium to Iraq. On March 14, Senator Jay Rockefeller IV, the ranking Democrat on the Senate Intelligence Committee, in response to the IAEA's exposé of the Niger documents, wrote a letter to FBI chief Robert Mueller asking for an investigation because "the fabrication of these documents may be part of a larger deception campaign aimed at manipulating public opinion and foreign policy regarding Iraq."

But none of this could stop the rush to war. The Pentagon's PR juggernaut had devised the brilliant strategy of "embedding" reporters as part of the dazzling high-tech war machine, and it was signing up credulous reporters who were ready for the adventure of a lifetime.

On *Meet the Press,* Dick Cheney said critics had "consistently underestimated or missed what it was Saddam Hussein was doing," and went even further than other proponents of the war. He added, "We know [Saddam] has been absolutely devoted to trying to acquire nuclear weapons. And we believe he has, in fact, reconstituted nuclear weapons."

On March 19, 2003, Bush went to the White House Situation Room, where he got on the line with his field commanders. "For the peace of the world and the benefit and freedom of the Iraqi people," he said, "I hereby give the order to execute Operation Iraqi Freedom. May God bless our troops."

And so the Iraq War began. Which meant Rove was now committed to a narrative that was ultimately ruled by the most unpredictable and ungovernable force of all: war.

Soon enough, Saddam's quick defeat provided Rove with his finest public relations moment. To be sure, critics carped when no WMDs were found immediately after the American invasion, and Rove knew the failure to find WMDs could undermine Bush's credibility in the 2004 elections. But for now that was overshadowed by the lightning quick overthrow of Saddam Hussein, a brutal dictator right out of central casting. All of which gave Rove an opportunity to transform Bush, whose National Guard service years earlier was filled with unanswered questions, into a war hero.

On May 1, 2003, just six weeks after the invasion, Rove staged a true Hollywood media spectacle, with George W. Bush emerging from the cockpit of a fighter jet after a dramatic tailhook landing on an aircraft carrier; then, clad in fighter pilot regalia, striding triumphantly across the deck of the USS *Abraham Lincoln,* the "Mission Accomplished" banner at his back. The scene was shot at dusk, and the lighting had that special glow that comes when the sun is just above the horizon. It was so cinematic that the *Detroit Free Press* asserted that Bush was bringing his "daring mission to a manly end."

Soon, however, Iraq was beset by massive looting, murders, assassinations, sectarian strife, chaos, and fear. The United States had disbanded the Iraqi police and military, more than half a million strong, and many were still armed. Further, the United States had alienated the Sunnis by banning anyone affiliated with Saddam Hussein's Ba'ath Party from participating in the government. It was the perfect recipe for civil war.

A few days after Bush's aircraft carrier landing, Rove's triumphant script began to unravel. On May 6, 2003, *New York Times* columnist Nicholas Kristof, citing unnamed sources, broke the story of Joe Wilson's trip to Niger the previous year, writing that "a former US ambassador to Africa was dispatched to Niger . . . and reported to the CIA and State Department that the information was unequivocally wrong."

Kristof was not the first mainstream journalist to question the veracity of the documents. Earlier, on March 31, in *The New Yorker,* Seymour Hersh had flatly called them forgeries. But now the White House was starting to take note. Vice President Cheney's office made inquiries at the State Department and quickly figured out that Kristof's unnamed source was Joseph Wilson.

At the time, Rove, and most of America, was still exulting over the quick U.S. victory. This was a time to celebrate—and gloat. Bush's approval rating soared to 77 percent, according to an ABC News/ Washington Post poll, his highest rating since 9/11. The media lionized Deputy Secretary of Defense Paul Wolfowitz, one of the neocon architects of the war, as "Wolfowitz of Arabia."

Rove himself was giddy. During a surprise visit to the Middle East with President Bush and top White House aides that spring, Rove offered to snap photos for soldiers who wanted their pictures taken with high-level Bush officials. "Step right up," Rove shouted. "Get your photo with Ari Fleischer—get 'em while they're hot. Get your Condi Rice."

Then, suddenly, things changed.

On Sunday, July 6, 2003, Karl Rove, as he did on most Sundays, headed outside in pajamas and an old T-shirt to get the papers. First, he skimmed the front page of the *New York Times* before jumping to the op-ed section of the Week in Review. There he came upon the piece by Joe Wilson that reverberated throughout the world. Titled "What I Didn't Find in Africa," the piece concluded that "it was highly doubtful that any such transaction [of uranium to Iraq] had ever taken place."

Rove had never even heard of Wilson before, but by the time he finished reading, he knew he had to act fast. He made two calls right away: one to the White House communications shop and the other to the National Security Council, asking what to make of Wilson's charges. "I was told that at that point, no one knew exactly what to think," Rove recalled. "Wilson's op-ed hit them like it hit me, a lightning bolt out of a clear blue sky." Here was hard evidence available to the general public that the Bush administration had knowingly twisted evidence to rush to war.

Later that morning, Rove watched Wilson on NBC's *Meet the Press* and judged his newfound nemesis to be "pompous and more than a little sanctimonious."

"[I]t was clear to me he meant to do the president grave harm," Rove wrote in *Courage and Consequence*. "His charges came at a critical moment: no weapons of mass destruction had been found in Iraq, and now a former ambassador was saying he advised the vice president's office—nine months before the State of the Union and a year before the United States invaded—that Saddam had not tried to acquire African uranium."

After *Meet the Press,* Rove spoke to White House aide Dan Bartlett and picked up what details he could. Specifically, Rove was told that Cheney had not initiated Wilson's mission, which, of course, raised the question of who had.

Next, Rove turned on CNN. Wilson was telling the nation that when he heard the president's State of the Union address he believed the United States had already "effectively debunked the Niger arms uranium sale. . . . [T]hat information was erroneous and that they knew about it well ahead of both the publication of the British white paper and the president's State of the Union address."

Acutely aware that damaging information was circling the globe and he didn't have all the answers, Rove was almost sick to his stomach. This was the kind of story that could spread like an uncontainable virus. "The White House press corps was ready to pounce on the story," Rove recalled. "Its members were on a long-scheduled trip to Africa with the president and had little to do but get worked up over Wilson. . . . As for us, we were caught not knowing all the facts right away."

Over the next two days, Rove says he received "the key rebuttal points" at the early morning White House senior staff meetings, learning, specifically, that Wilson had not been sent to Africa by Cheney or his office, that no report about Wilson's trip had been sent to the White House, and that the CIA was dubious about Wilson's information.

In his memoir, Rove characterizes himself during this period as a largely passive observer who was gathering as much information as he could about Wilson. What were the real facts behind Wilson's trip? How reliable was Wilson? What was his background? And it is clear, as the public record shows, that Vice President Dick Cheney and his aide Scooter Libby played principal roles in going after Joe Wilson and Valerie Plame Wilson. As White House press secretary Scott McClellan put it, "Under the cloak of anonymity, the vice president and trusted aide Scooter Libby soon began an effort to discredit Wilson with selected journalists. Unknown to anyone else in the compartmentalized, internally secretive White House—including the White House chief of staff, the national security adviser, and the CIA director—the president declassified key portions of information from the October 2002 NIE [National Intelligence Estimate on Iraq] for the vice president and Libby to use in this effort."

Nevertheless, Rove was very much an active partner in implementing a strategy to discredit Wilson as a way to protect the president.

"It is impossible for any of us to believe that this happened without Karl knowing about it," said author James Moore, not long after the investigation began. "When you cross this man in the political arena, he gets even; and he gets even in a way that he doesn't just defeat you, he is compelled to destroy you. He doesn't know how to do a measured response when he is angry, and so he leaks information about people that destroys them."

According to Scooter Libby's subsequent grand jury testimony, which contradicts Rove's memoir, on Monday, July 7, the morning after Wilson's op-ed piece, Rove emphasized that the White House needed to get the word out that Vice President Dick Cheney did not send Joseph Wilson to Niger. Libby's notes also indicate that the "Uranium story is becoming a question of the President's trustworthiness," and it was a story that was leading all the newscasts.

"[N]ow they have accepted Joe Wilson as [a] credible expert," Rove complained. Cheney and others agreed with him that that had to change.

At the press briefing later that morning, Rove's talking points gave White House press secretary Ari Fleischer plenty of ammo with which to belittle Joseph Wilson's op-ed, protect Cheney, and shift the blame to the CIA.

"Well, there is zero, nada, nothing new here," Fleischer said. "Ambassador Wilson, other than the fact that now people know his name, has said all this before. But the fact of the matter is in his statements about the vice president—the vice president's office did not request the mission to Niger. The vice president's office was not informed of his mission and he was not aware of Mr. Wilson's mission until recent press accounts—press reports accounted for it. So this was something that the CIA undertook as part of their regular review of events, where they sent him."

The next day, on Tuesday, July 8, the Bush White House, which rarely, if ever, admitted error, made an extraordinary concession. In the *Washington Post*, Walter Pincus published a story headlined "White House Backs Off Claim on Iraqi Buy," which included a quote: "Knowing all that we know now, the reference to Iraq's attempt to acquire uranium from Africa should not have been included in the State of the Union speech." The *New York Times* also quoted a senior official who said, "We couldn't prove it, and it might in fact be wrong."

Wilson's column had been the tipping point. Until its publication, the media had raised questions about the failure to find WMDs in Iraq, but had been largely supportive of the war. But now CNN, CNBC, Associated Press, NPR, MSNBC, and the British media had all raised questions about whether the Niger documents indicated that the United States had manipulated intelligence to start the war.

This admission was a sop that was intended to quiet them down. "It was the first public acknowledgment that the White House should not have made the uranium allegation in his State of the Union address and that the information on which it had been based was incomplete or inaccurate," wrote Scott McClellan, who replaced Ari Fleischer as White House press secretary that chaotic week, in his memoir, *What Happened: Inside the Bush White House and Washington's Culture of Deception.* "At the White House, everyone hoped the acknowledgment would put the sixteen-word controversy to rest. The reality was the opposite."

Even though the White House appeared to concede Wilson's most elemental point, in fact, its statement was vague, general, and left too many questions unanswered. Did Iraq have a nuclear program or not? Was Iraq getting uranium from elsewhere? Did the administration know the Niger documents were flawed before the speech and use them anyway? Had it knowingly used disinformation to start the war?

Rather than answer those questions, Rove and Scooter Libby escalated the battle with Wilson and Plame Wilson. According to McClellan, at roughly the same time, Rove, Libby, and other high-ranking administration officials, including Deputy Secretary of State Richard Armitage and then press secretary Ari Fleischer shared another piece of classified national security information—"the identity of Joe Wilson's wife, Valerie Plame, and her role as a CIA employee in helping to arrange Wilson's investigative trip to Niger."

Astoundingly, in his memoir, Rove dismisses this last detail as "almost an afterthought. Everyone's focus was on the substance of Wilson's charges, not the sponsor for his African junket."

But in fact, the leaking of Valerie Plame Wilson's identity as an undercover CIA operative was the single biggest detail in launching a federal investigation that dealt a devastating blow to the Bush administration. And at the time, inside the White House, as presidential press secretary Scott McClellan explained, exposing Plame Wilson's identity was vital to the scheme "to discredit Wilson, by undermining his public assertions that he had been sent to Niger by the CIA at the vice president's request. . . . These decisions—to defend the president and to launch a stealth campaign to discredit Joe Wilson and expose his wife's CIA role as part of that campaign—would have profound long-term implications for the credibility of the Bush administration."

And so the leaking began in earnest.* The information was not something syndicated columnist Bob Novak was seeking. "I didn't dig it out, it was given to me," he told reporters. "They thought it was significant, they gave me the name and I used it."

A crusty, cantankerous conservative who embraced his nickname as the "Prince of Darkness" (he used it as the title for his autobiography), Novak immediately decided he wanted to discuss the issue with Karl Rove. He and Rove had been close friends for more than two decades. It happened that Novak's mother-in-law lived in Hillsboro, Texas, and when Novak and his wife spent their Christmas holidays there he had made a point of getting together with Rove. The two men occasionally socialized together, and talked two or three times a week—but always off the record.

"Karl and I had grown close since he began plotting Bush's path to the presidency as early as 1995," Novak wrote in his memoir, *Prince of Darkness: 50 Years of Reporting in Washington.* "In four decades of talking to presidential aides, I never had enjoyed such a good source inside the White House."

---

* The leaking of Valerie Plame Wilson's identity had already begun, in a tentative way, in June, after Nicholas Kristof's column, when Deputy Secretary of State Richard Armitage, who was second-in-command to Colin Powell, leaked the story about Plame Wilson to *Washington Post* reporter Bob Woodward. But Woodward didn't bite. Likewise, Scooter Libby had told *New York Times* reporter Judith Miller that Wilson's wife "may have worked on unconventional weapons at the CIA." But she also declined to do a story.

Novak considered Rove "a grade A-plus source. While he did not dispense state secrets, confidential political plans, or salacious gossip, Rove always returned my phone calls. He knew everything, and while he did not tell me all that he knew, he never lied or misled me and often steered me away from a bad tip."

But Novak was well aware that the relationship was a two-way street: "Rove obviously thought I was useful for his purposes, too."

That was the way things worked between reporters and high-level sources in Washington, and to Novak it also meant that "[w]hat you did not find in my columns was criticism of Karl Rove. I don't believe I would have found much but reporters—much less columnists—do not attack their sources."

It was also clear that if Novak was to be "useful for [Rove's] purposes" the information being leaked to Novak was intended to damage Wilson's reputation. Indeed, later that day, a friend of Wilson's named Howard Cohen saw Novak on the street in downtown Washington. According to Valerie Plame Wilson, Cohen, who did not know Novak but recognized him from his TV appearances, began walking with Novak and asked him what he thought about Joe.

"Wilson's an asshole," Novak told Cohen. "The CIA sent him. His wife, Valerie, works for the CIA."

Cohen immediately told Wilson. "It was pretty clear to me [at that point] . . . that the nature of the smear campaign they were going to run against me was going to include the betrayal of her identity as a covert CIA officer," Wilson said.

Novak's next step was to follow up by calling Rove.* There were two topics on Novak's mind. "I think that you are going to be unhappy with something that I write," he told Rove, "and I think you are very much going to like something that I am about to write."

The "unhappy" news Novak wanted to discuss was the appointment of a former Clinton official to a national security position, a move about which Novak was quite critical. This, in fact, appears to have been the principal reason for Novak's call.

---

* According to Novak's court testimony, it is unclear whether this phone call took place on July 8 or 9.

But then Novak switched to the topic he thought Rove would like. He told Rove he had learned that Joe Wilson's wife "worked at the CIA in counterproliferation and that she—not Vice President Cheney—had suggested Wilson be sent to Niger."

Rove acknowledged familiarity with the subject. He added that Wilson's report was oral, and that Wilson had given an oral report to the CIA, which summarized it in another report that the White House wanted to declassify. Rove told Novak that Wilson's account "lacked meaning and was inconclusive."

The entire conversation, according to Novak, lasted about ten minutes.

As Rove saw it, he added nothing to Novak's story—and he certainly did not confirm it. "I didn't know or think I was his second source," Rove wrote. "After all, he hadn't asked for confirmation. If he had, I would have said that I couldn't do so."

But the exact words that Rove uttered are open to question. According to Rove's memoir, "All I had done was offer up the tentative 'I've heard that, too.'"

Novak's memory was slightly different. As he recalled the conversation, Rove said, "You know that, too."

The difference was slight. But it was enough to have real significance.

On the morning of Friday, July 11, Rove got a call from *Time* magazine's Matt Cooper. Once again, his memory is hazy. In his memoir, Rove goes so far as to say "to this day, I have no recollection" of their conversation. Nevertheless, it was important enough that immediately after the phone call, both he and Cooper wrote emails about it.

At the time of the conversation, Rove had already talked to Novak, but no one had yet written about Plame Wilson's identity. The best record of what transpired comes from Matt Cooper, who, at 11:07 a.m. on July 11, 2003, immediately after the conversation, wrote an email about it to his editor.

"Spoke to Rove on double super secret background* for about

---

* "Double super secret background" was, Cooper later said, "a play on a reference to the film *Animal House*, in which John Belushi's wild Delta House fraternity is placed on 'double secret probation.'"

two mins [sic] before he went on vacation..." Cooper wrote, adding, "Please don't source this to rove or even WH."

According to the email, Rove pointedly tried to discredit Wilson. Specifically, Cooper wrote, Rove gave him a "big warning" not to "get too far out on Wilson,"* and said Wilson's report should not be taken seriously because CIA director George Tenet or Vice President Dick Cheney had not authorized his trip. Rather, "it was, KR said, Wilson's wife, who apparently works at the agency on WMD issues who authorized the trip."

Rove added, the email said, that "not only the genesis of the trip is flawed an[d] suspect but so is the report. [H]e [Rove] implied strongly there's still plenty to implicate Iraqi interest in acquiring uranium fro[m] Niger."

Later, Cooper recalled that Rove concluded by saying, "I've already said too much."†

The entire conversation was on background, but Rove's message was clear: Don't believe Joe Wilson.

Even though Rove repeatedly professed not to remember the conversation, including in his subsequent grand jury testimony, he did something that might be interpreted as an effort to cover his tracks.

Rove sent an email to Deputy National Security Adviser Stephen Hadley about his talk with Cooper. That way, in the event that the conversation was discovered, Rove would have his own version of what transpired. "[Cooper] immediately launched into Niger?" he

---

* Cooper's original email has a number of typographical errors—"get too war out" instead "get too far out"—which he later corrected in the interests of clarity. The text quoted reflects those corrections.

† That afternoon, Cooper sent a more cogent account of the conversation to his editors: "A startling charge from a senior administration official that we need to handle with some caution.... The senior administration official warns that we shouldn't get too far ahead of ourselves on Wilson. The official says that Wilson was not sent by the director of the CIA or by Dick Cheney and when it comes out who sent him, it will be embarrassing. When I pressed the official, he said it was somebody in the agency involved in WMD, Wilson's wife. This guy was not an emissary, the source claimed. His report is nowhere near the truth, the official added; in fact, it may be totally wrong. The Iraqis, this person said, probably were seeking Niger uranium. He said the documents will be declassified in the next few days and eople [sic] will see a different side to Wilson."

wrote Hadley. "Isn't this damaging? Hasn't the president been hurt? I didn't take the bait, but I said if I were him I wouldn't get *Time* far out in front of this."

But in his email to Hadley, Rove conspicuously omitted one rather salient detail about his conversation with Cooper—namely, that he had leaked Valerie Plame Wilson's name.

Meanwhile, Rove was optimistic. He believed Novak's piece might help the White House regain control of the narrative. Later that day, Scooter Libby dropped by Rove's West Wing office. "Rove told me that Bob Novak had run into Ambassador Wilson in a Green Room at some point and . . . somehow Ambassador Wilson sort of turned him off," Libby later testified. Rove added that Novak thought Wilson had "an axe to grind." And, according to Libby, Rove mentioned one other significant detail—namely, "that Ambassador Wilson's wife worked at the CIA."

As Libby saw it, Rove clearly was happy about Novak's piece. "[H]e thought it was a good thing that somebody was writing about it," Libby testified. "But it was more body language and the tone in which he said things rather than any words he used. . . . I didn't know what Mr. Novak was going to say in his column, so if he said the right things, I'd be happy about it. I was glad . . . it was going to be clear in the column that it wasn't us, that it was the CIA who sent [Wilson], that would have been a good fact."

Of course, not everyone felt the same way about Novak's forthcoming piece. After he talked to Rove on July 8, Novak had called Wilson about Valerie's ties with the CIA. Wilson declined to talk about his wife, but now he and Valerie knew what Novak was up to. "I was uneasy knowing that a journalist had my name and knew my true employer," Valerie wrote in *Fair Game.* She quickly informed her supervisors in Counterproliferation, who assured her that "it would be taken care of."

Less than a week later, on the morning of July 14, Wilson woke early, got the newspaper, and went back to the bedroom where Valerie was just waking up.

"Well, the SOB did it," he said.

Novak had finally published. Asserting that Wilson's mission was initiated "at a low-level" and that his report from Niger was "regarded by the CIA as less than definitive," Novak defended the Bush administration from allegations that it had deliberately used forged documents to invade Iraq.

But Novak's real bombshell was buried in the sixth paragraph. "Wilson never worked for the CIA, but his wife, Valerie Plame, is an agency operative on weapons of mass destruction," he wrote. "Two senior administration officials told me that Wilson's wife suggested sending him to Niger to investigate the Italian report. The CIA says its counterproliferation officials selected Wilson and asked his wife to contact him."

Rove was trying to change the narrative. He was destroying the messenger. Equally important, he was putting forth a message to whistle-blowers: If you dare speak out, we will strike back. To that end, the cover of Valerie Plame Wilson, a CIA operative specializing in WMDs, had been blown by a White House that was supposedly orchestrating a worldwide war against terror.

Plame Wilson was devastated. "I felt like I had been sucker-punched, hard, in the gut. Although we had known for several days that he had my name and knew where I worked, we never believed for a moment he would actually print it or that the Agency would allow it. It was surreal."

There were national security consequences that far transcended issues about Plame Wilson's career and her family's personal safety. To her friends, relatives, and neighbors, she was the suburban mother who worked as an energy analyst at a firm called Brewster Jennings. Now her cover was blown. "What about the many people overseas I had met under completely innocent circumstances?" she wrote. "They too could come under a cloud of suspicion if their governments learned of our contact. . . . The next instantaneous thought was for my family's security. There are many disturbed people out there who hate the CIA or anyone associated with it. I didn't want to deal with a stranger on my doorstep or worse. Furthermore, Al Qaeda now had an identified CIA operative to put into their target mix."

Astoundingly, Rove and other administration officials were so obsessed with discrediting Wilson that it did not occur to them that leaking Plame Wilson's identity was a major security breach—this at a time when the nation as a whole, especially the Bush administration, was obsessed with national security. Later, a senior official in the White House told the *Washington Post* that the leaks of Plame Wilson's identity were "[c]learly . . . meant purely and simply for revenge." The official added that the leaks were "wrong and a huge miscalculation, because they were irrelevant and did nothing to diminish [Joseph] Wilson's credibility."

Now the unintended consequences of the leaks began to take on a life of their own. It started slowly, largely because many key figures in the Washington press corps simply liked Bush, Rove, and company too much to act as watchdogs. "Let me disclose my own bias . . ." wrote David Broder, the lead political columnist for the *Washington Post* and celebrated dean of the Washington press corps. "I like Karl Rove. In the days when he was operating from Austin, we had many long and rewarding conversations. I have eaten quail at his table and admired the splendid Hill Country landscape from the porch of the historic cabin Karl and his wife Darby found miles away and had carted to its present site on their land."

But on July 16, two days after Novak's column, journalist David Corn posted a piece on *The Nation*'s website called "A White House Smear." It asked if Bush officials decided to blow the cover "of a US intelligence officer working covertly in a field of vital importance to national security—and break the law—in order to strike at a Bush administration critic and intimidate others?"

The article explained that the leak may have violated the Intelligence Identities Protection Act, and noted that if the leak was accurate, Valerie Plame Wilson was apparently working as a NOC—an acronym for nonofficial cover, a term used by intelligence services to refer to agents or operatives who assume covert roles in organizations without ties to the government and are therefore working without a safety net and are subject to the risk of criminal prosecution and possibly execution by foreign governments. The Long Island newspaper *Newsday* soon followed, raising similar questions.

Even though most of the press was still silent, at last a pivotal point in the national conversation had arrived. For nearly two years in the aftermath of 9/11, George W. Bush had been lionized for bravely launching the War on Terror. When his approval rating inevitably descended from its stratospheric highs, he was able to send it soaring again by invading Iraq.

But already in Iraq the rosy glow of a quick victory was giving way to the realization that a sectarian conflict and growing insurgency were leading to a bloody civil war and a quagmire with no exit strategy. Bush's approval ratings were in near free fall. And now that Plame Wilson had been outed, it looked as if a vindictive White House was willing to go to extraordinary lengths to destroy those who disagreed with it. There were intimations of a federal investigation.

UPI's Nicholas Horrock compared the deceit to Watergate. The battle to control the narrative had been joined. And, of course, as Rove knew all too well, a presidential election was in the offing, Bush's numbers were plummeting, and something had to be done.

Fortunately, Karl Rove had other irons in the fire.

SIX

The Turn of the Screw

As the Plame Wilson affair bubbled to the surface in the summer of 2003, another project was under way, but one with a much lower profile. In fact, it was so far under the radar that it did not generate the slightest blip of media attention—even though it ultimately may have changed the course of American history.

Team Rove's latest feat took place in July 2003, when Mike Connell snared yet another government contract for GovTech, this time with the Office of the Secretary of State of Ohio. The deal did not seem particularly noteworthy at the time, especially in light of the highly sensitive contracts GovTech had already won. Nor was the amount of the contract—$132,995—of any real consequence.

Specifically, the contract called for GovTech to develop a "new interactive Election Night Web site" for 2003 and 2004, including a "Mirror site" of Ohio's election returns "to provide a failover solution in the event of failure of the primary installation on Election Day."

As usual, SmarTech would provide the actual hosting, as it did for most of GovTech's clients. There is no evidence that Rove played any role whatsoever in engineering the deal or discussed it with the principals on either side. But on both sides of the contract, the signatories just happened to have ties to Rove.

For GovTech, of course, there was Connell, Rove's cyber guru. Exactly how often he had contact with Rove during this period is unclear. His wife, Heather, says she does not know, and Connell himself was not terribly forthcoming about his relationship with Rove. "Good ideas will go as high as they have to [to] get approval," he told a reporter. But according to Stephen Spoonamore, the computer security expert who was friends with Connell, "Mike had a direct relationship with Rove. He told me so. He discussed meetings he had with Rove."

Connell also had close ties to Rove through Barry Jackson, his college roommate, fraternity brother, and the best man at his wedding, who had become deputy senior adviser to the president of the United States, tasked with running the portentously named White House Office of Strategic Initiatives. Jackson was, in effect, Karl Rove's Karl Rove, and charged with coordinating the planning and development of long-range strategies for the president. That meant, as Bush White House spokesman Dana Perino later put it, that Barry Jackson was "the most important person you don't know."

On the other side of the contract was Ohio secretary of state Ken Blackwell, who held two seemingly inimical positions. On the one hand, as secretary of state, Blackwell's job was to ensure that the 2004 presidential election in Ohio was conducted in a fair, nonpartisan manner. On the other hand, as honorary co-chairman of the Bush campaign in Ohio (Blackwell said the position carried no responsibilities, was merely honorary, and was shared by other statewide officials), Blackwell was Karl Rove's man on the ground leading a no-holds-barred campaign to win the most vital state in the Electoral College.

As a conservative African-American, Blackwell came to Rove's team from an unusual background that included liaisons with black militants, marginal left-wing parties, and professional football before launching a career as a movement conservative. A dashiki-clad lefty as a youth, Blackwell invited a Black Panther Party leader to speak on campus at the same time he was playing college football at Xavier University in Cincinnati. After graduating, Blackwell made it as far as the Dallas Cowboys training camp before giving up the sport. Then, as a member of the left-leaning Charter Party, he was elected to the Cincinnati city council and became mayor in 1979. It was not until he began considering statewide and national offices that he became a Republican.

From 1989 to 1990, Blackwell served in the administration of President George H.W. Bush as undersecretary in the Department of Housing and Urban Development. Following his defeat in an Ohio congressional race, Bush appointed him ambassador to the United Nations Human Rights Commission. In 1998, he was first elected secretary of state of Ohio. A strict fiscal and social conservative, Blackwell, as an activist Christian evangelical, was a strong proponent of gun ownership rights and the banning of same-sex marriage. But it was his position as secretary of state that made him so useful strategically to Rove as the presidential election approached.

On February 24, 2003, more than a year and a half before the presidential election, Blackwell was summoned to the White House to meet with Rove, who told him and other Ohio Republicans that their state would play a crucial role in the 2004 election. Immediately afterward, Blackwell said he resolved to make sure Ohio's election machinery could handle a down-to-the-wire 2004 presidential contest, and vowed to use federal money allocated for Ohio's elections to overhaul the state's voting machines. He added that the state's election results would be "under a microscope" and there would be "zero tolerance for error."

The next day, according to the *Cleveland Plain Dealer*, Blackwell's office announced that it would be awarding contracts for new voting machines throughout the state. Exactly which manufacturer would get the contract was unclear, but, the *Plain Dealer* reported, "Several county elections officials also have voiced concerns that Blackwell appears to favor Diebold Inc., an Ohio-based voting-machine maker, and has touted the company in meetings with them."

However, two problems with Diebold soon emerged. For one thing, in July, Avi Rubin, a computer scientist at Johns Hopkins University in Baltimore, tested the Diebold system, which used touch screens and smart cards, and found it was highly vulnerable to tampering and using it created a risk of massive election fraud. "The people who developed that [software] code I wouldn't trust to run an election, regardless of whether that was a practice system," he said. "They showed a lack of any understanding of computer principles that I teach in Computer Security 101."

Questions about its technical expertise aside, critics also asserted that Diebold was a highly partisan, Republican firm—too partisan to be trusted to count votes. The previous three years, Diebold had made a total of $195,000 in campaign contributions, all of which, according to the Center for Responsive Politics, went to Republicans. In August, Diebold CEO Walden O'Dell, after attending a strategy session with wealthy Bush benefactors at the president's ranch in Crawford, Texas, sent out a fund-raising letter to fellow Republicans saying he was "committed to helping Ohio deliver its electoral votes to the president next year." Consequently, State Senator Jeff Jacobson, a Republican, asked Blackwell to disqualify Diebold, but was refused.

Over the next six months, charges and countercharges flew back and forth between Diebold and its critics. There were concerns about the integrity of its software, over whether its machines could be hacked, over the absence of a paper trail in the event that a recount was necessary, over whether Diebold was too partisan, over alleged conflicts of interest by a Diebold critic, and over a lawsuit by a Diebold competitor. But, ultimately, forty out of Ohio's eighty-eight counties selected Diebold as the voting machine they would use in the November 2004 elections.

As for GovTech, its contract with Blackwell's office received no such scrutiny, perhaps because it would serve merely as a more obscure "failover site" and would have no direct contact with the public. However, SmarTech would provide the actual hosting of the site, as it did for most of GovTech's clients.

During the rest of July 2003, the saga of the forged Niger documents and the leaking of Valerie Plame Wilson's identity continued to dribble out. Initially, in the media, serious criticism of the White House was confined to outlets such as *The Daily Show with Jon Stewart*, HBO's *Real Time with Bill Maher*, MSNBC's *Countdown with Keith Olbermann*, and hundreds of liberal blogs on the Internet.

But the Democrats had finally begun to see an opening. "This may be the first time in recent history that a president knowingly misled the American people during the State of the Union address," said Democratic National Committee chairman Terry McAuliffe. "Either

President Bush knowingly used false information in his State of the Union address or senior administration officials allowed the use of that information. This was not a mistake. It was no oversight and it was no error."

And so a counternarrative emerged in opposition to the official version put forth by the White House. In July, Senate Majority Leader Tom Daschle (D-S.Dak.) called for Congress to fully investigate the use and misuse of prewar intelligence. Senator Carl Levin (D-Mich.) asked how a "bogus" claim could have become so crucial to the case for war. Ted Kennedy suggested the Niger claims amounted to a "deliberate deception."

Then *Time* magazine, in an article by Matthew Cooper and two other reporters, asked: "Has the Bush administration declared war on a former ambassador who conducted a fact-finding mission to probe possible Iraqi interest in African uranium?"

With much of the Washington press corps still promoting Rove's line, a seesaw narrative-counternarrative battle held forth in the media. It was a game at which Rove was exceedingly well practiced. But with the Valerie Plame Wilson leak, he and Libby were in dangerous territory and wouldn't let go. "Scooter and Karl are out of control," deputy press secretary Adam Levine told White House communications director Dan Bartlett after the *Time* article appeared. "You've got to rein these guys in."

On July 17, Rove flew to San Francisco and drove north to Bohemian Grove, a rustic 2,700-acre camp in the California Redwoods that served as a retreat for a private gentlemen's club founded by railroad barons during the Gilded Age of California in the 1870s. The site of secret meetings for a global elite for decades, it had hosted Republican presidents Eisenhower, Nixon, Reagan, and George H.W. Bush, and guests such as James Baker, Dick Cheney, Donald Rumsfeld, David Rockefeller, William Casey, and Henry Kissinger.

Rove, of course, had long been comfortable in such august company, but the Bohemian Club had a certain exotic cache thanks to its legendary weekends during which members donned red, black, and silver robes and conducted a ritual in which they worshipped a giant stone owl.* In an earlier visit there, Rove had found himself seated next to Mickey Hart, the drummer for the Grateful Dead, while listening to a speech by Henry Kissinger.

On this occasion, however, Rove ran into Chris Matthews, the host of MSNBC's *Hardball*. When they began to discuss the Niger affair, Rove was on rapid-fire spin cycle and was appalled at Matthews's response. According to Rove, "[T]he cable TV host hadn't noticed the CIA's July 11 statement that said the White House had not sent Wilson on the mission to Niger. Nor did he know that the information Wilson returned with actually bolstered the case that Iraq had attempted to acquire uranium from Niger. Nor did Matthews seem aware that the CIA had concerns about how Wilson collected his information and therefore considered his conclusions uncertain. In short, Matthews appeared to know squat."

On Monday, July 21, back in Washington, Rove called Matthews again, and the conversation soon turned to Joe Wilson and his wife, Valerie. The precise words that were used during this phone call are not in dispute, but who uttered them is. In his memoir, Rove disavows using the offending phrase and attributes it to Matthews.

In any case, as soon as the conversation ended, Matthews called Joe Wilson. "I just got off the phone with Karl Rove. He says, and I quote, 'Wilson's wife is fair game.'"

Wilson hung up, saw that Valerie had arrived home, and relayed the news. "[Joe] had a look on his face that I had never seen before," she wrote.

Wilson took it as Karl Rove's declaration of "war on two citizens, both of them with years of government service."

Later that night, *Newsday* posted an article in which intelligence officials confirmed that Plame Wilson was an undercover operative. Now Valerie Plame Wilson knew that her CIA career was truly over.

On August 8, for the first time, the *New York Times* ran a page-eight story in which Wilson said his wife had been outed as a warning to others who might challenge the White House.

---

* Upon visiting the club in 1882, Oscar Wilde is reported to have said "I never saw so many well-dressed, well-fed, business-looking Bohemians in my life."

Even though the Wilson story had begun five weeks earlier, in the op-ed pages of the *Times,* by and large its news pages had been hospitable to the Bush administration, and had even trumpeted phony stories planted by the White House about WMDs in Iraq. Now those stories were being undermined in the very pages that had once given them legitimacy.

On August 12, PBS's *Frontline* gave the story a full hour on national television. The fact that Plame Wilson was an attractive blonde did not hurt the story's viability, and by September the dam had given way. Hundreds of outlets reported how the Bush administration twisted intelligence to start the war—and had begun to strike out against Wilson and Plame. Now the entire media ecosystem wanted to know who had leaked Valerie Plame Wilson's identity. On TV, there was ABC, CBS, NBC, and CNN; there were hundreds of newspapers, from the *Los Angeles Times* to the *Washington Post,* and thousands of websites.

Speaking at the Ensley Forum in Seattle, Washington, Wilson made it clear who he thought was the culprit. "At the end of the day," he said, "it is of keen interest to me to see whether or not we can get Karl Rove frog-marched out of the White House in handcuffs."

Why did Wilson name Rove? "People we knew claimed to have sources in the White House told us," he said. But at the end of the day, Wilson had no real hard evidence.

One person who was especially curious about these matters was President George W. Bush.* On an unspecified date in late August or early September, the president found himself in the Oval Office with White House chief of staff Andy Card and Attorney General Alberto Gonzales, who was particularly concerned about rumors that Rove may have been behind the leak. Gonzales advised Bush not to call Rove, but the president insisted.

There are some discrepancies between President Bush's account of their conversation and Rove's. But according to Rove, the president asked, "Are you the one behind this Novak column?"

---

* In his memoir, *Decision Points,* President Bush's discussion of the Valerie Plame Wilson affair makes no reference whatsoever to Rove's role in the scandal.

"I explained to Bush that I'd talked to Novak and said 'I've heard that, too' when the reporter told me about Wilson's wife, whose name and role I didn't know."

Rove then told President Bush, "Novak hadn't asked me to confirm anything."

In other words, Rove implied, Novak must have found confirmation elsewhere.

He further told Bush, "[I]t sounded to me like he had his story and was running with it, and had even talked with the CIA."

Rove was suggesting that Novak's second source was the CIA. Of course, that simply was not the case.

According to Rove, Bush asked specifically about Novak. Presumably, because Bush did not ask more generally about the Plame Wilson leak, Rove did not give the president extraneous information, such as the fact that he had leaked Plame Wilson's identity to Matt Cooper.

Again, according to Rove, Bush sounded annoyed with the conversation, but he took Rove at his word.

Rove was a "dear friend," Bush said, but he "wouldn't tolerate these kinds of leaks even if it was his good friend." If Rove had been the leaker, he would fire him. But "if Rove said he didn't do it, then he didn't do it. If he was involved, he'd tell me. I trust him."

Bush had been Rove's close friend for more than twenty years. The two men had an intense, symbiotic relationship that had taken them both from a failed congressional campaign all the way to the greatest seat of power in the world. It was hard to believe that Karl Rove would lie to his patron, the commander in chief.

Meanwhile, on September 16 the CIA recommended to the Justice Department that the FBI investigate the Plame Wilson leak. The Justice Department's counterespionage section supported the request, thereby suggesting that there was ample reason to believe a crime had been committed in the leaking of Plame Wilson's name.

That meant the scandal now merited a "gate" suffix, as in Plamegate, a label that neglected to take into account the fact that she used her married name. More important, the investigative and judicial machinery of the federal government jolted into action. There would be hearings, subpoenas, depositions, and evidentiary inquests—in short, all the mechanisms necessary to create an ongoing media spectacle with a ready-made narrative complete with heroes and villains, comedy and tragedy. A national whodunit was now under way in which the entire country wanted to know who outed the blond secret agent. Was it Scooter Libby? Karl Rove?

And the questions started coming fast and furious. On September 16, for the first time, a reporter asked Scott McClellan if Rove was the leaker.

"I haven't heard that," McClellan responded. "That's just totally ridiculous."

In fact, McClellan had not yet talked to Rove about the issue, and wanted to make sure he hadn't gone out on a limb. "Rove had known Novak for years and spoke with him from time to time, and of course he was known for playing hardball politics," wrote McClellan in *What Happened*. "But surely even he knew that leaking classified national security information would cross a line."

Shortly after the briefing, he saw Rove in the Roosevelt Room of the White House. "You weren't one of Novak's sources, right?" McClellan asked.

"Right," said Rove.

"Just wanted to make sure," McClellan said.

"You're right," Rove said.

But the story was just getting started.

On Saturday, September 27, Mike Allen of the *Washington Post* emailed Rove for a follow-up story on the Plame affair, and Rove dutifully informed McClellan's deputy, Claire Buchan, about it.

Buchan then told McClellan that "Rove had volunteered to her that Novak had called him about Plame. He hadn't confirmed Plame's CIA status because he didn't know about it."

"Karl spoke to Novak?" asked McClellan.

This was news—big news. About ten days earlier, Rove had told McClellan he was not Novak's source. He had not let on that he had had any conversation whatsoever with Novak.

Rove should have let him know, McClellan felt. So he called Rove, who repeated what he had told Buchan earlier that day: "He [Novak] said he'd heard that Wilson's wife worked at the CIA. I told him I couldn't confirm it because I didn't know."

That wasn't true, of course. McClellan had no way of knowing Rove was lying, but he could see where the new story line was heading. The White House was the target of the federal investigation. So McClellan went even further. He had already seen Rove parse the issue a little too finely for his taste. If he was to defend Rove, a prime target in the administration, he needed a categorical answer. So he asked Rove a completely "unambiguous, unqualified catch-all question."

"Were you involved in this in any way?"

"No," Rove replied. "Look, I didn't even know about his wife."

This was both untrue and different from what Rove claimed to have told the president. Rove kept the conversation short. He did not volunteer that he'd also had a conversation about Wilson's wife with Matt Cooper of *Time*.

But McClellan had no reason to believe that Rove was less than forthcoming. He knew the press might come after the White House, but because he trusted Rove he felt confident that he could push back convincingly if necessary.

However, the next day, Sunday, September 28, 2003, the *Washington Post* had another story citing an unnamed senior administration official who characterized the leak as part of a very deliberate scheme to discredit Joe Wilson. According to the source, before Novak's column ran, "two top White House officials called at least six Washington journalists and disclosed the identity and occupation of Wilson's wife. . . . 'Clearly, it was meant purely and simply for revenge,'" the senior official said of the leak. The source added that the leaks were "wrong and a huge miscalculation, because they were irrelevant and did nothing to diminish Wilson's credibility."

Novak's column had cited "senior administration officials." As Rove saw it, that probably ruled out the CIA. Astoundingly, it did not even occur to him that he might be one of the sources himself—or so he said. "I couldn't accept the idea it was someone in the West Wing; I thought Novak's sources were more likely in the State Department."

But why on earth would Karl Rove think the State Department was behind the leak? That would have been counterintuitive in the extreme. The White House viewed the State Department, under

Colin Powell, as reluctant warriors who would be naturally sympathetic to Wilson's plight.

Rove would suspect State only if he had a specific reason to think they were involved.

By this time, the press smelled blood in the water. Before meeting with the press the next morning, Scott McClellan touched base with President Bush, as he frequently did "to get his thoughts on how to respond to a particular issue, to make sure I was keeping him fully abreast of what was on reporters' minds."

"Hey, Scott," the president said. "What's on the press's mind today?"

"The reports of a Justice Department investigation into the leak of Valerie Plame's name," McClellan replied. "I want to talk to you about it before I gaggle."

"Karl didn't do it," the president said, clearly referring to accusations that Rove had disclosed her identity.

"I know . . ." McClellan began.

"He told me he didn't do it," the president continued, cutting off McClellan, then shifting his gaze to Chief of Staff Andy Card, who was gesturing with his hands to get the president to stop talking.

Bush looked at Card as if he were irritated.

"What?" Bush said. "That's what Karl told me."

"I know," Card said. "But you shouldn't be talking about it with anyone, not even me."

At the press conference that day, McClellan told reporters the president considered the allegations "a very serious matter" and that he would fire anyone who had leaked Plame Wilson's name.

But, at the same time, McClellan also had Rove's back. He made it clear that "the President knows" Rove is not involved, then continued. "I've made it very clear, from the beginning, that it is totally ridiculous," McClellan said. "I've known Karl for a long time, and I didn't even need to go ask Karl, because I know the kind of person that he is, and he is someone that is committed to the highest standards of conduct."

Then he added, "I have spoken with Karl about this matter. . . . I've made it very clear that he was not involved, that there's no truth to the suggestion that he was."

There was just one problem, McClellan later explained: "What I'd said was not true. I had unknowingly passed along false information."

And McClellan had gotten that false information from Rove himself.

McClellan wasn't the only one looking out for Rove. According to a report in the *National Journal* by investigative reporter Murray Waas, Robert Novak called Rove, also on September 29, "to assure him that he would protect him from being harmed in the investigation."

"You're not going to get burned," Novak reportedly told Rove. "I don't give up my sources."

During the same conversation, Novak reportedly referred to a 1992 incident in which Rove had been fired from President George H.W. Bush's reelection campaign for allegedly leaking to Novak information about the inside workings of the campaign.

According to Rove, Novak told him things would be different with the Plame Wilson affair. "I'm not going to let that happen to you again," he said.*

Later that same day, as if to make good on his promise, Novak changed his story dramatically. In July, he had told reporters for *Newsday* that he didn't dig out the information about Plame Wilson, that "it was given to me. . . . They thought it was significant. They gave me the name, and I used it."

That quote suggested the White House was actively trying to out Plame Wilson.

Now, on his CNN program, *Crossfire,* Novak gave a very different spin to the same episode, which suggested exactly the opposite. "Nobody in the Bush administration called me to leak this," he said. "In July, I was interviewing a senior administration official on Ambassador Wilson's report, when [the official] told me the trip was inspired by his wife, a CIA employee working on weapons of mass destruction. Another senior official told me the same thing."

* Later, in front of a grand jury, Rove characterized the phone call as a "curious conversation," and said he did not know what to make of it. He chose to omit any mention of it in his memoir.

Novak continued in the same vein. Two days later, on Wednesday, October 1, 2003, he had another column out on Plamegate:

> During a long conversation with a senior administration official, I asked why Wilson was assigned the mission to Niger. He said Wilson had been sent by the CIA's counterproliferation section at the suggestion of one of its employees, his wife. It was an offhand revelation from this official, who is no partisan gunslinger. When I called another official for confirmation, he said: "Oh, you know about it."

As Rove saw it, the column contained good news and bad news. The good news: "Novak was telegraphing to the world that I wasn't the original source for his story." The phrase *partisan gunslinger* needed no translation. Novak was also asserting that Plame Wilson's outing was merely the result of "an offhand revelation," not a devious plot to out her as revenge against her husband.

But Novak was also indicating, in a way only Rove could understand, that Rove was his second source. Here is where the difference of a few words had enormous significance—enough, potentially, to send Karl Rove to jail.

On the one hand, there was Rove's version, "I've heard that, too," as opposed to Novak's "Oh, you know about it," or, as Novak later "distinctly" recalled, "You know that, too."

The two men were clearly referring to the same conversation. But Rove's "I've heard that, too" offered Novak almost nothing if that's what he was using to confirm Plame Wilson's identity. In an interview with the *National Journal,* Geneva Overholser, a journalism professor at the University of Missouri, raised questions about the propriety of Novak's writing a story of such importance if that were the case. "A comment like that could mean it's just gossip going around," said Overholser, who is a former chair of the Pulitzer Prize board and a former editor of the *Des Moines Register.* "That means something different than an affirmation to go with a story. If that was the basis for Novak's story, it was the slimmest of reeds."

On the other hand, Novak's version—"You know that, too"— suggests, unlike Rove's account, that Rove had not merely heard a rumor but had knowledge—real knowledge, not mere hearsay—that

Plame Wilson worked for the CIA. In other words, Novak was saying he felt Rove had confirmed the story.

When Rove read that, he was in a panic. Their stories were so close—but not close enough. "Novak treated my offhanded 'I've heard that, too' as a confirmation—and that was really bad. And while it had sounded to me in our conversation that Novak had been in touch with the CIA, that's not the impression his column left. I was sick to my stomach."

At the time, no one understood all this except Rove and Novak. Nonetheless, it presented a serious problem for Rove. According to his memoir, he had given the president a somewhat similar account. But that wasn't good enough because he had clearly told Bush that he was not Novak's source. In his first conversation with McClellan, Rove had simply said he was not one of Novak's sources, period, without mentioning that they had talked. Later, when pressed, he told McClellan he *had* talked to Novak but claimed not even to know about Valerie Plame Wilson. That was an outright lie. Rove had repeated that lie to the press at various times. And by withholding the fact that he had confirmed Plame Wilson's identity to Matt Cooper of *Time,* Rove had lied yet again to both McClellan and the president.

So far, he had gotten away with it. That was because McClellan and President Bush had both gone to bat for him and said unequivocally that Rove was not Novak's source.

But Novak had made it clear, albeit in a coded way, that Rove *was* the confirmation source.

And now the feds were coming.

At 9:30 a.m. on Friday, October 10, 2003, FBI inspector John C. Eckenrode and two special agents, Jeffrey Stetler and Kirk Armfield, came to the White House to interview Rove. He appeared to be relaxed, and offered "to help in any way I can."

A highly experienced fifty-year-old agent, Eckenrode had investigated leak cases before—one involved a confidential congressional briefing—and he knew how difficult they were to prosecute. He made a point of starting out with a broad, open-ended remark. "It sounds like there's stuff you want to tell us," he said.

Rove responded with essentially the same story he told President Bush about Novak's call: "I told him everything about my call with Novak. In detail. That he'd called July 7. . . . That I'd returned Novak's call the next day. . . . I went through it all, point by point."

Eckenrode then asked Rove if he had spoken to any other journalist about Valerie Plame Wilson before Novak's column was published.

"No," said Rove. He added that the issue had come up only when he talked to Novak.

In light of his talk with Matt Cooper, this last answer, of course, was indisputably untrue, though Rove did not see it that way. "I had told them the truth, and I knew I hadn't committed any crime," he wrote in *Courage and Consequence.* "Yet I was still being drawn into a story that I knew, even then, was going to weigh on me.

"I decided I needed to toughen up. I was letting the press chatter and Wilson's comments eat away at me. I felt my concerns and stress were becoming visible to colleagues and affecting my work." Rove's wife, Darby, told him he "needed to give this all over to a Higher Power."

It was good advice, thought Rove, but hard to do.

According to the *National Journal,* several weeks after they began investigating Plamegate, FBI agents informed Attorney General John Ashcroft that they believed Rove was conspiring with Robert Novak to hide Rove's role in the leak. The reason: Before his September 29 call to Rove, Novak, in his interview with *Newsday,* had all but said the White House was jamming Valerie Plame Wilson's identity down his throat. But after the call Novak changed his story dramatically, asserting repeatedly that the White House didn't call him and that it was simply an offhand remark.

During an October 5 interview on *Meet the Press,* Novak once again emphasized the second version. "I know when somebody's trying to plant a story," he said. "This thing—this came up almost offhandedly in the course of a very long conversation with a senior official about many things, many things, including Ambassador Wilson's report."

There was that word again: "offhanded." Both Novak and Rove

used it repeatedly to describe the outing of Plame Wilson. In fact, Rove alone used it three times, in various forms, in his memoir. The term also had potential legal significance. The Intelligence Identities Protection Act of 1982 makes it a federal crime for those with access to classified information to *intentionally* identify and expose the identity of a covert agent affiliated with U.S. intelligence agencies. In part because proving intent was so challenging, prosecutors had found the act so difficult to prosecute that it had been used in only one successful prosecution in its entire history.*

When asked about the discrepancy between his two very different accounts, Novak accused *Newsday* reporter Timothy Phelps of misquoting him. But Phelps stood by his story. Moreover, Phelps's story was consistent with others written by *Time*'s Matt Cooper and Judith Miller of the *New York Times.*

So now it appeared that investigators were looking into whether Rove had conspired with Novak to obstruct justice. According to Dan Richman, a professor of law at Fordham University and a former federal prosecutor for the Southern District of New York, "It's possible that prosecutors would view their [September 29] conversation as the beginning of a conspiracy to obstruct justice, given that [Rove and Novak] had reason to believe that an investigation would soon be under way."

But Richman added that obstruction of justice cases are difficult cases to make, because "you almost have to literally take the jury inside a defendant's head to demonstrate their intent."

On December 31, 2003, Attorney General John Ashcroft recused himself from the investigation. The reason was simple: Ashcroft was a longtime political client of Rove's. Their relationship went back to the mid-eighties, when Ashcroft successfully ran for governor of Missouri, and later when he was elected senator. Representative John Conyers (D-Mich.) called Ashcroft's apparent conflict of interest a "stunning ethical breach that cries out for an immediate investigation."

---

* In 1985, CIA agent Sharon Scranage was sentenced to five years, and served eight months, for espionage and giving the names of other agents to her boyfriend. But the letter of that law set a very high bar: the violator had to have knowledge of the agent's covert status as well as the fact that the CIA was concealing the agent's identity.

For the Wilsons, "it was a belated but welcome Christmas present," Plame Wilson wrote. "Ashcroft had clearly given some thought to his extensive financial and personal ties to Karl Rove."

But to Rove, it was an unwelcome development. Rove had been responsible for getting Ashcroft his job as attorney general, and it would have been reassuring to have the nation's senior law-enforcement official, who was so deeply indebted to him, overseeing the investigation. Privately, out of view, Rove continued to obsess about the case. He was "determined not to let White House colleagues, the press, the public, anyone else—up to and including Darby—see me suffer. Stiff upper lip, soldier on, all that. . . . But behind the mask, the whole thing was scaring the hell out of me."

For all his clout in the Justice Department, when it came to appointing federal prosecutors Rove did not always get his way. One trouble spot had been Illinois, where, in 2001, Republican senator Peter Fitzgerald had earlier unilaterally announced that Patrick Fitzgerald (no relation) would be the new U.S. attorney for the Northern District—without waiting for White House approval.

Rove had been incensed at the time. "Talk about a power grab! The Constitution says the president appoints U.S. attorneys, the Senate exercises the power of advise and consent. Not this time. In the name of comity, the White House went along with the headstrong senator."

As it turned out, the Illinois case now had particular relevance. Since Ashcroft had recused himself from the Plame Wilson investigation, it fell to Deputy Attorney General James B. Comey Jr. to appoint a special prosecutor to lead the Plame Wilson investigation, and, much to Rove's dismay, Comey was appointing Patrick Fitzgerald to take the lead. "Nearly three years later, the man I'd failed to dissuade Senator Fitzgerald from supporting was now in charge of an investigation that would shortly focus on me."

The appointee, Patrick Fitzgerald, came from an Irish immigrant background—his father was a doorman on Manhattan's Upper East Side—and by dint of hard work and persistence he had gone to a Catholic high school, Amherst College, and Harvard Law School before eventually being appointed deputy U.S. attorney for the Southern District of New York.

At the age of forty-three, Fitzgerald had already made a name for himself working on high-profile organized crime and terrorism cases—winning a guilty plea from Mafia capo John Gambino and the conviction of Sheikh Omar Abdel Rahman for the 1993 World Trade Center bombing. He had built the first criminal indictment against terrorist Osama bin Laden and, in late 2003, won an indictment against former Illinois governor George Ryan, a Republican, on conspiracy and fraud charges.

By all accounts, Fitzgerald was an earnest, nonpartisan, and uncompromising model of moral rectitude, the polar opposite of some of the more pliable appointees Rove and his team had been able to insert in Alabama and elsewhere throughout the country. He played by the rules, not politics. "Fitzgerald was not easily intimidated by wealth, status, or threats . . ." Plame Wilson wrote. "He was universally described by friends and critics alike as a man of integrity and zeal for pursuit of truth."

Not surprisingly, Karl Rove saw Fitzgerald very, very differently. To him, the new prosecutor was "cold, calculating, and relentless . . . like a bird of prey, circling his victim and driving him to open ground. . . . I did fear his hunter instincts: if he locked in on you, he had the need to destroy you."

Fitzgerald did not wait long before making his presence felt. On January 14, 2004, he arrived at an interview at the Washington law offices of Swidler Berlin, the law firm representing Robert Novak, bearing waivers of confidentiality signed by, among others, Karl Rove.

As Novak later put it, signed waivers "constituted a shock too severe for a seventy-one-year-old man." It meant the feds had identified his sources.

Already, Novak had talked to the FBI, but without disclosing his sources. Now he was uncomfortable, but on the advice of his attorney he began answering questions about Rove.

Meanwhile, a grand jury had been empaneled. On February 13, Karl Rove was called to testify at the Prettyman Federal Courthouse, a massive postwar building on Pennsylvania Avenue between the Capitol and the White House. The grand jury had assembled in a dingy, windowless room resembling a college classroom. Rove's lawyer Robert Luskin waited in the hallway outside. Rove had the right to invoke his Fifth Amendment right against self-incrimination, which he never did. Or he could ask for a break to use the restroom or confer with Luskin, which he did on occasion. Otherwise, he recalled, "[I]t was Rove v. Fitzgerald, with lots of questions, some exhibits, and bored grand jury members looking on."

In the course of Fitzgerald's interrogation, Rove explained his relationship with Robert Novak. Then came one of the most important moments in Rove's testimony.

"Fitzgerald asked whether I had had contact with reporters other than Robert Novak, running through a string of them. One name was Matt Cooper of *Time*."

Rove's simple response was that he "didn't recall talking to him."

Later, he explained, "Remembering any particular White House phone call is like grabbing one drop out of a rain shower."

SEVEN

All Roads Lead to Rove

For Rove, justice was now a double-edged sword. On the one hand, he lived in fear of being indicted, booked, arraigned, and tried. His home computers—and those of his wife, Darby—were being subpoenaed. The family's finances, photos, letters, and personal documents were being read by strangers. He faced hundreds of thousands of dollars in legal fees. Darby was already so drained by the ordeal that she sought solace in her women's Bible study group. And the grand jury appearances had just begun.

On the other hand, from his office in the West Wing of the White House Rove still had his hands on the levers of power. When it came to the electoral process, he knew the judiciary could be used both to affect who could run for office as a viable candidate and who was allowed to vote. And with John Ashcroft, his former client, as attorney general, the Justice Department was just a phone call away.

As we have seen, before Bush became president Rove had been a powerful force in transforming the judiciary in Texas and Alabama from Democratic to Republican. And after Bush took office, he was able to make sure U.S. attorneys were appointed in Alabama who were in sync with his political vision.

Even in the heat of the Plame affair, under the radar, Rove's team resumed in late 2003 its battle against former Democratic governor Don Siegelman, after the *Mobile Press-Register* published a poll showing that Siegelman would beat Rove's man, Republican governor Bob Riley, in a rematch. Hoping to thwart a Siegelman comeback, the Republicans went back into action using the most partisan U.S. attorneys as attack dogs. In May 2004, Siegelman was indicted by U.S. Attorney Alice Martin, who, as *Harper's* put it, appeared to be going "after Governor Siegelman as part of a Republican political vendetta."

At the heart of the case were allegations that Siegelman's former chief of staff, Alabama physician Phillip Bobo, had been the beneficiary of bid rigging for health care contracts.* But the prosecution failed to produce any substantial evidence against Siegelman and the charges were soon dropped. "They kept looking for a hook into the governor's office," said Doug Jones, Siegelman's lawyer. "But ultimately it became clear that [Phillip Bobo] was just using the name of the governor." The judge even suggested prosecutorial misconduct.

As Jones saw it, Siegelman had been under investigation for years, but he was finally out of the woods. Alice Martin's case against him in the Northern District was dead. In Montgomery, in the Middle District, Leura Canary's office was still pursuing allegations against Siegelman, but Jones had heard that the case wasn't progressing, either, and in late 2004 he wasn't terribly concerned about it. "I'm a real Department of Justice guy," said Jones. "I'm giving all these people the benefit of the doubt. . . . There is no way they are going to let [Siegelman] get indicted. They are giving me the clear impression this case is winding down."

But Jones had misjudged what was happening with Siegelman. In fact, the case against him was just getting started. And although it had not yet come to a head, the prosecution of Don Siegelman had huge implications in that Karl Rove was using the power of government, specifically, the Department of Justice, for political ends.

"One of the critical indications of the health of a democratic state is that political parties don't use the criminal justice system for political purposes," said Scott Horton, a lecturer at Columbia Law School who covered Rove's role in the Siegelman case and, more broadly, in the U.S. attorneys scandal for *Harper's* magazine.

But that was precisely what was going on. As a measure of the extent to which that was true, during the Clinton administration only four people in the Clinton White House—the president, the vice president, the White House counsel, and the deputy White House

---

* Bobo was later acquitted on all charges.

counsel—were empowered to take part in discussions with the Justice Department regarding pending criminal investigations and criminal cases, and only three Justice Department officials were allowed to talk to the White House. But, as Senator Sheldon Whitehouse (D-RI) later pointed out, in the Bush administration 417 White House officials and at least 30 Justice Department officials were so empowered—a staggering increase.

With Don Siegelman being prosecuted by the Bush Justice Department, the larger question was, who else was the department going after?

The answer was that the Bush Justice Department had a striking propensity for going after Democratic politicians and their contributors. In 2003, Mississippi attorney Paul Minor and several Mississippi judges were indicted on charges that Minor tried to bribe the judges, largely by guaranteeing their campaign loans. The charges against Minor were unusual in that both Republicans and Democrats frequently guarantee loans for political campaigns. But Republican contributors in Mississippi, such as Richard Scruggs, who allegedly engaged in the same practice, were *not* indicted. Indeed, Senator Trent Lott, the Republican from Mississippi who happened to be Scruggs's brother-in-law, acknowledged that he spoke to prosecutors about the case and came away assured "that Mr. Scruggs had nothing to worry about."

On the other hand, Paul Minor made an interesting target for Republican prosecutors in that he was a high-profile trial lawyer who had won widely publicized lawsuits against Bridgestone-Firestone, Ford Motor Company, and the tobacco companies, and was a major contributor to the Democratic Party who had donated more than $500,000 to local and national Democratic candidates. As a result, prosecuting him for bribery had the potential to curtail contributions to the Democrats by taking him out of the picture and intimidating other possible donors.

Minor was eventually convicted, but not everyone was convinced he was guilty. "I am still not sure what they did was illegal under the weak laws governing such activities, nor am I sure the government really proved its case," wrote David Hampton, editorial director of the *Jackson Clarion-Ledger,* a conservative paper. "[T]here was too much of a political smell to this case. The extent the Republican Justice Department went to in going after a wealthy influential Democratic trial lawyer just seemed over the top. I've never seen anything like it. It was extraordinary."

But, like Siegelman, Minor was just one of many. To be more precise, during the period between Bush's inauguration and Ashcroft's recusal at the end of 2003, federal prosecutors in the Bush administration initiated investigations of no fewer than two hundred public officials on charges including bribery, bid rigging, influence peddling, mail fraud, tax evasion, extortion, and more.

The targets of these investigations were largely people who held or sought positions of significant power. They included mayors of at least fifteen major cities—San Francisco; Los Angeles; Atlanta; Las Vegas; Honolulu; Chicago; New Orleans; Detroit; Cleveland; Portland, Oregon; Philadelphia; Pittsburgh; Memphis; Nashville; and Dallas. They included governors and lieutenant governors from five states—Alabama, Hawaii, Michigan, New Jersey, and Maryland. They included congressmen from Kentucky, Louisiana, New Mexico, and Nevada. They included senators and senatorial candidates from New York, New Jersey, Minnesota, and Nevada.

What was most striking about the subjects of the investigations listed above was that they were *all* Democrats. Amazingly, according to "The Political Profiling of Elected Democratic Officials," a study of the Bush Justice Department by Donald C. Shields and John F. Cragan, out of two hundred officials under investigation at that time, only thirty were Republicans—15 percent—a disparity so great that the authors compared it to racial profiling of African-Americans. "The real Pulitzer Prize–winning story," the study said, "is the extent of the politicization of Justice Department investigations and/or indictments of local elected and office-seeking Democrats vis-à-vis their Republican counterparts across the nation."

In other words, being elected to a noteworthy office as a Democrat carried with it the significant risk of federal prosecution.

What made this phenomenon particularly pernicious was that it took place almost unnoticed. That's because in virtually every instance the prosecution appeared to be an isolated case that was only of local interest. "We believe that this tremendous disparity is politically motivated and it occurs because the local (non-statewide and non-congressional) investigations occur under the radar of a diligent national press," the Shields-Cragan study said.

As a result, the larger pattern in which U.S. attorneys appointed by the Bush administration went after Democratic candidates all over the country was barely discernible.

Meanwhile, Rove, of course, had not neglected the coming 2004 presidential campaign. Far from it, he had begun strategizing nearly two years before the election. Rove's first step, in early 2003, was to talk to White House chief of staff Andy Card to clarify who was in charge: "There would be one person at the White House through whom all information to and from the campaign must pass, and that person would be me."

Or, as Ken Duberstein, Ronald Reagan's chief of staff and a prominent Washington insider, put it: "All roads lead to Karl." Such was the nature of Rove's power, even after he became a target in the Plame investigation.

And so, once a week, beginning February 2, 2003, on Saturday mornings or early Sunday afternoons, Rove's "Breakfast Club," consisting of top campaign aides and various White House officials, began meeting at his townhouse on Weaver Terrace in Washington. Rove served his special cream and cheese "eggies," pastries, fruit, bacon, and exotic sausages including venison, wild boar, and nilgai—the last an antelope from India that now runs wild in South Texas.

Rove appointed Ken Mehlman campaign chairman, and, along with campaign aides Mark McKinnon and Matthew Dowd, they developed a strategy focused on creating an image of Bush as a strong wartime leader. But by the time the primary season began in 2004, Bush's approval ratings had plummeted a full forty points from his 90-point rating just after 9/11. Democratic voter registration soared. Rove felt that Bush would win, but it was going to be a tight race.

Far from abandoning his vision of a permanent majority, Rove went into action. One by one, he assembled his weapons: there was the Justice Department; there were "independent" third-party groups that might come to Rove's aid; and there were tech resources such as

SmarTech in Chattanooga and Mike Connell's New Media in Rich-field, Ohio.

When it came to the judiciary, in addition to prosecuting Democrats Rove had another favorite issue that could be vital to winning elections, and he made sure it was being pursued by U.S. attorneys: voter fraud.

For Rove, voter fraud was an issue very much like tort reform. On the surface, no reasonable person could argue against it. After all, who could possibly be *for* fraud? Yet, like tort reform, a campaign to fight voter fraud had within it a hidden agenda that offered untold riches, in electoral terms, for the Republican Party.

Here the dirty secret was that voter fraud—sneaking into the polls to cast an illicit vote, dead people voting, illegal aliens voting—was virtually nonexistent. Indeed, according to a piece in the *Washington Post* by Michael Waldman and Justin Levitt of the Brennan Center for Justice at New York University School of Law, "[T]he notion of widespread voter fraud . . . is itself a fraud. . . . Before and after every close election, politicians and pundits proclaim: The dead are voting, foreigners are voting, people are voting twice. On closer examination, though, most such allegations don't pan out."

Nevertheless, all over the country U.S. attorneys had been instructed by the Bush administration to keep a keen eye out for voter fraud and to prosecute whenever possible. More often than not, however, they had little to show for it. Thanks to what he called "Karl Rove's obsession with voter fraud issues throughout the coun-try," New Mexico U.S. attorney David Iglesias, a Bush appointee, established an election fraud task force in September 2004 and spent more than two months probing claims of voter fraud in his state.

The result? "After examining the evidence, and in conjunction with the Justice Department Election Crimes Unit and the FBI, I could not find any cases I could prosecute beyond a reasonable doubt," Iglesias said. "Accordingly, I did not authorize any voter fraud related pros-ecutions."

Iglesias was not alone in finding scant evidence of such crimes. According to the *New York Times,* between October 2002 and Sep-tember 2005, the federal government convicted a grand total of eigh-teen people for the crime of voting while ineligible—out of more than

120 million votes in the 2004 presidential election, and another 80 million who voted in the 2002 midterms. "The Truth About Voter Fraud," an in-depth study on the subject by the Brennan Center published in 2007, concluded, "It is more likely that an individual will be struck by lightning than that he will impersonate another voter at the polls."

So why the hue and cry about voter fraud?

Because just as Rove had built tort reform into a cleverly disguised movement to allow Republicans to take over the judiciary and build a GOP funding machine, he wanted to build voter fraud into an issue that could disenfranchise millions of Democratic voters. In 2002, the Justice Department launched a new Voting Integrity Initiative, which, on the surface, sounded like a commonsense good-government policy. But according to the Brennan Center report, 11 percent of Americans lack government-issued photo IDs, as opposed to 25 percent of African-Americans, 16 percent of Hispanics, and 18 percent of elderly voters. As a result, the ultimate effect of such policies was to disenfranchise minorities and the poor, most of whom voted Democratic. Not surprisingly, Democratic blogs referred to voter fraud as "Jim Crow 2.0."*

According to an op-ed piece in the *Los Angeles Times* by Joseph Rich, formerly chief of the voting section in the Justice Department's Civil Rights Division, thanks to such policies the Bush administration "shirked its legal responsibility to protect voting rights . . . and skewed aspects of law enforcement in ways that clearly were intended to influence the outcome of elections." Starting in 2001, Rich wrote, "no voting discrimination cases were brought on behalf of African-American or Native American voters. U.S. attorneys were told instead to give priority to voter fraud cases, which, when coupled with the strong support for voter ID laws, indicated an intent to depress voter turnout in minority and poor communities."

Meanwhile, Rove wasted no time in going after the presumptive Democratic nominee, Senator John Kerry (D-Mass.). The fact that

---

* Significantly, according to Daily Kos, the term *voter fraud* did not even exist to a meaningful degree until after the Voting Rights Act of 1965—that is, it came into widespread use only *after* it became illegal to disenfranchise minority voters.

Kerry was a Vietnam War hero who had won multiple combat medals created a real conundrum for Rove. The Democrats had a genuine combat veteran who was critical of Bush's Iraq War, while the Republicans had a president who had never seen combat himself and had presented fraudulent intelligence to start an increasingly controversial war.

At the Breakfast Club, Rove decided to attack by launching ads characterizing Kerry as a "flip-flopper" for having voted first to authorize the war in Iraq and then having voted to cut spending for it. "Then Kerry gave us the line that perfectly encapsulated who he was. . . . He said, 'I actually did vote for the $87 billion before I voted against it.'"

Rove went on, "I was dumbfounded. . . . In thirteen words, he told Americans he was an unreliable, inconsistent, weak flip-flopper unfit for the Oval Office."

But at the same time, an even bigger problem for Kerry came to life thanks to millions of dollars of ads from Swift Boat* Veterans for Truth, an "independent" 527[†] political group that launched an aggressive media campaign claiming Kerry lied to get his medals. Media Matters, Factcheck.org, and nine major newspapers later uncovered a slew of inaccuracies, falsehoods, and outright lies in the charges leveled against Kerry. But the damage was real, and Kerry had been slow to correct it.

The campaign smacked of similar efforts against former governor Ann Richards of Texas, of Bush's South Carolina primary race against John McCain, or any number of Karl Rove campaigns in which the opponent was accused of lesbianism; fathering out-of-wedlock, racially mixed babies; or pedophilia. Rove said, "The Swifties did a damned good job."

But Rove also asserted, repeatedly, that he and the Bush-Cheney campaign had nothing to do with it. "Of course, I was blamed for the Swift Boat ads, accused of helping to organize the group, orchestrat-

---

* In Vietnam, Kerry had been the commander of a patrol craft fast (PCF), also known as a swift boat.

† A 527 organization is a type of tax-exempt organization, named after Section 527 of the IRS code, that is generally set up to influence elections for federal, state, or local public office.

ing its activities, and creating its messages," he wrote in *Courage and Consequence.* "I had no role in any of it."

He neglected to say, however, that Mike Connell's New Media Communications had built the Swift Boaters' site, and, perhaps more important, more than half of the reported contributions to the group came from three Republican donors in Texas: Houston builder Bob Perry, an early contributor to Rove's causes, who donated $4.45 million; Harold Simmons, another longtime Rove supporter, who donated $3 million; and oilman T. Boone Pickens Jr., who donated $2 million.

But thanks to a lack of diligence on the part of the media, the electorate knew none of that, and Rove was successfully able to draw a line between the Swift Boaters and the Bush campaign as if they were completely unrelated.

One of the more astute analyses of what was going on came from Joshua Green, in *The Atlantic*:

> Early in the summer, as Bush was struggling, even Rove's allies professed to doubt his ability to control the dynamics of the race in view of an unrelenting stream of bad news from Iraq. . . . Yet by August, when attacks by the anti-Kerry group Swift Boat Veterans for Truth were dominating the front pages, such comments had become rarer. Then they died away entirely.
>
> If this year stays true to past form, the campaign will get nastier in the closing weeks, and without anyone's quite registering it, Rove will be right back in his element. He seems to understand, indeed to count on, the media's unwillingness or inability, whether from squeamishness, laziness, or professional caution, ever to give a full estimate of him or his work. It is ultimately not just Rove's skill but his character that allows him to perform on an entirely different plane. Along with remarkable strategic skills, he has both an understanding of the media's unstated self-limitations and a willingness to fight in territory where conscience forbids most others.
>
> Rove isn't bracing for a close race. He's depending on it.

Merciless on offense, Rove could be equally brutal, cunning, and effective on defense. That became clear on September 8, 2004, two months before the election, when CBS's *60 Minutes Wednesday* aired a segment by Dan Rather, the iconic CBS News anchor, and produced by Mary Mapes, that was critical of George W. Bush's military service. Rather, of course, had long been considered no friend of the Bush administration, ever since a combative interview in 1988 between Rather and then vice president George H.W. Bush. More recently, in April 2004, he and Mapes had broken the story of human rights violations at the Abu Ghraib prison in Iraq in the form of psychological, physical, and sexual abuse including torture, rape, sodomy, and homicide. It was not the kind of thing Rove and the Bush White House appreciated.

Specifically, Rather's latest report alleged that in 1968 George H.W. Bush had used his political clout to get his son into the National Guard and avoid Vietnam, and that once George W. was in the National Guard he shirked his duty and got away with it. Coming at the height of the savage Swift Boat attacks on Kerry, and in the midst of Abu Ghraib and increased concerns that the Iraq War was devolving into a quagmire, the report was so explosive that it had the potential to tip the balance in the presidential race.

Among the documents CBS used to back up its allegations were four memos said to be from Bush's commanding officer, Lieutenant Colonel Jerry Killian. One of them, dated August 1973, a period during which Bush had earned a reputation as a hard-drinking "badass" flyboy, was labeled "CYA" (Cover Your Ass) and in it Killian described the political pressure he was under to "sugarcoat" Bush's performance reviews. "I'm having trouble running interference and doing my job," the memo said. "[Colonel Walter 'Buck'] Staudt is pushing to sugarcoat it. Bush wasn't here during rating period, and I don't have any feedback from the 187th in Alabama. I will not rate. Austin is not happy today either."

The documents were just one component of a complex report by CBS that included a long-sought-after exclusive interview with Ben Barnes, the former lieutenant governor of Texas, who described, on camera, how he pulled strings for the elder George Bush to get George W. into the National Guard.

The piece had all the earmarks of a story that could be a memorable capstone for Rather's legendary career. If they got traction, the charges could eviscerate the image Rove had crafted of Bush as the heroic leader of a nation at war. For John Kerry, they were the perfect antidotes to the Swift Boaters.

But when the report aired on September 8, as Joe Hagan put it in the *Texas Monthly,* "it blew up in [Rather's] face, tarnishing his career forever and casting a dark cloud of doubt and suspicion over his reporting—and that of every other journalist on the case."

In other words, this was one of Karl Rove's finest hours.

Over the next two weeks, Rove wrote, he went from feeling "alarm and anger at the smear—it was clearly meant as a knockout blow against Bush—to watching with delight as bloggers, not reporters, dethroned one of America's most prominent anti-Bush journalists."

Exactly what happened?

Within hours of the broadcast, Harry MacDougald, a GOP lawyer and conservative activist who was known as Buckhead on the message boards, downloaded the documents CBS had posted online, logged on to the conservative online site freerepublic.com, and wrote, ". . . every single one of these memos is in a proportionally spaced font. In 1972 people used typewriters for this sort of thing, and typewriters used monospaced fonts. I am saying these documents are forgeries. This should be pursued aggressively."

With that, the spark had been struck, the Internet caught fire, and Rathergate was born. Because the piece had been crashed and aired so quickly, it was not without flaws. One source, former guardsman Bill Burkett, was easily discredited as a disgruntled Bush hater. Another problem was that the memos in question were photocopies, which have no forensic value when it comes to proving the date of origination. As a result, it was impossible to corroborate or refute their authenticity with 100 percent certainty, and CBS was slow to answer the ensuing barrage of questions. To make matters worse, Rather's ratings were low and CBS had regulatory issues that the Bush administration was about to rule upon, so top brass at the network were none too eager to stand up for Rather.

Over the next twelve days, the attacks on CBS were relentless, coming from right-wing bloggers "who had been part of meetings or conference calls organized by Karl Rove's political operation," according to Sidney Blumenthal in Salon.

At the White House, Rove protégé Dan Bartlett tirelessly coordinated former National Guardsmen to counterattack and served as the front man on the story. But the way it was handled bore all the hallmarks of his master. "There is absolutely no way that Karl Rove was not involved in [orchestrating] the reaction to the story," said Mary Mapes, who produced the CBS segment and was fired as a result. "It is the beauty of Rove's evil genius that we do not know exactly what he did. But I do know that Rove set the psychological tone for the Bush administration's response to many, many things they didn't like.

"Rove was the guy who taught people how to respond to negative stories, who developed the scorched earth policy. He was terrifically adept. He was the master of the symphony, the orchestra director, and he could get everyone to play exactly what he wanted. There is a dark and terrible beauty about what he does. He is incredibly good at it and it is incredibly dangerous and damaging to the country."

Four years later, in 2008, Mike Missal, a lawyer for the firm that CBS hired to investigate Rather's report, conceded, "The blogs were actually wrong. . . . We actually did find typewriters that did have the superscript, did have proportional spacing. And on the fonts . . . there were some typewriters that looked like they could have some similar fonts there. So the initial concerns didn't seem as though they would hold up."

All of which meant it was possible, but not conclusive, that the documents were real. Harry MacDougald, who made the original charge, acknowledged as much in an interview with Hagan that appeared in April 2012 in the *Texas Monthly,* and answered many of the questions of how Bush shirked his duty and covered it up.

Hagan advanced the story considerably, but the question of whether the documents were real was still unanswered. In fact, some of Hagan's reporting suggested that even though fonts were not the issue, Rove's team may have set Rather up, or allowed him to be set up, with fake documents so he would then get creamed. Before commenting on the documents, Rove protégé Dan Bartlett had taken the precaution of emailing copies of the memo to Albert Lloyd, Bush's longtime National Guard expert, who immediately told Bartlett they were forgeries. "I looked at them and I said, 'Don't do a damned thing with these, because these are fake,'" Lloyd said.

But Bartlett ignored Lloyd's evaluation of them, presumably, Lloyd speculated, because "I guess he was trying to set Rather up for getting mauled."

The Bush family had long harbored animosity against Rather. Wouldn't it be deliciously tempting to see him get what appeared to be a smoking gun but have it explode in his face?

As for the revelations that the fonts were not an issue, they came too late. By then, the term *Rathergate* had appeared on hundreds of thousands of web pages. The apologia from Mike Missal appeared on only about a hundred. It was a case of shouting the accusation and whispering the apology. Not to mention the fact that the political impact of the CBS piece, and the counterattack against it, was all geared to the 2004 presidential election.

In the immediate aftermath of the CBS report, the *Washington Post* collated the critiques from the right-wing blogosphere and fueled the controversy further. On September 10, 2004, the *Washington Post,* the *New York Times,* and *USA Today* ran stories in which the legitimacy of the documents was questioned. The right smelled blood. Dan Rather was on the defensive. Instead of simply reporting the news each night for CBS, he was under continuous siege, and went on CNN to defend the story.

On September 13, CBS backed off a bit. Rather acknowledged that some questions about the legitimacy were being raised by "people who are not active political partisans," though, he insisted, document analysts and other experts said "the documents *could have been created* in the 70s."

A week later, network executives were in full-scale retreat. "Based on what we now know, CBS News cannot prove that the documents are authentic, which is the only acceptable journalistic standard to justify using them in the report," CBS News president Andrew Heyward said. "We should not have used them. That was a mistake, which we deeply regret."

CBS then appointed a panel, chaired by Dick Thornburgh, former attorney general of the United States under George H.W. Bush, to review the matter. Mary Mapes and two of her associates were fired, and Dan Rather was eventually forced into early retirement.

Most significant, even though the substance of the story was later corroborated, according to Walter V. Robinson, a *Boston Globe* reporter whose 2000 investigation had led to much of the subsequent reporting, the furor "buried the story so deeply that you couldn't possibly disinter it in 2004. Inevitably, the only candidate who ended up with a serious credibility problem about his military service was John Kerry, who had absolutely nothing to hide or be ashamed of. To me, in a close election—and it was a close election—who knows, that could have been the difference."

All of which left Karl Rove more than comfortable with perpetuating, in his 2010 memoir, *Courage and Consequence,* the myth that the memos used fonts "unavailable in typewriters of that day but commonly used later on personal computers."

"The revelation that a liberal journalist used fake documents to damage the president actually energized Bush's supporters," he wrote. "My sense was that some voters still up for grabs moved a little our way, too. Bush . . . came off as the victim of a dirty trick."

Even though the elemental facts about Bush's failure to serve had been corroborated, they had been obscured by the unsolved mystery about the legitimacy of the documents.

As Mary Mapes put it in her book about her ordeal, *Truth and Duty,* "Karl Rove was the mastermind of the Republican attack against the story, and I think he was, as always, brilliant. While White House officials scrupulously avoided saying that they thought the Killian memos were forged, in case they were later proved to be true, Rove's minions attacked every element of the documents in an attempt to knock the story down. They came after us under cover of darkness, swarming like a computer-age re-creation of Custer's last stand. And it worked, long enough to get through the election, long enough for it to cost me my reputation, Dan Rather his position, and the entire CBS News division its pride."

EIGHT

Lady Luck

As election day approached, Mike Connell's job was to make sure the Ohio secretary of state's computer system held up under high traffic for just one night—November 2, 2004. During the summer, he had begun meeting regularly with techies in Secretary of State Ken Blackwell's office to that end. While SmarTech programmers set up the servers to handle the load, their Ohio counterparts built a replica of their Oracle database so that updates on the secretary of state's computers would be mirrored on the backup at SmarTech. Then the SOS (secretary of state) network administrator gave SmarTech the protocols necessary to establish a connection between the two sites.

To explain how things worked, Bob Mangan, the director of information technology for the Secretary of State's Office, put together an elaborate multicolored diagram with an equally baroque name, "SOS [Secretary of State] Election Production System Configuration for Web Results Entry, EN [Election Night] Staff Results Entry and Web Queries." In late summer, several months before the election, testing indicated that once the onslaught of queries hit, the Secretary of State's Office could easily redirect millions of queries to SmarTech's servers from people going to their site to find out the Ohio election results.

A veteran civil servant who had plenty of experience dealing with political partisans, Bob Mangan saw himself as "guardian of the gates" when it came to the technology behind the election. He had assembled a cohesive staff that had seen both Republican and Democratic administrations come and go. "We all had a firm belief that nobody but nobody messes with the elections," said Mangan.

Determined to build a database that could not be hacked, Man-

gan used Oracle RAC (real application clusters) software, a highly idiosyncratic program that is protected by no fewer than seventeen security protocols. "We all knew that SmarTech was a heavy, heavy Republican shop," Mangan said. "Ex-Oracle people could have done something [to penetrate the secretary of state's computers]. But not Mike Connell or the SmarTech people. I built those databases with complete security in mind."

There were also safeguards at the most local level of all. To prevent hacking, individual electronic tabulators at the precinct level were prohibited from having connections to local area networks (LANs). Instead, tabulators were given to the county election boards, each of which had two Republicans and two Democrats to ensure fairness. In other words, it was impossible for SmarTech to steal the election.

Or so it seemed.

At the time, the Internet was, relatively speaking, still in its infancy, and was just beginning to play a key role in political campaigns. In that regard, SmarTech was all but invisible to the public at large, but the impact of its technology, its clients, and the people affiliated with its various forms was everywhere. As mentioned earlier, Mercer Reynolds, a principal investor in SmarTech's precursor, had been tasked by Rove with delivering Ohio's twenty electoral votes for the president and was named finance chairman of the Bush-Cheney reelection campaign. The result? The most successful political fundraising campaign in history, bringing in more than $260 million to GOP coffers.

Likewise, New Media and SmarTech designed, built, and hosted the Republican National Committee's website, www.gop.com, www.georgewbush.com, and dozens of related sites. SmarTech's vast video streaming capabilities were also put to use. In May, the Bush-Cheney campaign launched its ad campaign, and as many as 100,000 Internet users began simultaneously downloading ads from Smar-Tech. "We were pushing more than 250,000 megabytes per second, which is far more than any previous outbound data transmission ever in Chattanooga," said Jeff Averbeck, the company's CEO.

SmarTech was also behind another high-tech tool in which Rove took special pride: microtargeting. In his memoir, Rove compares the

GOP strategy to that of Billy Beane, the general manager of the Oakland Athletics, who used statistical analysis to assemble a winning team and became the subject of Michael Lewis's bestselling book *Moneyball*. As Rove explains it, the GOP database drew upon "as many as 225 pieces of information we could collect on an individual household to help identify which members were likely to support Bush and turn out to vote for him. Among the pieces of information we sought were whether they owned a gun, whether their children attended private schools, what kind of magazines they subscribed to, what kind of car they owned, even what kind of liquor they preferred."

Rove added, "No one piece of information was a reliable indicator by itself. The complicated algorithms that made sense of the relationships among these data points were prized secrets."

Rove didn't name the computer database, but he was apparently referring to the Republican National Committee–funded Voter Vault, the GOP's much vaunted data-mining tool run out of Smar-Tech, which has instantly retrievable data on every single household in the country and is capable of pulling together at a moment's notice the voting history of any precinct in the country.*

Now Rove's voter fraud campaign came back to life. With the help of Mark Hearne, national counsel to the Bush-Cheney campaign, Rove initiated aggressive efforts to suppress Democratic voting in the battleground states, particularly Ohio, Florida, and Pennsylvania. According to his law firm's website, "Hearne traveled to every battleground state and oversaw more than 65 different lawsuits," challenging voter registration drives by pro-Democratic groups, popularizing claims about widespread voter fraud, and demanding stricter voter ID laws.

The Republicans were not always wrong about voter fraud. In October, Chad Staton of Defiance County, Ohio, was charged, and later convicted, with filling out more than a hundred phony voter registration cards for the NAACP National Voter Fund, using such

---

* In *Courage and Consequence,* Rove also salutes the work of e-campaign manager Chuck DeFeo, an associate of Mike Connell's who ultimately replaced Connell when the latter died in a plane crash.

names as Dick Tracy, Mary Poppins, Jeffrey Dahmer, Michael Jordan, and George Foreman.

But the practice was not nearly so widespread as the Republicans alleged, and the end result of their campaign was to suppress the vote of minorities who voted heavily for Democrats. One voter suppressor tactic they relied on was known as "caging," a technique that typically starts with direct mail being sent to voter rolls so that lists consisting of addressees from which the mail is returned undelivered can be compiled.

In Ohio, according to a report by the House Judiciary Committee, the state Republican Party decided "to engage in pre-election 'caging' tactics," selectively targeting 35,000 predominantly minority voters* whose letters had come back as undeliverable. For the most part, the report said, that included voters who were homeless, serving abroad, or who simply chose not to sign something concerning the Republican Party.

Meanwhile, an event took place that, had it been widely known, might have changed the outcome of the coming presidential election. It occurred on October 15, 2004, when Rove returned to the dingy confines of the Prettyman Federal Courthouse in Washington to face yet another interrogation by Patrick Fitzgerald before the grand jury in a room lit by fluorescent lights that looked, as Rove put it, "vaguely Third World."

At the time, Rove had not told anyone about his conversation with *Time*'s Matt Cooper. He had lied outright about it to Scott McClellan. And he had told President Bush, the FBI, and Fitzgerald's grand jury he had no recollection of such a conversation. His grand jury testimony had taken place under oath, under penalty of perjury.

Given that the Intelligence Identities Act was a famously difficult

---

* The Third Circuit Court later found these activities to be illegal and in direct violation of consent decrees barring the Republican Party from targeting minority voters for poll challenges. Likewise, the U.S. District Court for the Southern District of Ohio later found these procedures to violate the Due Process Clause of the Constitution and ruled that the notices were sent so late that many voters did not even receive them before the election and "the court found that ineffective notice must have been the intent" and that would-be voters could not possibly have responded.

tool for prosecutors, it was far more likely that Fitzgerald would pursue indictments for perjury or obstruction of justice. All of which made the question of whether Matt Cooper would testify especially vital. His notes of his conversation showed Rove saying, "Wilson's wife, who apparently works at the agency . . . authorized [Wilson's] trip." If disclosed, they could be devastating to Rove.

To make matters more complicated, whether or not Cooper would testify was the subject of an ongoing yearlong dance taking place between the media and the law. Fitzgerald's investigation had come to a near standstill because he needed the testimony of Judith Miller of the *New York Times* and Cooper of *Time*.

But the reporters had refused to cooperate because they were holding fast to the sacred journalistic credo of protecting confidential sources. In this case, however, as Scott McClellan has pointed out, there was an unusual twist to their position. "By refusing to divulge the names of their sources in the leak case, the two reporters were not protecting courageous whistle-blowers revealing government wrongdoing in the public interest," McClellan wrote. "Rather, they were shielding government officials who administration critics believed had used leaks as weapons of partisan warfare."

And so, for more than a year, a series of subpoenas, contempt citations, and appeals ensued. Whether Cooper would testify hung in the balance.

But, at the same time, yet another secret drama regarding Karl Rove's fate was being played out. In this case, his fortune was determined not by his guile but by a stupendous stroke of luck.

The story began early in the Plame Wilson investigation, when *Time* reporter Viveca Novak, a colleague of Matt Cooper's and no relation to Bob Novak, got a call from Rove's lawyer Bob Luskin. A partner at the high-powered Washington law firm Patton Boggs, Luskin was a specialist in white-collar crime and government investigations who blended his impeccable establishment credentials with colorful tastes. A graduate of Harvard College, Harvard Law School, and a Rhodes Scholar, he was buff, bald, and rode to work on a black Ducati Monster motorcycle, the stylish vehicle of choice among Hollywood celebrities and top designers. In 1995, he is said to have become the first male lawyer to argue a case before the U.S. Supreme Court while wearing an earring.

Novak had known Luskin for about seven years as a friendly source with whom she would occasionally have drinks.

"Well," Luskin had told her several months earlier, "you're sitting next to Karl Rove's lawyer."

Novak "was genuinely surprised, since Luskin's liberal sympathies were no secret, and here he was representing the man known to many Democrats as the other side's Evil Genius."

As the investigation unfolded, Novak began spending more time with Luskin to keep on top of things. At one of their meetings, they discussed Rove's talks with *Time*'s Matt Cooper.*

Luskin looked at Viveca. "Karl doesn't have a Cooper problem," he told her. "He was not a source for Matt."

Viveca thought Luskin was spinning her. "Are you sure about that?" she replied. "That's not what I hear around *Time*."

Luskin looked surprised. "There's nothing in the phone logs," he said.

Novak was taken aback by Luskin's reaction: "I had been pushing back against what I thought was his attempt to lead me astray. I hadn't believed that I was disclosing anything he didn't already know. Maybe this was a feint. Maybe his client was lying to him. But at any rate, I immediately felt uncomfortable."

Luskin walked Novak to her car.

"Thank you," he said, or words to that effect. "This is important."

Immediately afterward, Luskin called Rove at home to share the news and to inquire again whether Rove had talked to Cooper. "It didn't jar any recollection; I was still drawing a blank," Rove recalled—or, rather, failed to recall.

Nonetheless, he did not hesitate to take marching orders from his lawyer: "So Luskin told me it was important to get [administrative assistants] Ralston, Hernandez, and Goergen to scour the office records to see if they might confirm the contact."

---

* The exact date of the meeting is open to question. In *Courage and Consequence*, Rove said it took place in November 2003. Various other accounts place in the summer or fall of 2004. Viveca Novak initially told Patrick Fitzgerald that it took place in May 2004, but, according to her final testimony, the meeting probably took place in March 2004.

Rove did exactly that the next morning, and his staffers ransacked the office for several days. But they did not find what they were looking for.

In the fall, however, in the heat of the presidential race, Rove was subpoenaed to appear before the grand jury again. This time, Fitzgerald told Luskin that Rove's status had changed and that Rove was now a "subject." In the lingo of prosecutors, a "subject" of an investigation is someone whose conduct is within the scope of the grand jury's investigation. A "target" is a person about whom there is substantial evidence linking him or her to the commission of a crime.

In addition, Matthew Cooper had met privately with Scooter Libby, a principal target in the investigation, gotten a signed release from his confidentiality pledge, and, in August, given a deposition to Fitzgerald, which, by previous agreement, concerned only his conversations with Libby.

But Cooper was still under subpoena to give more information. Rove wasn't off the hook.

Luskin had already gone through all of Rove's emails from April through September 2003—a herculean task, given that Rove often got several hundred emails a day. Nevertheless, this was important enough to call for a do-over. According to *Tangled Webs,* by James Stewart, Luskin sat on the floor of his office going through three or four boxes of documents of Rove's correspondence when he came across an email dated July 11, 2003, from Rove to Deputy National Security Adviser Stephen Hadley:

Matt Cooper called to give me a heads-up that he's got a welfare reform story coming. When he finished his brief heads-up, he immediately launched into Niger/isn't this damaging/hasn't the president been hurt? I didn't take the bait but said, if I were him, I wouldn't get TIME far out in front on this.

Luskin later described finding the email as "a holy shit moment."

Rove's email conspicuously omitted one salient detail about his conversation with Cooper—namely, that he had leaked Valerie Plame Wilson's name. Nonetheless, it was explosive evidence. So when Rove appeared before the grand jury on October 15, less than three weeks before the presidential election, the stakes were astronomically high.

On a personal level, Rove found these grand jury appearances devastating emotionally, and described them as leaving him "mentally beaten to a pulp." He had now been told explicitly that he was a "subject" of the investigation.

Within the FBI, no one thought they had sufficient evidence to reach the high bar set for prosecution by the Intelligence Identities Act. But perjury, false statements, obstruction of justice was another matter. At least one FBI agent felt there was enough evidence to indict and convict Rove based on what they had.

Rove realized there was now documentary evidence that contradicted sworn testimony he had given before Fitzgerald's grand jury. Evidence that *he* had written. In Rove's earlier appearance before the grand jury, Fitzgerald had not let on that he had the email. But according to Rove, Luskin surmised that he had it. Rove had no choice but to set the record straight.

After being sworn in before the grand jury, Rove told Fitzgerald he wanted to correct a statement he had made in his previous appearance. "While I still had no recollection of talking to Matt Cooper, I told Fitzgerald, I had written Steve Hadley the morning of July 11 to say I had talked to the *Time* reporter," Rove wrote.

When Rove finished, he felt "as if I'd detonated a bomb in the shabby little room." After examining the email, Fitzgerald recessed the grand jury and rushed out to meet Luskin in a nearby corridor, anxious to find out how Luskin had come to have it. Fitzgerald was almost "quivering," Luskin recalled.

After eight and a half hours of testimony, Rove left the grand jury room exhausted because Fitzgerald had pummeled him mercilessly, but ecstatic that he had set the record straight. Yet it was not immediately clear if he had strengthened or weakened his case. Coming forward with the email was Rove's way of showing Fitzgerald he was not trying to mislead the grand jury when he concealed the Cooper conversation from them in February. It also shored up Luskin's credibility with Fitzgerald.

On the other hand, in turning over the Hadley email, Rove had just provided Fitzgerald with hard evidence that may have reinforced any suspicions Fitzgerald had. "I did not understand then that by [turning over the email] I had painted a target on my back," Rove wrote. Fitzgerald's suspicions would nag him for more than a year "and lead him to within inches of indicting me. For now, though, I was in blissful ignorance."

Not surprisingly, without knowing the details of what had just happened, the Kerry campaign insisted Rove and Bush should disclose everything about the Plame Wilson scandal. "With two weeks to go before the election, the American people are still in the dark about how it is that their White House leaked the name of an undercover CIA operative to the press, jeopardizing the life of this agent and possibly violating federal law," Kerry spokesman Joe Lockhart said. "Instead of hiding behind the lawyers he so often likes to criticize, George Bush should direct Karl Rove and anyone else involved to go to the White House briefing room and come clean about their role in this insidious act."

If it had been made public at that time, eighteen days before the election, there is little doubt that Rove's testimony would have changed the dynamics of the campaign—and that Rove himself and his role in leaking Valerie Plame Wilson's name would have dominated the last days of the presidential campaign. But a federal rule of criminal procedure prohibits the disclosure of grand jury testimony from just about everyone—except the witness himself.

And Karl Rove was not about to talk.

NINE

As Goes Ohio

Increasingly, Ohio was center stage. That was not particularly surprising. No Republican had won the White House since the Civil War without winning Ohio; hence the aphorism "As goes Ohio, so goes the nation." It was also, of course, the home of Rove's favorite president, William McKinley, and of his hero, Mark Hanna.

For this election, Rove had had the foresight to have Ken Blackwell, who was serving both as Ohio's secretary of state and as honorary co-chairman of the Bush-Cheney campaign in Ohio, oversee an aggressive campaign to disenfranchise blacks, minorities, poor people, and those who lived in largely Democratic precincts. Exactly what took place there, in one of the ugliest electoral campaigns in American history, has been chronicled at length by Representative John Conyers (D-Mich.) in his House Judiciary Committee Report, in an extended article by Robert F. Kennedy Jr. in *Rolling Stone,* David Earnhardt's documentary *Uncounted,* and in various books, articles, and blogs.

Astoundingly, according to the House Judiciary Committee Report, there were at least 3,300 incidents of voting irregularities. This was hardball politics Karl Rove style. Flyers and phone calls provided Democrats with misleading information about when and where to vote. Uneven distribution of voting machines ensured that voters in heavily Republican precincts could zip through the voting booths, while those in Democratic ones had to wait for hours.

By not sending out absentee ballots to tens of thousands of Ohio voters who requested them, Blackwell made sure that thousands of employees who could not get off work to vote would be disenfranchised. Though African-American himself, Blackwell attempted to enforce idiosyncratic Jim Crow–like laws demanding that voter applications be printed on eighty-pound unwaxed white stock paper, similar to the thickness of a postcard. As a result, local newspapers that had printed registration forms, county election boards, and even Blackwell's office distributed lighter-weight forms that violated Blackwell's rule. (The regulation was later dropped, after a public outcry.)

Likewise, according to the House Judiciary Committee Report, Blackwell decided to restrict the use of provisional ballots—those given to voters whose eligibility is in question—and that led "to the disenfranchisement of tens, if not hundreds of thousands of voters, again predominantly minority and Democratic voters."

Blackwell also decided to prevent voters who requested absentee ballots but did not receive them in a timely fashion from being able to receive provisional ballots, a decision that, the Judiciary Committee Report said, "likely disenfranchised thousands, if not tens of thousands, of voters, particularly seniors."

Meanwhile, Rove had vowed that Bush would draw 4 million more evangelical voters than he had in 2000. Figuring that supporters of a proposed constitutional amendment to ban same-sex marriage and civil unions would also vote for Bush, Blackwell led the Ohio Campaign to Protect Marriage, an under-the-radar campaign orchestrated by Rove, in fifty-seven rural counties to mobilize Christian evangelicals.

Then, on Monday, November 1, 2004, the day before the election, Karl Rove himself went on Fox News to hammer home the message about voter fraud. "Particularly in Ohio, but in a lot of the other key battleground states, there has been a lot of voter registration fraud. We don't want that to turn into voter fraud on election day . . ." Rove said. "[T]here are multiple registrations on the rolls. There are felons who are ineligible to vote who are registered on the rolls."

As election day dawned, most polls showed Bush with a slight lead in Ohio, though some showed Kerry ahead. The tightness of the race prompted pundits to say that Ohio could be to 2004 what Florida was to 2000, and compare Blackwell to the woman who won notoriety as his Florida counterpart. "I'm glad I'm not in Ken Blackwell's shoes," said Kentucky secretary of state Trey Grayson. "Ken could be the next Katherine Harris."

* * *

Monday, November 1, was supposed to be the final full day of campaigning, and Rove made sure that it was a full one for President Bush. Between 6:30 a.m. Monday and 1:40 a.m. Tuesday, according to Rove, Bush delivered seven speeches in five critical battleground states—Ohio, Pennsylvania, Wisconsin, Iowa, and New Mexico—before heading home to a late-night event at Southern Methodist University in Dallas.

When Rove took his seat at the SMU rally, the crowd began applauding. "I wondered what was going on until I realized some people were chanting my name. I appreciated the sentiment and did my best to keep my emotions in check."

But moments later it was off to Crawford, Texas, where Bush had his ranch. At about one a.m. on election day, Rove began receiving the final tracking data, which showed that Bush was ahead by four points in Ohio and even in Florida—too close for Rove's comfort. "I decided we would add two election day stops onto the trip back to Washington: one in the I-4 corridor of Florida and the other in Columbus, Ohio. By 1:30 a.m., Deputy Chief of Staff Joe Hagin, who was in charge of Air Force One, called to say only one stop was possible. I asked Mehlman to choose. He picked the Buckeye State. . . . Mehlman and I had the same instinct: the race in Ohio felt closer than Florida."

Early the next morning, election day, Rove told the president the bad news. Bush had thought the campaign was over, but he stoically agreed to one more day. The president and first lady, accompanied by their daughters Jenna and Barbara, went to the Volunteer Fire Department in Crawford, where they cast their votes. Then they boarded Air Force One.

Just before they landed at Andrews Air Force Base outside Washington, Rove got a call with the first wave of exit polls. "I took the numbers down on a note card balanced on my knee," Rove reported. "They were bad: We were losing Ohio. We were dead even in Florida. North Carolina was gone. Minnesota was out of play. Arizona, South Carolina, and Colorado were too close to call. Mississippi—Mississippi!—was close. State after state would fall to the Kerry campaign, according to the exit polls. The president was on his way to a crushing defeat."

Even though Air Force One was just seconds from touchdown, Rove went forward to Bush's cabin. "The exit polls are dreadful," he told Bush. He went through the numbers state by state. "If they're accurate, we're not going to win."

Bush was stunned. "That doesn't sound right to me. What happened?"

Rove didn't know. He was sick to his stomach.

The press would be there when they arrived at the White House. "Everyone put on your game face," said Bush.

Rove tried to pull it off. But the photos didn't lie. He looked grim.

Meanwhile, voter turnout in Ohio was at a historic high, with more than 5.6 million voters—65 percent of those eligible—coming to the polls.

Going to the polling booth was one thing; voting was something else. Throughout the state, polls didn't open on time in many precincts, and scores of voting machines were broken, particularly in the inner-city areas. Voters waited up to fifteen hours in some precincts. In Columbus, Ohio, the *Washington Post* reported, twenty-seven of the thirty wards with the most machines per registered voter were in areas that were pro-Bush. At the other end of the spectrum, six out of the seven wards with the fewest machines were in neighborhoods that were heavily for Kerry. At liberal Kenyon College, there were only two voting machines for thirteen hundred registered voters, which meant a wait of eleven hours for some voters. But conservative voters at nearby Mount Vernon Nazarene University, a fundamentalist college, had no lines at all. Most of the irregularities, concluded the House Judiciary report, were "caused by intentional misconduct and illegal behavior, much of it involving Secretary of State J. Kenneth Blackwell."*

Among those who had difficulty voting was Bob Fitrakis, the Columbus attorney who is co-counsel with Cliff Arnebeck in the *King Lincoln Bronzeville* lawsuit that was later filed against Blackwell. "We immediately went down to the Franklin County Board of Elections

---

* Blackwell declined to respond to phone calls by the author.

to complain about the lack of machines," Fitrakis said. "It was like it was braced for a terrorist attack. There were concrete bunkers and you had to go through a phalanx of armed sheriffs just to get inside."

Now Rove's team saw the fruits of its preelection "caging" efforts. Tens of thousands of would-be voters, most of whom resided in heavily Democratic precincts, arrived at their polling places to find that their registrations were being challenged because it appeared that they did not reside at the address in question. Voters who were consigned to this electoral limbo—college students, servicemen, the homeless, and people with more than one residence—were given provisional ballots, ballots for people whose eligibility was in question, when they arrived at the polls. But because there were no clearly defined standards for counting provisional ballots, thousands of such ballots went uncounted.

To further hamper Democratic voting, Rove was reportedly responsible for assembling the Mighty Texas Strike Force, consisting of some fifteen hundred volunteers who were deployed in Ohio, Florida, Pennsylvania, New Mexico, Michigan, Wisconsin, and other battleground states. Officially, the group was tasked with persuading voters to reelect President Bush, but incidents of voter intimidation were widely reported.

Over the course of the day, Edison Research's National Election Pool (NEP), the sole provider of exit poll data to ABC, CBS, CNN, Fox, NBC, and the Associated Press, had questioned voters as they left the voting booth about whom they pulled the lever for.

Because exit polls are based on interviews with actual voters who are questioned as they are leaving the polling place, rather than probable voters or registered voters, they have historically been regarded as so authoritative that major TV networks have used them to project winners in various states before all the votes are counted. In the 1980 presidential election, NBC came under criticism when it accurately predicted victory for Ronald Reagan at 8:15 p.m. EST based on exit polls of twenty thousand voters. Because the polls were still open on the West Coast, there was widespread speculation that many people didn't bother to vote after hearing the results. Since then, the major networks have adopted a policy of not announcing the winner in a given state until all polls have closed in that state, and not declaring the winner nationally until voting has ended on the West Coast.

In Ohio, the polls closed at 7:30 p.m. By this point, members of the National Election Pool—that is, the major TV networks and the Associated Press—had been told that preliminary exit polls* showed Kerry leading Bush in the popular vote nationally by 3 points, and Kerry taking Ohio, 52.1 percent to 47.9 percent, a significant lead of 4.2 points in what would arguably be the most important state in the Electoral College. Nationally, the same polls showed John Kerry winning the Electoral College, with 309 votes to Bush's 174. Only 270 were needed for victory, and fifty-five votes were still too close to call.

The major networks refrained from calling Ohio for Kerry, however, presumably so as not to influence voting in the West, where the polls were still open. But the polls were so persuasive they did have a considerable impact on election night coverage. Pollster John Zogby found the data so impressive that he immediately called the race for Kerry. Television broadcasters began speculating about who might serve in President Kerry's cabinet. Prime Minister Tony Blair went to sleep in London assuming he would soon be dealing with President-elect John Kerry. At eight p.m., a Fox News analyst put it succinctly: "Either the exit polls, by and large, are completely wrong, or George Bush loses."

* * *

* Edison/Mitofsky, the firm that did the exit polls, later released revised data that was aligned with final election results and showed Bush beating Kerry by three points. Needless to say, the revisions and unanswered questions about them created a heated controversy.

Asked to explain how and why it revised the numbers, a spokesperson for the National Election Pool issued a statement: "Exit polls, by standard procedure, incorporate many pieces of data that we continually collect throughout the day—including the responses of voters, the tallies from our sample precincts and, eventually, the actual state voting results. The exit polls are updated at various times throughout the day and evening, and after polls close, using all this information until they are final. Therefore, someone viewing an exit poll at any point earlier in the process, before all of it was finished, would be looking at an incomplete exit poll that would not—and should not—necessarily be expected to reflect its final results."

But the statement did not explain why the National Election Pool would release incomplete and misleading numbers to the national press corps.

Meanwhile, Rove had arrived at his office in the West Wing and had dived into a huge stack of exit poll data. "What I found shocked and profoundly angered me. An imbecile could see these reports were trash," he wrote. Wherever he looked, the figures seemed impossible. According to Rove, the polls showed Bush losing white men in Florida. Impossible. They showed Bush losing Pennsylvania by 18 points, when he had been down by just 2 a week earlier.

On and on it went. The more Rove immersed himself in the numbers, the more convinced he was they were wrong. He called the president and then briefed Andy Card. "I had gone from being sick to steaming. I knew the networks and cable channels would shape their evening coverage based on erroneous numbers and, just as in 2000, what was said on the air early could have an effect on turnout in the Midwest and West. I called Darby to tell her to forget everything I had told her earlier: the numbers were crap. We were going to win. I didn't know that for certain just yet, but the corrupted exits made me defiant."

By 7:30 p.m., voting was over in Ohio, but the election returns were not yet in. At eight p.m., the polls closed in eighteen states, mostly on the East Coast, including Florida. CNN all but called Florida for Bush, saying Kerry was ready to concede there. But broadcasters stopped short of a final pronouncement. It was going to be a long night.

After his trip to Ohio, President Bush had returned to the White House to watch the election returns with his family. Rove and his staff—Susan Ralston, Israel Hernandez, and B. J. Goergen—had set up their own temporary office on the State Floor of the White House, the first floor of the presidential residence, where they worked the phones and the computers.

This was Rove's own private war room, and it was filled with two large-screen TVs, a bank of phones, and four computers. Ken Mehlman, director of the White House Office of Political Affairs, had made sure the code jockeys at the RNC, whose tech operations were hosted at SmarTech in Chattanooga, wrote a program for Rove that allowed him to monitor election returns in real time. "My computer screen featured a map of the country. All I had to do was click on a state, and a map and its statewide returns would pop up. Click on a county and its returns appear."

Rove also kept a closely guarded notebook next to him that had the numbers of votes and percentage Bush needed for every county in every battleground state. "All I had to do was compare results for a county or state from the computer screen against the notebook figures, and I could quickly get a sense of how well we were doing. Susan, Israel, and B.J. sat to my left with terminals and phones. They tracked down anyone I needed to talk to and kept an open line to Mehlman at headquarters."

As the returns came in, the eyes of the nation were fixed on Florida and Ohio. For most of the day, the atmosphere "was almost like the Super Bowl," said Robert Destro, a professor at the Columbus School of Law at the Catholic University of America, who had been invited to be an observer at Blackwell's Secretary of State's Office in Columbus. He, other observers, and Blackwell's staff spent most of the time in a large conference room with big TVs on and Doritos, chips, and soda on a table for refreshments. "Most of the election returns were being sent by fax to the secretary's office and the office took care of the data entry and processed the information as fast as it came in. And then they would try to get it on the website as quickly as possible."

At nine, Bob Mangan, director of information technology, left the State Office Computer Center in Columbus and headed home. There were still more than thirty people in the office working overnight, including at least one technician from SmarTech—Mike Henry. Mangan would resume his duties at eight the next morning.

The smaller counties reported first in Ohio. At 9:30 p.m., Allen County came in with 48,121 votes. Fayette came in at 9:49 with 11,704; Adams at 10:26. These socially conservative rural areas strongly favored Bush, especially in light of the initiative prohibiting gay marriage. The big cities—Cleveland, Cincinnati, and Columbus—with a high percentage of African-Americans, favored Kerry, and they would come later.

Half an hour later, the last polling booths began closing on the West Coast. As a result, exit polls were finally available throughout almost the entire continental United States. They showed Kerry ahead in ten out of eleven battleground states. If the exit polls were correct, Kerry would win the popular vote by a million and a half votes nationally.

But from his war room in the White House, Rove had a very different perspective. As soon as the polls closed in Florida, he began clicking on the counties north of Tampa Bay, such as Pasco and Hernando. In 2000, Bush had won Pasco by fewer than 1,000 votes, but now he had a lead of 18,000 plus. Likewise in Hernando. Rove called Jeb Bush, who saw a similar pattern. Bush appeared to be beating his targets in Duval, St. Johns, Volusia, Brevard, Seminole, and Indian River counties. According to Rove, "Even in the big Democratic strongholds of Palm Beach, Broward, and Miami-Dade, the president was doing better than he needed to carry the state. I gave up worrying about Florida. For the rest of the evening, I returned to the Sunshine State only if I needed to feel really good."

Not everyone felt the same way, particularly when it came to Florida. John Kerry's team was seething with frustration at the Sunshine State because of its apparent inability to count absentee ballots. At 9:55, Democratic consultant Paul Begala went on CNN saying that three primarily Democratic counties—Broward, Palm Beach, and Dade— would not be able to count their absentee ballots until Thursday.

"How on God's Earth do we not have absentee ballots counted in Florida?" Begala said at 10:42. "Jeb Bush and Glenda Hood—the Republican secretary of state playing the part of Katherine Harris— are making the state look like a banana republic run by a bunch of banana Republicans. I've been talking to Kerry campaign operatives in Ohio and Florida. The Kerry folks are pretty optimistic in Ohio; in Florida they are pretty angry that they can't get ballots counted."

Worse, the numbers were trending toward Bush. If he won Florida, everything depended on Ohio. With 77 percent of the vote counted in Florida, CNN reported, Bush had a lead of more than 250,000 votes over Kerry.

But that was still not enough to call Florida for Bush.

At eleven p.m., on CNN, Democratic strategist James Carville repeated his mantra: "Ohio, Florida, Ohio, Florida."

Then, Carville added, "And if the president carries both Ohio and

Florida, it is extremely difficult, almost impossible . . . for Senator Kerry to win." Carville was clearly glum.

In Columbus, outside observers, techies, and staffers in the Secretary of State's Office watched the news stream over the Internet. By eleven p.m., the tide had clearly shifted. CNN had not officially called Florida for Bush yet, but a report said the president was doing unusually well along the corridor between Orlando and Tampa, and that would likely offset Kerry's strength in unreported areas.

To the extent that that meant Florida was going for Bush, the entire election would now be in Ohio's hands. In the Computer Center in Columbus, the IT department anticipated getting over 40 million hits in a twenty-four-hour period, but the SmarTech linkup had still not been activated. Now that all the attention was shifting to Ohio, traffic on the secretary's site shot up dramatically. "Almost instantly, our load on the Internet increased six or seven times," said a technician who was present. "We had two boxes accepting queries and they exceeded our load factor and one of them failed. This is the mysterious switchover."

Now SmarTech's "failover" site in Chattanooga went into action. This was the moment Mike Connell had prepared for. "In order to keep running," said the techie, "we split our load for queries so that half the queries went to SmarTech and half to the Secretary of State's Office." That meant millions of queries were channeled to the SmarTech database for the first time.

In other words, the highly partisan GOP tech company that was the successor to the firm started by Rove's fund-raisers Mercer Reynolds and Bill DeWitt, the firm that hosted RNC.com, georgewbush.com, the Swift Boat Veterans for Truth, Karl Rove's emails, and the RNC's Voter Vault database with its secret algorithms that Rove prized so dearly, was now wired into the incoming Ohio election results—at the exact moment when Ohio held the fate of the nation in its hands.

It was 11:14 p.m.

TEN

11:14 P.M.

R eturns from other counties in Ohio continued to roll in. At 11:56 p.m., Butler County reported 163,668 votes. Cuyahoga County came in at thirty-one seconds after midnight with 665,334 votes from Cleveland and its suburbs. Election day was over. Lorain, Mahoning, and Montgomery counties all reported less than a minute later with 139,069, 131,938, and 279,801 votes, respectively.

At 12:21 a.m., on November 3, CNN finally posted the exit polls that had been released nearly five hours earlier. They showed John Kerry winning Ohio by 4.2 percentage points. To the public at large, it now appeared that John Forbes Kerry had an excellent chance of winning Ohio's twenty electoral votes and, with it, the presidency of the United States.

But exactly seventeen minutes later, a very different reality emerged in the White House. Rove got off the phone with the Ohio campaign headquarters and made an important announcement: Ohio was "cooked," he said, "and in our column."

Three minutes later, Fox News called Ohio for President Bush. Andy Card congratulated Rove. Hugs, handshakes, and laughter broke the tension. Fox News put up the graphic awarding Ohio to Bush. As it was being displayed, Rove's wife, Darby, snapped a photo of Karl on the phone with President Bush. "I've got a phone to my ear and [my son] Andrew standing next to me giving two thumbs-up with a big grin," she said. "Take it from me, there's nothing like shepherding two winning presidential campaigns and celebrating both with your son."

With Ohio, Bush now had 269 votes in the Electoral College. He needed exactly one more vote to win, so any of the states that were outstanding would put him over the top. The 2004 election was over.

To Rove's dismay, however, the media would not the call the election for Bush. He continued to work the phones. From the private White House quarters above the war room, Bush repeatedly called Rove, asking for the latest news, until, finally, at 2:30 a.m., he couldn't stand it any longer, came down, and joined his consigliere. A victory would mean that he had outdone his father, who had failed to win a second term.

By four a.m., the Associated Press and the major networks called Nevada for Bush. Rove wanted to declare victory, but cooler heads prevailed, asserting it would look rushed and unpresidential to do so in the middle of the night. He had been up for twenty-four hours and had slept but four hours or so in the previous two days. The announcement could wait.

In the end, it had all come down to Ohio. If the Democrats had taken the state, John Kerry would have won the White House, with 272 electoral votes to Bush's 266. Thanks to Bush's victory there, he had been reelected president of the United States.

Or had he?

Allegations that the Republicans stole the 2004 presidential election are nothing new. In 2005, the investigation by the House Judiciary Committee concluded that Ohio, the most crucial swing state of all, conducted its election in a way that had so many "massive and unprecedented" irregularities that it raised "grave doubts" about the legality of the outcome of the entire presidential election.

In addition, the case that the election was stolen in Ohio has been made by a quixotic assortment of bloggers, journalists, lawyers, and academics. But for the most part they have been ignored or scorned— often by presumably friendly left-of-center critics, including Salon, *Mother Jones,* and even, at times, by the Democratic Party itself.

Among the most striking telltale signs that the Ohio election results were questionable was the fact that Kerry fared significantly better in the much-vaunted exit polls—6.7 percent—than he did in the final official results. And Ohio was not the only anomaly. According to a study by Steven Freeman, who is an MIT PhD and a visiting scholar at the University of Pennsylvania, in ten out of the eleven battleground states—Colorado, Florida, Iowa, Michigan, Minnesota, Nevada, Ohio, Pennsylvania, New Hampshire, and New Mexico— "the tallied margin differs from the predicted [exit poll] margin, and in every one, the shift favors Bush."

But exactly what did that mean? Could it be that the exit polls were correct and the final results were wrong? If that were the case, of course, it would raise a question that was all but taboo: Had the 2004 presidential election been stolen?

For Karl Rove, the answer was simple. He derided the exit poll consortium as those "geniuses in New Jersey" who, at various times, produced polls that were "stupid," "flawed," "shoddy," "unreliable," "trash," "terribly wrong," and "corrupted." The final election results merely proved how wrong the exits were.

On the left, however, many argued that the exit polls had such an extraordinary history of accuracy that, as Freeman asserted, the unexplained discrepancies make "systematic fraud or mistabulation . . . an unavoidable hypothesis, one that is the responsibility of the media, academia, polling agencies, and the public to investigate."

But there was also a third possibility. In recent years, other polling experts who are in no way linked to Karl Rove, including highly regarded bloggers such as Nate Silver of fivethirtyeight.com and the *New York Times* and Mark Blumenthal, polling editor of the Huffington Post and founder of pollster.com, have offered compelling critiques of exit polls and various flaws in their methodologies.*

Blumenthal, for example, argues that exit polls have a history of unreliability thanks to a host of logistical problems and methodological issues that make it hard to put together a statistically valid sample. Exit pollsters must take breaks to tabulate responses and call in results.

---

* Those seeking a more complete discussion of this issue might examine the works of Steven Freeman, whose paper "The Unexplained Exit Poll Discrepancy" can be found at http://www.appliedresearch.us/sf/ and Mark Blumenthal at http://www.mysterypollster.com/main/2004/11/the_freeman_pap.html.

Freeman argues that the odds of having three critical battleground states (Florida, Pennsylvania, and Ohio) in which Kerry does far better in the exit polls than he does in the final results is a statistical anomaly the odds of which are 250 million to one. For his part, Blumenthal argues that methodological flaws in exit polls mean they are not nearly as accurate as they are said to be, so that Freeman overstates his case.

They must stop polling an hour before the polls close. They must try to interview voters who sometimes emerge in packs all at once. When they miss potential respondents, they end up using "cluster sampling" as opposed to "simple random sampling." Where telephone pollsters have quotas for women interviewees, exit pollsters do not, even though women historically skew toward Democratic candidates. And if several precincts vote at a single polling place, the interviewers have no way of identifying which precinct the voter is from. All these factors, Blumenthal says, can contribute to a higher degree of error.

Certainly the discrepancies between the exit polls and the final count were highly suggestive, especially insofar as the final count consistently favored Bush. But until all those methodological flaws could be accounted for, it was hard to say they conclusively proved systematic fraud.

All of which suggests that the exit polls are, to a certain degree, a red herring in any discussion of the 2004 election results because it is altogether possible that Karl Rove was right in saying exit polls were flawed, *but* that does not eliminate the possibility that there was electoral fraud as well. "I have never argued that the exit polls can be used to *rule out* or *disprove* the possibility that vote fraud may have occurred in Ohio," Blumenthal concluded.

At the heart of the issue of fraud in Ohio is the question of exactly what role SmarTech played on election night. That's because after SmarTech's servers in Chattanooga kicked in at 11:14 p.m., the returns from Ohio were characterized by many different anomalies involving the tabulation of punch cards, electronic voting machines of various types, spectacularly high turnouts in pro-Bush precincts, and turnouts in pro-Kerry precincts that were astoundingly low. Virtually all the irregularities favored Bush, and the vast majority of them remain unexplained.

How and why all this happened is central to the lawsuit filed on behalf of the King Lincoln Bronzeville Neighborhood Association against J. Kenneth Blackwell by Cliff Arnebeck and Bob Fitrakis to protect the election rights of blacks, young voters, and others whose voting rights were allegedly violated by irregularities in Ohio's 2004 election process.

A key point raised by the lawsuit is whether 11:14 p.m. was the time at which SmarTech began to change the election results. "If you think about manipulating the election," says Arnebeck, "it seems to me that SmarTech had to have a program that was guiding the way things had to be manipulated in order to win without being obvious."

In other words, putting Ohio in Bush's column was not simply a question of flipping enough random votes. The fraud would have to be done in a *believable* way. That meant enough votes had to be changed in the *right* precincts to swing the state to Bush without triggering widespread suspicion. There were only so many voters in each of Ohio's 11,360 precincts. Some areas, the African-American wards in Cleveland's Cuyahoga County, for example, had a long history of being so heavily Democratic that a Bush landslide there would simply not be credible. Making such changes was difficult enough, but doing so in any of Ohio's thousands of precincts, each of which has its own unique voting history, presented hundreds of decisions that would have to be made, and executed, instantly in the dead of night, beginning at 11:14 and continuing for the next few hours.

To make matters more complicated, because each of Ohio's eighty-eight counties was allowed to establish its own voting procedures and tabulate the votes at the county board of elections, rigging the election presumably would have to be coordinated at both the statewide level and the county level, or even the precinct level. Some counties used electronic voting machines made by Diebold, whose CEO, Warren O'Dell, had vowed to help deliver Ohio for the Republicans. Others used optical scanning machines made by ES&S. Many chose punch card ballots tabulated by Triad. Each methodology was potentially vulnerable to fraud in various ways, before, during, and after the voting process, but executing such an operation without detection would have been an extraordinarily daunting task.

"They had to have formulas saying you could swing this many votes, that would be plausible given historic voting patterns," said Arnebeck. "SmarTech had to have oversight of the entire process. I'm assuming that the data was coming into the Secretary of State's Office, that SmarTech would get it immediately and that they would use that information to determine what additional votes were needed, and they would convey that information to the counties they were in a position to manipulate."

How could that be done?

Arnebeck concedes that there are many unanswered questions, but he points out that in the basement of the Pioneer Bank Building in Chattanooga, SmarTech had a network operations center consisting of racks of servers that hosted sites for George Bush, the Republican National Committee, the Swift Boat Veterans for Truth, and scores of other GOP sites. SmarTech also hosted the RNC's Voter Vault, which, as noted before, was a database cross-referencing phone numbers, driver's licenses, hunting and fishing licenses, property records, and, most important, the voting history of every precinct in the United States.

According to Arnebeck, the Voter Vault or a similar resource—perhaps the database from another company working with the secretary of state—could have served that purpose. "We were informed that state of the art software and communication technology was being utilized to coordinate all adjustments necessary to produce the desired margin of reported victory for Mr. Rove's candidate.

"You are dealing with millions of votes in a process that unfolds in a matter of hours," said Arnebeck. "It's like flying a plane on autopilot. You want to be able to make hundreds of calculations instantly. It's the difference between computer trading in the stock market and manual trading in the stock market."

In *Courage and Consequence,* Rove himself refers to unnamed programs written by the "RNC's computer wizards," presumably Voter Vault, that appear to fulfill Arnebeck's conditions by allowing "us to monitor election returns in real time," as Rove puts it.

However, one problem with Arnebeck's theory was that the secretary of state's computer system had been designed so SmarTech could post results from the SOS computers but could not input new data. "SmarTech was just a mirror site," says Robert Destro, the law professor who served the Secretary of State's Office as outside counsel for the election. "I don't know how mirror sites work, but the idea that people could manipulate data is absurd."

In other words, according to Destro, SmarTech did not have the capacity to change election results—or, at least, that was the plan. As designed by Bob Mangan, head of IT for the Secretary of State's

Office, information flowed only one way. Political operatives at SmarTech or GovTech would not be able to change the results.

But once Mike Connell gained access to the secretary of state's servers, that could have changed. Indeed, in his deposition for the *King Lincoln* case, Connell testified that Ohio needed a backup server precisely because the Oracle database software it used was "a resource hog" that allowed its clients, many of whom were banks, to have an audit trail for all activity. Several computer experts believe that in bypassing that system Connell could have made the Ohio servers easy to penetrate by what is known as a man-in-the-middle attack.

One of them is Harri Hursti, a Finnish computer expert best known as the man behind the so-called Hursti Hack, in which he collaborated with the election reform group Black Box Voting for the HBO documentary *Hacking Democracy* and, on camera, exposed serious flaws in the voting system of Diebold Election Systems.

"Anytime you are hauling traffic from one location to another, that is the kind of place where man-in-the-middle attacks can be applied," Hursti said. "Your computer tells you [that you] are talking to [one computer] when you are really talking to a rogue server. At any point in time, it can modify the information."

He added that such attacks are easy to do, like "taking a lollipop from children."

Nor is Hursti alone in his critique of the Ohio-SmarTech setup. In addition, a source who was intimate with SmarTech's technology corroborated Hursti. "The Ohio system was pretty secure until it started flowing through SmarTech," says the source. "At that point, SmarTech was the man in the middle, and they could have done anything they liked."

Finally, a similar assessment came from Stephen Spoonamore, who not only knew Connell but also discussed the 2004 election system with him. A cyber security expert who specializes in defending massive computer systems against hackers, Spoonamore, who is an expert witness testifying in the *King Lincoln* case, asserted in a sworn affidavit for the case that the system set up by the office of Secretary of State Blackwell was so insecure that that "would be cause to launch an immediate fraud investigation into any of my banking clients."

"This computer placement, in the middle of the network, is a defined type of attack," said the affidavit. "It is called a MIM (Man in the Middle) Attack. It is a common problem in the banking settlement space. A criminal gang will introduce a computer into the outgoing electronic systems of a major retail mall, or smaller branch office of a bank. They will capture the legitimate transactions and then add fraudulent charges to the system for their benefit.

"Any time all information is directed to a single computer for consolidation," the affidavit continued, "it is possible, and in fact likely, that a single computer will exploit the information for some purpose. In the case of Ohio 2004, the only purpose I can conceive for sending all county vote tabulations to a GOP managed Man-in-the-Middle site in Chattanooga BEFORE [sic] sending the results onward to the Sec. of State, would be to hack the vote at the MIM."

But did that happen? Not all critics of the Ohio election are sure. Bev Harris, founder of the election reform group Black Box Voting, sees a man-in-the-middle attack as a remote possibility in view of the fact that results in many counties were collected at the local level and faxed in. As a result, she said, "It's more likely that they were getting 'first look' so they could figure out how much they needed; then, using more old-school tactics like stickers over punch cards, ballot stuffing and spoliation, they worked with counties that had not yet reported and were 'open for business' to achieve what was needed."

Finally, in his affidavit Spoonamore spoke about his friendship with Mike Connell, who had contracted with the Secretary of State's Office to build the "failover site" at SmarTech. "While he has not admitted to wrongdoing, and in my opinion he is not involved in voting theft, Mike clearly agrees that the electronic voting systems in the US are not secure. He further made a statement that he is afraid that some of the more ruthless partisans of the GOP may have exploited systems he in part worked on for this purpose. Mr. Connell builds front-end applications, user interfaces and web sites. Knowing his team and their skills I find it unlikely they would be the vote thieves directly. I believe however he knows who is doing that work, and has likely turned a blind eye to this activity."

Spoonamore's account of his conversations with Connell is vital to the *King Lincoln* case, and the author has not been able to corroborate it independently. However, Spoonamore's affidavit is signed, "I declare under penalty of perjury that the foregoing is true and correct."

But if SmarTech had seized control, surely there would be evidence. If Arnebeck is right, that would suggest that the Ohio counties that reported *before* the SmarTech connection kicked in at 11:14 would have reported results that were relatively untouched. And if Smar-Tech was indeed tampering with the results, counties that reported *after* 11:14 presumably would be the ones that were full of irregularities.

To test the hypothesis, the author gave a list of Ohio's counties and their reporting times to Richard Hayes Phillips, who served as an expert witness specializing for the *King Lincoln* case.

A former college professor with a doctorate in geology, Phillips is an unlikely expert on electoral fraud. He is a self-described singer/ songwriter who spends several months a year clearing trails in the Adirondacks, a wandering minstrel who actually does play the mandolin, and a "detective" who is also trying to unravel an epic mystery—the alleged theft of a presidential election, no less. He is also the only person to have spent three years researching the 2004 election in Ohio, putting together a team of sixteen people who analyzed more than 120,000 ballots, 127 poll books, and 141 signature books from the election.

In his audit of the Ohio election, *Witness to a Crime,* published in 2008, before SmarTech's role came into question, Phillips examined data from ten of the counties that reported before 11:14—Adams, Ashtabula, Crawford, Fayette, Hancock, Henry, Medina, Muskingum, Preble, and Wayne.

The result? "None of the counties that reported before 11:14 ever raised any red flags with me," said Phillips. "None were suspect."

Of the counties reporting after 11:14 p.m., Phillips had investigated fourteen—Butler, Clark, Clermont, Cuyahoga, Delaware, Geauga, Hamilton, Lorain, Lucas, Mahoning, Miami, Montgomery, Van Wert, and Warren.

The result? "All fourteen of the counties reporting after 11:14 *are* suspect," said Phillips. Then he added, "How's that for a pattern?"

* * *

But how could any of this have been executed? One important clue could be found in Cleveland's Fourth Ward, which had striking aberrations in its final election results.

Historically, when it came to delivering votes for Democrats, Benedictine High School, in Cleveland's Fourth Ward, was as true blue as it gets. In 2000, Al Gore got fully 95 percent of the vote. Ralph Nader got just eight votes and was the only non–major party candidate to get any at all.

When the 2004 returns came in for Benedictine, Kerry and the Democrats still had a majority. But their share had shrunk to 59.8 percent—a 35 percent drop—because obscure new third-party candidates were suddenly polling well.

Astonishingly well.

In Precinct 1814 at Benedictine, for example, Libertarian Michael Badnarik polled 164 votes, more than thirteen times as many votes as Bush.

Even harder to believe, in Precinct 1806, the other precinct at Benedictine, Michael Peroutka, an obscure "Christian/Constitutionalist" with white nationalist support, got 40 percent, 215 votes—roughly ten times as many votes as Bush.

How was it possible that in one of the most liberal areas in the state more than 40 percent of the voters, many of whom were highly disciplined African-American voters, had picked Peroutka? Anyone with knowledge of the area was astounded. "I can't believe it," Fourth Ward city councilor Kenneth Johnson told Juan Gonzalez of the *New York Daily News*. "It's obviously a malfunction."

But a malfunction seemed unlikely as well. Like voters in forty-one of Ohio's eighty-eight counties, Benedictine used Triad voting machines, the most widely used means of voting in the state. Triad machines used punch card ballots, which were made of paper, of course.

How could paper ballots possibly be hacked?

The answer, Ohio voters later discovered, could be found in a technique known variously as cross-voting, "vote migration," or the "caterpillar crawl," which was both extraordinarily effective and hard to detect because of the unique way in which it exploited two idiosyncrasies in Ohio's voting procedures.

One such practice was that the order in which candidates appear on the ballot rotates from one precinct to another. This is the result of a 1975 Ohio law that was passed to make sure that no candidate had an unfair advantage by having the top position on the ballot.

In 2004, there were five presidential candidates on the ballot in Ohio, and that meant five possibly different ballot orders. The order in one precinct had Bush, Kerry, Ralph Nader, Michael Anthony Peroutka of the right-wing Constitution Party, and Michael Badnarik of the Libertarian Party. The next was Kerry, Nader, Peroutka, and Badnarik, with Bush going to the last position. The sequence was always the same, but the starting point shifted from one precinct to the next.

The intent of ballot rotation was to ensure fairness. But there were unintended consequences thanks to another common practice in Ohio voting, namely, that voters from two or more precincts often voted at the same location. This practice of "collocation" is so common that fully seven out of eight voters in Cleveland's Cuyahoga County vote at sites that serve more than one precinct.

Together, those two practices—ballot rotation and collocation—created a problem, namely, a susceptibility to cross-voting or the caterpillar crawl. The electoral equivalent of three-card monte, it was stunning in its elegance and simplicity. But, most important, it was an ingenious means by which the tabulation of punch card ballots—ballots made of paper—could be manipulated on a mass scale.

Yes, paper ballots could actually be hacked.

In any event, here's what happened:

Benedictine hosted voters from two precincts. After arrival at the polling station, voters signed in and were given punch cards corresponding to the precinct in which they were registered. Voting machines were available for both precincts, but voters were unaware that there was any difference between the two ballots. "There was no distinction between precincts," said Katie Daley, a Democratic observer who spent election day at Benedictine. "Voters were being told to go to any machine that was open."

And that was the problem. Because, according to Phillips, if voters were given the right punch card, but went to a voting machine for a different precinct, "their votes would be shifted one or two positions, and their votes would be counted for the wrong candidates." The ballots were later tabulated at the county level by tabulators contracted by Triad GSI, a small Ohio company that provides election hardware and software.

Brett Rapp, president of Triad, backs up Phillips's assessment. "I have no question that situation took place," Rapp said.

Similarly, the House Judiciary report came up with a straight-forward conclusion: "It appears that hundreds, if not thousands, of votes intended to be cast for Senator Kerry were recorded as being for a third-party candidate."

Steering voters to the wrong voting booth, said Phillips, "worked best in urban, blue counties where Kerry's support was so strong, he was sure to be the net loser. And in big cities they had voting places with multiple precincts, so it was easy to do." So for Republicans, the beauty of cross-voting was the stronger Kerry's support, the more damage it did to his chances.

In the case of Benedictine, of course, electronic fraud played no role whatsoever. "Those ballots were not altered," said Phillips. "The voters themselves punched the wrong hole, being wrongly induced to do so."

Nonetheless, Benedictine was significant because it was the "tell" that exposed cross-voting in Ohio. More to the point, in other precincts the same scam could take place by other means—for example, by swapping votes from one precinct to another, or by tabulation—almost undetected, by flipping a small percentage of votes, say 5 or 10 percent, from Kerry to Bush or another candidate. "That is the most likely method for wholesale vote-shifting by computerized intervention," says Phillips. "If one shifts a certain percentage of the vote in every precinct countywide, there will be no 'irregular' precincts. Every single one will have results that are consistent with historic voting patterns."

But there were many, many ways in which cross-voting might take place, and because more than 70 percent of the votes cast in Ohio that year were via punch cards, Triad had the power to change the outcome.

Exactly what role did Triad play?

From his office in the small town of Xenia, Ohio, Triad president Brett Rapp, whose company built the tabulators used in 2004, asserted that it was difficult "to corrupt the election without someone finding out," because an examination of the ballots would reveal any fraud.

But within that context, Rapp added, things could go wrong. Even before the voting began, he says, election officials in each county were entrusted with inserting the appropriate page frame in the voting machines so that the ballot sequence would be properly aligned in each precinct. "If I wanted to mess up an election," said Rapp, "I might switch the page frames so that the [sequence] in the voting machine is different from what appears on the ballot."

If that happened, he said, the vote would go to a different candidate than intended. In effect, it was a variation on the cross-voting that took place at Benedictine High School. In this case, however, the same goal could be accomplished by switching page frames instead of sending voters to the wrong machine.

But that was just one weakness. According to Rapp, after the polls closed, the punch cards were taken out of the machines, bundled by poll workers, put in a locked bag, and brought to the board of elections in each county, where stacks of ballots from different precincts might be swapped. "If you took exactly the same number of ballots and swapped them so the ballot counts came out properly, you could do that," he said.

But that type of fraud, Rapp said, would easily be detected, because each ballot was identified by precinct.

In addition, Rapp said the Triad tabulating machines had programs "that would accept all the precincts and know the ballot rotations," so at each county board the person running the tabulator could have effectively instituted cross-voting merely by intentionally using the wrong ballot rotation.

But again, it would be difficult to do that without being caught because, he said, "There are usually multiple people, Republican and Democrats, watching the tabulation process."

Finally, according to Rapp, there is a card called the "header card" that is inserted into the tabulator to identify the correct ballot sequence to tabulate each precinct properly. "Can you count the wrong stack of ballots with the wrong header card?" Rapp said. "The answer is yes."

But again there was a safeguard, and Rapp said the fraud would surely be discovered, because "each precinct doesn't have the same number of votes."

Benedictine wasn't the only place where clues suggesting cross-voting surfaced. According to Phillips, in Cuyahoga County alone "there are at least 16 precincts where votes intended to be cast for Kerry were shifted to other candidates' columns." In Warren County, the returns were suspect because the vote totals for the amendment to ban gay marriage were completely at odds with the returns for the presidential race. Here the "tell" was that ballot initiatives do *not* rotate by precinct. That meant if that cross-voting was implemented, votes for or against the marriage amendment remained unchanged.

So when a mysterious Homeland Security alert took place at the Warren County Board of Elections after one a.m., five hours after the polls closed, and officials summarily carted thousands of ballots off to an alternative building, investigators saw it as a fake lockout so that Republicans could manipulate the vote in peace and quiet. After the election, an audit of fifteen precincts in Warren County showed that more than half the supporters of gay marriage also voted for Bush—an extraordinarily unlikely outcome.* The simplest explanation, said Arnebeck, is that "ballots cast for Kerry were shifted to a precinct in which that position would be read by the tabulator as cast for Bush."

Equally unlikely—and, in some cases, impossible—voter turnout suggests rampant cross-voting took place throughout the state. According to the Judiciary Committee Report, in heavily Republican Perry County, for example, two precincts had 124 percent and 120 percent turnouts, respectively. In Miami County, also according to the Judiciary Committee report, "voter turnout was a highly suspect and improbable 98.55 percent." Inexplicably, nearly 19,000 new ballots were added after all precincts reported in the highly Republican county. At one voting site in Miami, 679 votes were counted even

* Issue One, the constitutional amendment prohibiting gay marriage, was not subject to ballot rotation, so gay-friendly Democrats whose ballots were switched would be counted as gay-friendly Republicans.

though just 547 had signed in. In one precinct, Gahanna Ward 1, precinct B, Bush received 4,258 votes even though there were only 638 registered voters.*

And so it went. In Franklin County, where Columbus is located, voters reported that their votes for Kerry faded from the screens of their electronic voting machines. In Mahoning County, touch screens had been programmed to default to candidate Bush so that if the voter did nothing at all, or failed to override the default, Bush got the vote. In Youngstown, the biggest city in the county, the *Washington Post* reported that twenty-five electronic machines transferred an unknown number of Kerry votes to the Bush column. Veteran voter Jeanne White stepped into the booth, pushed the button for Kerry—and saw her vote jump to the Bush column. "I saw what happened; I started screaming: 'They're cheating again and they're starting early!'"

Hundreds of irregularities—the vast majority of which favored Bush, not Kerry. Which, in turn, raised serious questions that remain unanswered: Did a man-in-the-middle attack actually take place? Were election results in Ohio manipulated by computer after the 11:14 link-up with SmarTech took place? Could results at the county level be manipulated by a computer controlling the statewide results? Did people at the county level manipulate ballots in an effort to match the statewide results? At the county level, were Triad's electronic tabulators similarly manipulated? And what about the electronic voting machines such as Diebold's and ES&S's?

"What they did was brilliant," claimed Stephen Spoonamore. "You have to admire that. They won. They changed the election. Kerry won, but they switched it to Bush. Trust me, that's what they did."

Spoonamore's certitude notwithstanding, for all these anomalies, many questions remained unanswered. "The Secretary of State doesn't do the counts, he just reports them," said Robert Destro. "The count itself takes place at the local level and you have more eyes than you can shake a stick at from both sides of the aisle."

So for many counties, making the subtotals mesh by working

---

* The numbers were later adjusted to show President Bush's true vote count at 365 votes and Senator Kerry's at 260 votes.

backward was impossible, because the computer servers in the Secretary of State's Office were not even connected to all eighty-eight county election boards. "[More than thirty] counties either call up and give us a series of numbers over the phone, or they are faxed and entered manually," said Bob Mangan.

On the other hand, McClatchy Newspapers reported, the election night "architecture map for Blackwell's office appears to suggest that as many as 51 of Ohio's 88 counties periodically sent their results to the secretary of state's office." The article said that computer technicians in the Secretary of State's Office "have been unable to determine how many, if any, counties transmitted results directly from vote tabulators, rather than from separate computers to shield against outside access to vote counts."

All of which meant that if there was electronic fraud at the statewide level, it would also have had to be done at the county level where the tabulation took place, and it would have had to happen not just in one county but in many counties.

Likewise, as Triad's Brett Rapp pointed out, if ballots had been tabulated by the wrong precinct setting, if the wrong page frame had been used, if the wrong header card had been used—if any such methods were used to manipulate the vote—all of that would be evident in an examination of the ballots. If these allegations were true, surely the vote manipulators could not possibly get away with it.

As the dust began to settle, John Kerry and the Democratic Party decided not to challenge the election. "Kerry heard all the disquieting stories" about voting irregularities in Ohio, said Jonathan Winer, a former deputy assistant secretary of state who had served as Kerry's counsel on the Senate Foreign Relations Committee. "But he didn't have the evidence to do more."

Nonetheless, voter-reform activists, progressives, and activist lawyers began to strategize. Netroot bloggers began to stir. Even though the Democrats did not demand a recount, the Libertarian Party and the Green Party did. The plaintiffs further sued to delay the seating of Ohio's Electoral College delegation until after the recount was finished, demanding as part of discovery access to Karl Rove's laptop.

But Secretary of State Ken Blackwell quickly rushed to certify the results of the election, thereby rendering the recount moot. And

as for the recount itself, even it was the subject of controversy and alleged fraud. A spokesman for the Ohio Democratic Party, Daniel Trevas, told the *New York Times* that county election officials sometimes ignored requests to see rejected or provisional ballots. "Some of these boards did not give us full access during the recount," Trevas said.

The story of what happened in Ohio was not over yet. But, ultimately, to get the answers to the questions raised by the anomalies in Ohio's voting, as Triad's Brett Rapp pointed out, one would have to examine the ballots themselves.

ELEVEN

Drawing an Inside Straight

In the immediate aftermath of November 2, the mainstream press, for the most part, either ignored or scorned the notion that the election had been decided by fraud. On November 10, the *Boston Globe* announced, "Internet Buzz on Vote Fraud Is Dismissed." Then came the *New York Times:* "Vote Fraud Theories, Spread by Blogs, Are Quickly Buried."

In truth, there seemed to be good reasons to dismiss cries of fraud. For one thing, there were both Democrats and Republicans on the board of elections overseeing the tabulation of the official votes in each county and the totals could not be released unless both parties agreed that the local count had been conducted in a fair and nonpartisan manner. If there were widespread fraud, surely Democrats would have been crying bloody murder.

But the reality was more complicated than that. For one thing, security violations were so pervasive that many violations likely went unseen. In county after county, Triad tabulators were left unsecured. According to the House Judiciary Committee report, at least one Triad employee and officials in several counties had remote access to Triad tabulators—even though protocol prohibited the servers from being connected to outside computers. "Tons of people have access to those tabulators," said Bob Fitrakis, a co-counsel to Arnebeck in the *King Lincoln* case.

In Miami County, at least ten unauthorized Republicans were allowed into the board of elections on election day during the counting of the ballots. Moreover, such irregularities were widespread because they seemed to come from the top. "Blackwell made Katherine Harris look like a cupcake," John Conyers told *Rolling Stone*. "He saw his role as limiting the participation of Democratic voters. We had hearings in Columbus for two days. We could have stayed two weeks, the level of fury was so high. Thousands of people wanted to testify. Nothing like this had ever happened to them before."

As a result, the Judiciary Committee largely blamed Blackwell and the Republican Party and concluded that the misallocation of voting machines led to "unprecedented long lines that disenfranchised scores, if not hundreds of thousands, of predominantly minority and Democratic voters"; that "Blackwell's decision to restrict provisional ballots resulted in the disenfranchisement of tens, if not hundreds, of thousands of voters, again, predominantly minority and Democratic voters"; that "the Republican Party's pre-election 'caging' tactics selectively targeting 35,000 predominantly minority voters for intimidation had a negative impact on voter turnout"; that the GOP's use of thousands of partisan challengers "in minority and Democratic areas likely disenfranchised tens of thousands of legal voters"; and that a variety of other tactics by Blackwell and the Republicans resulted in widespread violations "of the Voting Rights Act, the Civil Rights Act of 1968, Equal Protection, Due Process and the Ohio right to vote" that threw the legitimacy of the vote in Ohio into question.

The most basic question, of course, was whether these practices actually changed the outcome of the election, and it was hoped that the recount would settle that once and for all. But even when it came to the recount the irregularities continued.

First and foremost, the outcome of the recount was moot, because on December 13, 2004, the very day the recount began, Secretary of State Blackwell presided over a statehouse session of Republican Electoral College members to cast Ohio's twenty electoral votes for George Bush, thereby delivering the presidency to Bush.

Nevertheless, the recount continued—and was still problematic. Under Ohio law, a county must first hand-count 3 percent of the ballots in its county randomly selected and then run them through a machine count to see if they match. But there are many reasons to believe those standards were not rigorously observed. According to the Judiciary Committee Report, Triad "essentially admitted" that it provided election officials with "cheat sheets" informing election officials how many votes they should find for each candidate so they "could avoid doing a full county-wide hand recount mandated by state law." Likewise, the committee said that "Blackwell's failure to articulate clear and consistent standards for the counting of provisional ballots resulted in the loss of thousands of predominantly minority votes" in the recount.

When the recount was done, Bush still came out ahead—by 18,000 fewer votes—but it was unclear what, if anything, had been resolved.

The report from the House Judiciary Committee was searing, but when it was released on January 5, 2005, it was greeted with a yawn. All that remained were a few left-wing websites pushing for investigations while the Libertarian Party—not the Democrats, mind you—demanded a recount. "Latest Conspiracy Theory—Kerry Won—Hits the Ether," read the headline for a brief item in the *Washington Post*. Translation: The conspiracy nuts are at it again. Pay them no mind.

As far as Rove was concerned, of course, the election was over. His chief concerns had to do with Bush's second term. Immediately after the election, President Bush announced that he was nominating White House counsel Alberto Gonzales to replace John Ashcroft as attorney general. Even before Gonzales took office in February, the White House began to review all the U.S. attorneys with an eye to potentially replacing them.

Rove led the way. In January 2005, while Gonzales was undergoing confirmation hearings, Rove asked White House deputy counsel David Leitch "how we planned to proceed regarding U.S. Attorneys, whether we were going to allow all to stay, request resignations from all and accept only some of them, or selectively replace them, etc."

In response to Rove, Kyle Sampson, who was counsel to departing Attorney General John Ashcroft and about to take on the additional job of chief of staff to Alberto Gonzales, wrote an email back to Leitch that was clearly sensitive to the political upheaval that might result from Rove's suggestion. Noting that U.S. attorneys serve at the pleasure of the president, Sampson pointed out that none of the U.S. attorneys appointed by Bush had completed their four-year terms and it would be "weird to ask them to leave before completing" their terms. Consequently, he said, replacing the attorneys "would certainly send ripples through the U.S. Attorney community."

Sampson added, "The vast majority of U.S. Attorneys, 80–85 percent, I would guess, are doing a great job, are loyal Bushies, etc."

Of course, not every U.S. attorney was as aggressive in prosecuting Democrats or pursuing "voter fraud" as Rove had hoped. In deference to Rove, Sampson said, "We would like to replace 15–20 percent of the current U.S. Attorneys—the underperforming ones. (This is a rough guess; we might want to consider doing performance evaluations after Judge [Gonzales] comes on board.)"

Having pointed out the political repercussions that might ensue, Sampson concluded, "That said, if Karl thinks there would be political will to do it, then so do I."

In April 2005, Attorney General Alberto Gonzales, who had just been confirmed, made this new direction abundantly clear when all the U.S. attorneys in the country assembled in Scottsdale, Arizona. "His first speech to us was a 'you work for the White House' speech," said John McKay, a U.S. attorney from the state of Washington. 'I work for the White House, you work for the White House.'"

McKay and his colleagues were stunned at Gonzales's remarks, because they meant that the judiciary would be subject to partisan politics. At first, McKay thought, "He couldn't possibly have meant that speech. It turns out he did."

That such sentiments were being articulated at the highest reaches of the Justice Department gave enormous latitude to Don Siegelman's foes. That became evident in Alabama in early 2005, when Jill Simpson spoke to Rob Riley, the son of the Republican governor, and found that he was still concerned about a possible Siegelman comeback in the 2006 election. As Simpson later testified before the House Judiciary Committee, Riley said that his father, the governor, and GOP consultant Bill Canary "had had a conversation with Karl Rove again and that they had this time gone over and seen whoever was the head of [the Public Integrity Section of the Justice Department.]"

The Public Integrity Section is a part of the Criminal Division of the Justice Department that is charged with fighting political corruption at all levels of federal, state, and local government. Part of its mandate is to assure that political prosecutions do not take place. But, according to Simpson's testimony, Rob Riley said that Karl Rove had spoken to "the head guy there," Noel Hillman, who agreed "that he'd allocate all resources necessary" to prosecute Siegelman. (Hillman has stated that the Siegelman prosecution had "nothing to do with politics.")

So the barrier had apparently been breached again. Simpson asked Riley why the case would take place in Alabama's Middle District, as opposed to another jurisdiction. According to her testimony, "[Riley] mentioned Leura Canary, Bill Canary's wife, would be a good reason as to why to bring it."

In other words, even though U.S. Attorney Leura Canary had publicly recused herself from prosecuting Siegelman, they were making a point of going after Siegelman in her district so she could oversee the case. According to Simpson, Rob Riley also said that the judge in the case would be Mark Fuller, who had been appointed to the federal judiciary by George W. Bush in 2002, and who had attended the University of Alabama with Simpson and Riley. Such an assertion in itself was quite striking, as Alabama's practice is for federal judges to be selected for each case through a lottery process of random selection.

According to Simpson, Riley added that "Fuller would hang Don Siegelman. . . . Rob got to telling me that . . . Fuller just hated Don Siegelman" because Fuller had the impression "that Don Siegelman had caused [him] to get audited. That's what Fuller thought. He hated him for that."

Finally, according to Simpson's sworn testimony, Riley explained they had even come up with a new legal strategy to use against Siegelman. Richard Scrushy, the CEO of HealthSouth, a giant health care company based in Birmingham, had been charged with a $2.7 billion accounting fraud the previous year. The owner of two airplanes, dozens of automobiles, nine boats, and millions of dollars in jewelry, Scrushy had become a highly charged figure in Alabama when he became a televangelist in the middle of his 2004 trial. Because Scrushy had made hefty donations to Siegelman's lottery campaign, Simpson said, "They had come up with an idea to prosecute Don with Richard Scrushy. Because nobody likes Richard Scrushy, [Rob] thought that that would assure a conviction for Don Siegelman."

Now that the government was assembling a new case against Siegelman, it became increasingly clear to Siegelman's attorneys that Washington was behind it. When Doug Jones pressed for meetings with prosecutors, he was specifically told that Noel Hillman, the head of the Public Integrity Section, was playing an active role in the investigation and that key meetings would have to take place in Washington because Hillman did not have time to travel to Alabama.

"[T]he FBI and the feds now seemed to be taking control and they were casting a wider net than ever before," said Jones.

Earlier, Jones had been told that various charges had been "written off." Now they were back on the table. "For the first time it appeared that agents were not investigating any allegations of a crime, but were now fishing around for anything they could find against an individual," Jones wrote in an affidavit to the House Judiciary Committee. "New subpoenas were being issued for documents and witnesses. Anyone that was a major financial backer of Don Siegelman or who had done business with the state during his administration began receiving visits by investigators and subpoenas by prosecutors."

Finally, in October 2005, Leura Canary released a new indictment against Siegelman on twenty-nine charges, including bribery, mail and wire fraud, RICO, and obstruction of justice. The charges were based on alleged bribes and gifts such as the T-shirts and coffee mugs that had been given to Siegelman's campaign for promotional purposes. In addition, Siegelman was charged with accepting a $500,000 contribution from Richard Scrushy for his 1999 lottery campaign in exchange for a seat on a state health board.

"It's a joke," G. Robert Blakey, a law professor at Notre Dame and former prosecutor, told the New York Times. "A guy walks in, gives a contribution, and gets an appointment? Until Congress reforms this, this is the system we live under. They are criminalizing this contribution."

Indeed, if one applied such standards to all American politicians, hundreds of them, perhaps thousands, would be in jail—not least among them President Bush himself. No fewer than 146 contributors made or put together donations of $100,000 or more to the Bush-Cheney campaign and later received appointments from the administration.

* * *

Meanwhile, on Monday, August 29, 2005, Hurricane Katrina hit New Orleans. Winds reached 175 miles per hour, 53 levees broke, and 80 percent of the city was under water. Over 300,000 households had to be evacuated, 700,000 people needed housing, tens of thousands were trapped in the sweltering Superdome and the Convention Center under inhumane conditions, and the Bush administration's incompetence in dealing with a natural disaster was on display. Day after day, the nation was transfixed by the images of floating bodies and despairing people marooned on rooftops. Ultimately, Katrina was the costliest natural disaster in American history, destroying $108 billion in property and killing 1,836 people.

In response, President Bush, speaking to Michael D. Brown, the Federal Emergency Management Agency director in charge of relief efforts, uttered the three memorable words that would come to symbolize his administration's historic ineptitude: "Heckuva job, Brownie."

For his part, Rove immediately saw the emerging political fiasco, and went to work as soon as the levees were breached. The scene is best recounted by Democratic senator Mary Landrieu in an interview with journalist Paul Alexander, author of *Machiavelli's Shadow: The Rise and Fall of Karl Rove.*

At a press conference the day Katrina hit, with New Orleans in chaos, Senator Landrieu recalled, "[Louisiana Republican senator] David Vitter walked up to the mic and said, 'I just got off the phone with Karl Rove.'"

Landrieu was agog. She looked at Louisiana governor Kathleen Blanco, a Democrat, in astonishment. That Vitter was citing Rove's name meant only one thing: New Orleans faced catastrophe, but, even before relief and rescue had fully commenced, the blame game had begun. "[Vitter] could have been talking to generals, the president himself, but Rove is just a political hatchet man," said Senator Landrieu. "I said to myself, 'Oh my God, I can't believe the White House has already given David Vitter talking points to talk about this.' . . . I mean, is there a Republican talking point for how to get people water?"

The next day, Governor Blanco called Bush, but he declined to take her call. Blanco then tried White House chief of staff Andy Card, who also did not take her call.

Meanwhile, Rove came up with a plan. "They looked around," Landrieu said, "and they found a Democratic governor and an African-American Democratic mayor [New Orleans mayor Ray Nagin] who had never held office before in his life.

"I could see where Rove was going. Blame Blanco. Blame the levee board. Blame the corruption in New Orleans. 'The reason the city is going underwater is because the city is corrupt,' Rove was saying. 'But don't blame the Republicans or George W. Bush or David Vitter. We are the white guys in shining armor, and we are going to come in and save the city from years of corruption.' That was their story and they sold it very well."

But not *that* well. In the wake of Katrina, Bush's approval ratings plummeted to historic lows. And yet after all the mismanagement, the aftershocks still redounded to the long-range benefit of the Republican Party. That was because, after the storm, Bush turned to Rove to head the hurricane reconstruction effort, which meant that Rove was now distributing at least $200 billion in federal largesse. Among the major beneficiaries were firms with close ties to the Republican Party, such as Bechtel and Halliburton.

A year later, one could begin to evaluate the result of those reconstruction efforts: Less than half of the city's 460,000 residents had returned. Sixty percent of the homes still lacked electricity. Six out of nine of the city's hospitals were still closed. Eighty-four percent of the city's residents rated the reconstruction efforts negatively.

All of which added up to a huge win for the Republican Party, because it meant the permanent removal of about 250,000 voters, most of whom were blacks and Democrats.

According to Michael Brown, "Karl Rove became interested in Louisiana for the very practical reason that it had voted solidly Democratic when Bill Clinton won his two terms, and it had voted for George W. Bush in the election that followed."

Katrina, Brown asserted, presented a "wonderful opportunity to bring Louisiana solidly with the Republicans. . . . [It]was the first time in 160 disasters that I kept smelling politics. It was something I never saw anywhere else."

* * *

In addition to Katrina, Rove still had to deal with the Plame Wilson affair. On April 26, 2006, Rove testified for a fifth time before a grand jury in the federal investigation that had begun nearly three years earlier. Luskin had never had a client appear more than once—and here was Rove approaching thirty hours of testimony.

But this time testifying was relatively easy. Fitzgerald was focused on whether Rove had lied or obstructed justice in failing to disclose his conversation with Matt Cooper. He asked Rove if Luskin had told him about his conversations with Viveca Novak and had he then asked his staff to search his office records. The answer was yes, said Rove. Unlike Rove's other sessions with the grand jury, this was perfunctory—and it was his last.

When Rove left, eager reporters crowded the courthouse elevator assuming he was about to be indicted. By now, Scooter Libby had resigned as chief of staff to Vice President Dick Cheney after being formally charged with obstruction of justice, perjury, and making false statements. But in the public's imagination Rove—Bush's Brain—was a far bigger fish.

Inwardly, Rove chortled with delight that the public would not get what they wanted. "They didn't know what Luskin and I knew about the purpose of my visit, that it was to answer the prosecutor's last remaining concern," he wrote in *Courage and Consequence*. "They assumed my indictment was likely and imminent. I wanted to grab them, shake them hard, and tell them I was out, free, in the clear— that they weren't going to get a story under their byline on page one, above the fold, in large type, about a White House aide's indictment and fall from grace."

The news became public the next day: Karl Rove was off the hook. There was no question he had leaked Plame Wilson's identity as a CIA agent to Matt Cooper, and that he had been the second source who confirmed Bob Novak's story. There was also no question he had lied to Scott McClellan, and misled the FBI, the president, and the grand jury about it. As Pete Yost of the Associated Press wrote, "The decision not to charge Karl Rove shows there often are no consequences for misleading the public."

So why did he get off? The bar set for proving a violation of the

Intelligence Identities Act was so high that Fitzgerald never really had much of a case. But building an airtight case for perjury or obstruction of justice can be extraordinarily difficult as well. Proving *intent* was not easy to do. And according to law professor and former federal prosecutor Dan Richman, the fact that Rove, in his last two appearances before the grand jury, "ultimately cooperated and told what he knew" made it difficult for Fitzgerald to prove Rove intended to lie.

And those final appearances before the grand jury came about as the result of only one freakishly lucky happenstance for Karl Rove that probably saved him from being indicted: Viveca Novak's conversation with Luskin in which she let on that Rove did, in fact, have a Matt Cooper problem.

When she wrote about it in *Time* the previous year, Viveca Novak asked, "Will it make the difference between whether Rove gets indicted or not?" Answering her own question, Novak said she had "no idea."

But the answer was unequivocally yes. As Luskin himself said, their conversation is precisely what led him to find the email Rove wrote right after talking with Cooper, thereby initiating the process that led Rove to acknowledge he had indeed spoken with Cooper. "I hadn't intended to tip Luskin off to anything," Novak wrote. "I was supposed to be the information gatherer. It's true that reporters and sources often trade information, but that's not what this was about. If I could have a do-over, I would have kept my mouth shut."

Immediately after her grand jury appearance, *Time* put Viveca Novak on a leave of absence from which she never returned. Her editors were furious that she had disclosed the confidential workings of the news organization to Rove's lawyer. In the end, she may have unwittingly sacrificed her job to save Rove from going to jail.

Nor was the Viveca Novak episode Rove's last stroke of luck with regard to the Plame Wilson scandal.

In the summer of 2006, one great mystery remained unsolved: Who was Bob Novak's primary source? Everyone knew that Rove had confirmed Plame Wilson's identity for Novak. But who told Novak first?

In fact, Karl Rove found out nearly a year earlier, on October 24,

2005, when Bob Woodward was at the White House for an interview and happened to run into Rove in the West Wing. According to James Stewart's *Tangled Webs*, Rove struck up a conversation, mentioned the Plame Wilson investigation, made a reference to Novak's original source, then still unknown, and happened to use the phrase *alpha source*.

"You've got that right," said Woodward.

Rove was perplexed—and it showed. What didn't register immediately to him was that Woodward was a navy veteran to whom "alpha" meant the letter *A*.

Seeing Rove's bewilderment, Woodward cut to the chase. "Armitage," he said.

He meant Richard Armitage, the garrulous deputy secretary of state, and a long and highly valued source of Woodward's.

"Armitage?" asked Rove.

Then his face lit up.

"You've turned my world upside down!" he said.

For the first time, apparently, Rove knew the identity of Bob Novak's primary source—and he was filled with delight. He couldn't have put together a better scenario if he'd written it himself.

In any case, once the news of Armitage's role became public, it all redounded to the benefit of Cheney, Libby, and Karl Rove. The right-wing media—the *Wall Street Journal* editorial page, Fox News, the *New York Post*, *The National Review*, *The Weekly Standard*, and more—went ballistic. And so did the mainstream media. *New York Times* conservative columnist David Brooks joined in the attacks, calling the exposure of Plame Wilson "a piffle." In the *San Francisco Chronicle*, right-wing Debra Saunders argued that the entire affair was mere gossip, exculpated Rove, and asserted that the only "abuse of power" was the investigation itself.

And who could blame them?

Michael Isikoff's scoop in *Newsweek* effectively said the same thing: "The disclosures about Armitage . . . underscore one of the ironies of the Plame investigation: that the initial leak, seized on by administration critics as evidence of how far the White House was willing to go to smear an opponent, came from a man who had no apparent intention of harming anyone."

It was even more ironic that Isikoff's *Newsweek* story was timed to promote *Hubris,* a new book co-authored by Isikoff and David Corn of *The Nation.* In other words, the chief purveyors of this chronicle, a narrative that in some measure appeared to exculpate Scooter Libby and Karl Rove, were reporters not from Fox News but from one of the mainstays of the so-called liberal media, *Newsweek,* and the proudly leftist weekly *The Nation.*

It remained for Christopher Hitchens, the erstwhile leftist turned neocon rhetorician, to embrace this Rovian narrative. "We have the final word on who did disclose the name and occupation of Valerie Plame," he wrote in Slate, "and it turns out to be someone whose opposition to the Bush policy in Iraq has—like Robert Novak's—long been a byword in Washington. It is particularly satisfying that this admission comes from two of the journalists—Michael Isikoff and David Corn—who did the most to get the story wrong in the first place and the most to keep it going long beyond the span of its natural life."

From Rove's point of view, revelation of the Armitage leak could not have provided a more stirring coda to the entire episode. Rove had leaked the name of a covert agent for his own political reasons. He had lied about it to the press, the FBI, a federal grand jury, his colleagues in the White House, and even his longtime friend and patron, the president of the United States. It was the fall of 2006, and a significant part of Karl Rove's ordeal was over. Thanks, in large measure, to Viveca Novak, he had avoided jail, and now, thanks to Richard Armitage, the mainstream media was humming his tune.

TWELVE

The Verdict

As he campaigned for his party's gubernatorial nomination in the spring of 2006, Don Siegelman tried to shrug off the fact that he was going on trial just six weeks before the June primary against Lieutenant Governor Lucy Baxley. "I'm not the slightest bit concerned," he said, with a touch of bravado. "We'll blow the doors off the barn with a high-profile acquittal. I'll take a week off with my family and then come back, campaign for a week, and win."

But it wasn't that simple. For one thing, the political damage had begun the moment the indictments against Siegelman were released. As the *Birmingham News* reported, he stood accused "of turning his public office into a criminal enterprise to solicit more than $1 million in payoffs." The article did not explain in any depth the broader political context of the charges against Siegelman, nor did it make clear the fact that Siegelman personally received no funds from Scrushy.

Meanwhile, the ongoing investigation continued to generate devastating negative publicity. "Every bank record, every financial record, every investment record of the Governor, his wife, his campaign and his brother were being subpoenaed," said Siegelman lawyer Doug Jones. "All of this was done in a very public way. Every month there was a parade of new witnesses called to appear at the grand jury in Montgomery, all in front of the ever-present eyes of the Alabama media who chronicled each witness in every newspaper and every television station across the state."

As for the case itself, the government was trying to prove, among other things, a specific quid pro quo regarding the fact that Richard Scrushy was appointed to the Alabama Certificate of Need Board (the CON Board) after he made a $500,000 contribution to the Alabama Education Foundation. But the prosecution's argument was filled with uncertain premises, damning inconsistencies, and evidentiary problems. First of all, there was the rather dubious notion that Scrushy's donation was actually a bribe. Siegelman had not profited personally from the transaction. All Scrushy got was an unpaid appointment to a public service position. His company, HealthSouth, had no interests before the CON Board.

Even if one accepted the premise behind the government's case, prosecution attorneys were still plagued by the inconvenient fact that Scrushy had contributed to Siegelman's opponent as well. Moreover, Scrushy and his subordinates at HealthSouth had already been appointed to the CON Board by the three previous governors of Alabama.

Then there was the problem of the government's star witness, former Siegelman aide Nick Bailey. Because he had admitted to taking over $100,000 in bribes himself, Bailey's testimony was already somewhat tainted. But there was an additional factual problem that went to the heart of the case. In the trial, Bailey testified that he saw a $250,000 check, which represented half of Scrushy's donation, change hands at the very meeting at which Scrushy was appointed to the CON Board. But Bailey's testimony was false. The check had not been written until several days later. "Bailey had said he walked out of the meeting with Scrushy on the fourteenth or fifteenth of July [1999], and [Siegelman] showed me this check for $250,000," said Doug Jones. "But we knew that couldn't have been the case because the check had not even been cut until July 19. They had a real problem with their star witness, who was not credible at this point."

And the studied coaching of Bailey was obvious to observers in court. According to CBS's *60 Minutes*, Bailey said he had more than seventy meetings with prosecutors, and in some of them they demanded that he memorize key points of his testimony.

But the defense team became concerned that whatever holes there were in the case wouldn't matter. One reason was that the presiding judge was indeed Mark Fuller. Fuller was problematic as a judge not merely because he was a Republican who had been appointed by

Bush. The bench assumes that most judges belong to one political party or another and can put their partisan prejudices aside when the time comes. But Fuller had been an electoral strategist, an executive committee member, and a campaigner against Siegelman.

Worse, it turned out that Fuller held a 43.75 percent controlling interest in Doss Aviation, a government contractor with holdings in Alabama, California, Colorado, Florida, Maine, Texas, and elsewhere throughout the country, which did training, fueling, and maintenance jobs for the air force, navy, and other federal contractors, and had received hundreds of millions of dollars in government contracts.

When Siegelman's defense team filed a motion for Fuller to be recused, the judge ridiculed the "rather fanciful theory" that he could be swayed by such contracts. Karl Rove later dismissed the theory as "pure goofiness."

But Doss was awarded a contract for $178 million just as the trial was about to start. "This is not a run-of-the-mill criminal case where a judge's commercial side-dealings with the government would not raise a question about pro-government bias," legal ethicist David Luban, a law professor at Georgetown University, told *Harper's.* "This one is a politically charged case involving a former governor in which political leaders in Washington, D.C., who ultimately exercise tremendous control over the process of military procurement contracts, are likely to take great interest. Given the amount of money Judge Fuller's company gets from government contracts, any reasonable person would question how impartial he could be. He should not have taken this case. . . . [H]e had no option but to drop out."

But rather than drop out, Fuller made one ruling after another in favor of the prosecution throughout the trial, and saved his most controversial act for the end. On June 21, 2006, after the jurors had finished several days of deliberations without reaching a verdict, Fuller summoned them back into the courtroom. "To have deliberated for four days in a case this complex is not unusual," Fuller told the twelve jurors. "Discuss the case and do not hesitate to change your mind if you believe you were wrong, but do not give up your honest opinion."

He also reminded the jurors that they had the option of delivering a partial verdict if necessary, but he stopped short of delivering an "Allen charge" or a "dynamite charge"—formal directions to the jury in which the judge admonishes jurors that they must reexamine their opinions and attempt to reach a unanimous verdict if possible.

Two days later, however, the jurors sent Fuller a note saying they were unable to reach a unanimous decision on any of the thirty-four counts in the indictment. This time, Fuller resorted to the Allen charge. "Obviously, another trial would only serve to increase the cost to both sides," he said. He encouraged jurors in the minority to reconsider their positions, but not to change their minds just to bring the trial to an end.

According to Cloud Miller, a Chicago legal scholar who has researched more than a thousand cases in which it was used, the Allen charge is "prejudiced and biased towards a finding of guilt." Miller said a guilty verdict occurs 90 percent of the time after a judge gives the instructions.

But convincing the other jurors wasn't easy. In late June, after nine days of deliberation, jury foreman Sam Hendrix sent Fuller another note, this time complaining that they still had not reached a verdict and that some jurors showed "no interest in continuing the discussion." Asserting that declaring a mistrial from the deadlocked jury would be his "last resort," Fuller gave the jurors a second Allen charge, insisting that if they didn't reach a verdict that a second trial would be necessary.

For his part, Siegelman was stunned by Fuller's action. "It shocked me. The jury was deadlocked. . . . They're tired. The Fourth of July is coming up, and they're being told he can keep them there for a year. 'Bring me a partial verdict' translates to 'Give me a guilty verdict.'"

As one juror later put it in a sworn affidavit published on the Huffington Post, "The judge said that he could keep us until the next 4th of July and we needed to have a unanimous decision. Our whole objective changed at that point after nine days; we felt he applied extreme pressure on us to get us to make a unanimous decision. We all decided to agree with whoever was in charge so we could leave and go home. I told everybody I was through deliberating—do whatever you want to do. Just tell me which way I should vote so I can go home. The stake of [Siegelman's and Scrushy's] lives was totally irrelevant at this point for all of us, and we had a more pressing objective in mind—just to leave and go home for good. We did not vote our conviction. We voted based on the pressure applied by the judge."

Finally, on Thursday, June 29, 2006, both Siegelman and Scrushy sat silently on the edge of their seats but showed no emotion as the jury returned.

"I was emotionally numb," said Siegelman. "I couldn't believe I was hearing the word guilty instead of not guilty."

About six months after Siegelman was convicted, in December 2006, the Bush administration fired eight U.S. attorneys—Bud Cummins, Kevin Ryan, Daniel Bogden, Carol Lam, David Iglesias, Paul Charlton, John McKay, and Margaret Chiara. All eight were appointees of President Bush, and it later emerged that they either were pursuing corruption investigations of Republican public officials or had refused to pursue investigations of Democrats that would have been beneficial to Republicans in elections.

Typical was the case of David Iglesias of New Mexico, who received a call from Senator Pete Domenici inquiring about an investigation of a Democratic state senator. After Iglesias told Domenici that the indictment would not be handed down until at least December 2004, after the elections, the line went dead. Iglesias felt he was being pressured to expedite the indictment in time for the elections.

Then, according to the *New York Times,* in June 2005, Scott Jennings, one of Rove's top political aides, wrote a colleague that Republicans in New Mexico "are really angry over [Iglesias's] lack of action on voter fraud stuff."

But for his part Iglesias told the *New York Times,* "The amount of backstabbing and treachery involved is just breathtaking. It's astounding that without reviewing the evidence or talking to the FBI or anything, the White House would assume that these were provable cases and that I needed to file them for the political benefit of the party. That's not what U.S. attorneys do."

Finally, according to closed congressional testimony, a "very agitated" Karl Rove called Harriet Miers, a White House counsel under President Bush, and said that he wanted action taken against Iglesias. "It was clear to me that he felt like he has a serious problem and that he wanted something done about it," Miers said, referring to Rove. "He was just upset. I remember his being upset."

Rove told the *New York Times* that he saw himself as only passing on complaints about Iglesias to Miers. In any case, Iglesias had received a positive performance review, but he was fired anyway. Documents also showed that Rove was behind forcing Bud Cummins, a U.S. attorney in Arkansas, to resign and replacing him with Timothy Griffin, a Rove protégé who had served as opposition research director for the Republican National Committee.

In the months following Siegelman's conviction, Judge Fuller denied motions filed by the defense for a mistrial. After Siegelman was sentenced in June 2007, Jill Simpson, the Republican attorney and activist, signed a sworn affidavit about her conversations regarding Rove's role in Siegelman's prosecution, and forty-four state attorneys general asked Congress to investigate.

As we have seen before, thanks to the investigation of the House Judiciary Committee, Siegelman was not the only Democratic politician who was a target of the Bush Justice Department. Similarly, in 2006, U.S. Attorney Mary Beth Buchanan, a Bush appointee, brought an eighty-four-count indictment against Dr. Cyril Wecht, a prominent Democrat who was the coroner in Allegheny County, Pennsylvania. Among Wecht's alleged missteps were such crimes as misusing $3.20 worth of postage and twenty-four counts of using the office fax machine for private matters. Wecht was even charged with striking a deal with a local university to trade unclaimed cadavers for lab space.

The trivial and apparently selective nature of the charges was such that even former attorney general Richard Thornburgh, a lifelong Republican, testified before Congress on Wecht's behalf, saying, "We should not allow any citizen of the United States to proceed to trial knowing that his prosecution may have been undertaken for political reasons as opposed to being done to serve the interests of justice. Sadly, that appears to have been so in the case against Dr. Wecht."

After Wecht's criminal case ended in a mistrial, Buchanan immediately attempted to retry him but was blocked when the Third Circuit Court of Appeals issued an indefinite stay. University of Pittsburgh law professor John Burkoff characterized Buchanan's attempt as a disgrace. "It's beyond embarrassing," he said. "We're nearing humiliation."

As for Siegelman, astoundingly, he had been found guilty of bribery even though he clearly had received no money for personal gain whatsoever. His "crime" was to appoint a health care executive to a nonpaying position on a state hospital board after the executive made a large contribution to Siegelman's campaign for a state lottery fund for universal education.

On June 28, 2007, Judge Fuller sentenced Siegelman to serve eighty-eight months in jail, a shockingly severe punishment for a white-collar crime. It was the end of his political career. "I was told by my probation officer that being locked up immediately after sentencing, that that wasn't going to happen," said Siegelman. "He said, 'In your kind of case, if you were a murderer, had a propensity for violence, or were a mafia figure, they might take you away immediately. Maybe. But don't even think about that.'"

But his probation officer was wrong. "So we were taken ... out of court immediately and kept in solitary confinement in the maximum security prison in Atlanta until one morning at about three o'clock, there was a knock on the door that had housed Al Capone and John Gotti."

Siegelman's lawyers had originally been told he was being flown to Texarkana, but Siegelman found out that the plans had changed. "I was flown to New York and then from New York to Michigan, from Michigan to Oklahoma City, where I stayed in isolation for about six days. For a period of about six days, I was not allowed to talk to anybody. . . . I was manacled, handcuffed behind my back, treated like a violent criminal. I asked, 'Why am I being separated?' and they said for my own safety, and I said, 'If it's for my own safety, why am I being handcuffed behind my back?'

"It never occurred to me that I might go to jail for raising money for the state lottery."

Ultimately, Siegelman was sent to clean latrines in a federal penitentiary in Oakdale, Louisiana, and saddled with a gag order. Then, in March 2008, he was finally released on bond, pending appeal.

In the meantime, the House Judiciary Committee, chaired by Representative John Conyers, had been investigating the Siegelman affair for close to nine months and had heard testimony from Dana Jill Simpson and a number of other witnesses speaking on behalf of Siegelman.

But getting Rove to testify was another question. On July 1, 2008, in response to a Judiciary Committee subpoena, Rove declined to testify, citing executive privilege. Rather than submit to potentially hostile questions by Democrats, Rove took questions from Lamar Smith, a Republican from Texas on the committee who happened to be a former client, and released a nine-page document titled "Answers to House Judiciary Committee Ranking Member Lamar Smith from Karl C. Rove Regarding Allegations of Selective Prosecution in the Case of Former Alabama Governor Donald E. Siegelman."

In the document, Rove said he has "never communicated, either directly or indirectly, with Justice Department or Alabama officials about the investigation, indictment, potential prosecution, prosecution, conviction, or sentencing of Governor Siegelman, or about any other matter related to his case, nor have I asked any other individual to communicate about these matters on my behalf. I have never attempted, either directly or indirectly, to influence these matters."

He further said that he has had no contact whatsoever with Jill Simpson about the Siegelman case "or another other matter whatsoever . . . I have never communicated, either directly or indirectly, with Simpson about any political campaigns before, during, or after 2001, or about any other matter whatsoever. . . . I do not and have never known Simpson personally. It is possible that Simpson may have met me at a public function, but I do not know her, I have never worked with her, and I have never communicated with her, either directly or indirectly. . . . I have never communicated, either directly or indirectly, with Simpson about taking photographs of any individuals whatsoever, including Governor Siegelman, and I have never asked her to undertake any task to discredit Governor Siegelman."

Yet for all his denials, Rove's finely parsed statement avoided the question of whether he communicated about Siegelman's prosecution with other people such as Bill Canary or Rob Riley, which were central to the allegations against him. In large measure, that was because Rove made sure he was questioned only by a friendly Republican rather than the committee itself, which was controlled by Democrats.

On July 30, 2008, with Rove still refusing to honor its subpoena, the Judiciary Committee voted to hold him in contempt of Congress. But the vote was only a recommendation, and, in the context of a presidential campaign promising hope and change, the Democrats deemed it more politic to look forward, as the Bush administration drew to an ignominious end. In effect, Rove was saved by the bell from even this relatively minor rebuke.

None of which was good enough for Siegelman, who was out on bail but still faced a long jail sentence.

In late August, at the 2008 Democratic National Convention in Denver, Siegelman pleaded with his fellow Democrats not to let Karl Rove off the hook. "If Congress does not act," Siegelman said, "we are essentially setting up two standards of justice, one for the powerful and those connected to the White House and another system for us. Congress must act in the first three weeks of September before they adjourn. History teaches us that Democrats in victory are too magnanimous. . . . I guarantee you . . . that if the Congress does not vote to hold Rove in contempt when they come back from recess, he will walk off into the sunset and it will be a great disservice to the country."

"One of the critical indications of the health of a democratic state is that political parties don't use the criminal justice system for political purposes, and that is one of the major barriers they crashed through here," said attorney Scott Horton, a Columbia Law School lecturer who specializes in human rights law. "What is really striking about this wave of political prosecutions is it's not just a matter of a rogue prosecutor here or there. These prosecutions are top down, systematic, widespread and part of a nationwide political campaign. It's not just a question of individual political attorneys involved in gamesmanship. There are cases in Georgia, Mississippi and on and on that have very similar traits. If we look at the U.S. attorneys scandal, it is very clearly being directed out of the White House with a centrally coordinated strategy. There are easily more than a dozen well-documented cases. The patterns are almost identical and the streams all lead back to Karl Rove."

THIRTEEN

The Vanishing

In the spring of 2007, Josh Bolten, who had replaced Andrew Card as White House chief of staff, told White House staffers that they should either leave shortly or be prepared to stay through to the end of George Bush's second term. Bolten's directive gave Rove an excuse to assess how long he should remain at the White House. The Plame Wilson investigation had exhausted him emotionally and burned through his financial reserves.

"More important than money, however, was the toll that my life had taken on my wife and son," he wrote. "I could see more clearly how the press attention, the protesters surrounding our house, the ugly anonymous letters, and the snarky Internet postings had weighed on them. . . . There are downsides to having 70 percent of the American people recognize your name and face, especially when some of them hate your guts and consider you the epitome of evil or Beelzebub himself."

Rove's teenage son, Andrew, had started to position himself ahead of his father when they went through airports, acting as a security agent of sorts. Karl thought it was funny, but Darby wasn't amused. "Don't you understand he's worried about your safety?" she explained.

Bush's ratings were lousy, and Rove didn't want to seem like he was deserting a sinking ship. But in June Ed Gillespie came in to run the White House communications shop, and Rove felt that a strong team was in place. He met Bush for lunch in the president's private dining room, with John Quincy Adams's portrait hanging above their heads. Bush ate a low-fat hot dog; Rove, a peanut butter and honey sandwich. Finally, Rove told the president that he thought it was time for him to go. He was angry "that financial circumstances were forcing me to leave. But I felt grateful the president had supported my complicated decision."

The two men hugged good-bye and Bush gave Rove a pat on the cheek. "That was enough. I didn't need or want to say any more." Then, Rove told Bolten he would go during the August break. He was leaving the White House.

But Rove's ordeal wasn't over yet. At roughly the same time, the House Judiciary Committee uncovered a potentially serious criminal violation regarding Rove. In March 2007, in the course of investigating the U.S. attorneys scandal, the Committee had subpoenaed emails from a number of White House staffers and learned that Rove aide Scott Jennings had used a non–White House email account to communicate with Justice Department officials concerning the appointment of Tim Griffin, another Rove aide, as U.S. attorney in Little Rock, Arkansas.

The use of an outside email account was a problem, because the Presidential Records Act requires the president to ensure that all his duties and those of his office "are adequately documented . . . and maintained as Presidential records." As a result, White House staff had been instructed to use only the official White House email system for official communications and to retain any official emails they received on a nongovernmental account. But Jennings, who worked with Rove at the White House at the time, used an email account registered to the Republican National Committee.

Democrats were suspicious that Bush officials used the off-site accounts as a way to avoid scrutiny. "Now we are learning that the 'off book' communications they were having about these actions, by using Republican political email addresses, have not been preserved," said Senator Patrick Leahy (D-Vt.), chairman of the Judiciary Committee.

In response, White House spokesperson Dana Perino initially assured the press that "only a handful" of White House officials had RNC email accounts. But even emails on the White House servers were missing. Where were they? Nobody seemed to know.

On April 11, 2007, the Bush White House acknowledged that the emails may have been lost, and Perino attributed it to "a technical issue."

Democrats were irate. "You can't erase emails, not today," said Senator Leahy. "They've gone through too many servers. Those emails are there—they just don't want to produce them."

Leahy then invoked the iconic imagery of Watergate. "Like the famous 18-minute gap in the Nixon White House tapes, it appears likely that key documentation has been erased or misplaced. This sounds like the administration's version of the dog ate my homework," he said.

How many emails had been destroyed? On April 12, 2007, a Washington-based public interest group, Citizens for Responsibility and Ethics in Washington (CREW), released a report detailing the loss of more than five million emails generated between March 2003 and October 2005.*

Later in April, Perino's estimate that "a handful" of officials used RNC email accounts jumped to twenty-two White House officials and "about 50 over the course of the administration." But when the House Committee on Oversight and Government Reform later investigated, it was found that, once again, Perino had understated the facts: At least eighty-eight White House officials had RNC email accounts, among them Karl Rove, Andrew Card, and political affairs director Ken Mehlman.

To make matters worse, a briefing by Rob Kelner, counsel for the Republican National Committee, raised special concerns about Rove, who used his RNC account for the vast majority of his emails. According to Kelner, the RNC had no emails prior to 2005 for Rove, meaning that at least four full years of Rove's emails were missing. A report by the House Oversight Committee found that the RNC preserved only 130 emails sent to Rove during all of Bush's first term.

---

* In late 2009, technicians finally recovered many of the missing emails and found that the number had been significantly understated: No fewer than 22 million emails were found. "We may never discover the full story of what happened here," said Melanie Sloan, CREW's executive director. "It seems like they just didn't want the emails preserved." Vast as that number is, it does *not* include what may well be the most interesting emails of all—those of Karl Rove and eighty or so other White House officials who used accounts hosted by SmarTech.

"Mr. Kelner did not give any explanation for the emails missing from Mr. Rove's account," said Congressman Henry Waxman (D-Calif.), chairman of the House Committee on Oversight and Government Reform, in a letter to Alberto Gonzales, "but he did acknowledge that one possible explanation is that Mr. Rove personally deleted his e-mails from the RNC server."

Rove's missing emails were relevant not just to the U.S. attorneys scandal investigation but also to the Plame Wilson investigation. Melanie Sloan, executive director of CREW, wrote Patrick Fitzgerald that "revelations about the destruction of Karl Rove's emails raise serious questions about the thoroughness of Mr. Rove's cooperation with your investigation as Special Counsel." Sloan urged Fitzgerald "to reopen your investigation" because to the extent "Mr. Rove continued to delete email with full knowledge of your investigation . . . would obviously raise very serious questions about the illegality of Mr. Rove's conduct."

But it was too late. In March, Scooter Libby had been convicted on four counts of perjury, obstruction of justice, and making false statements. The investigation was over and no one else would be charged. Unspoken was the fact that millions of missing emails had been hosted on SmarTech servers in the old Pioneer Bank Building in Chattanooga, Tennessee.

But not just emails were vanishing. The attempt to find out what really happened in the alleged 2004 Ohio election fraud was encountering similar problems.

In August 2006, Cliff Arnebeck and co-counsel Bob Fitrakis had filed the *King Lincoln Bronzeville* suit against Ken Blackwell, who was cited as "having conspired to deprive and continue to deprive Ohioans of their right to vote." A week after the suit was filed, on September 7, 2006, Judge Algenon L. Marbley ordered the county boards of elections to save all ballots from the 2004 presidential election.

Two months later, Democrat Jennifer Brunner, a Columbus, Ohio, attorney who specialized in election law and campaign finance, was elected Ohio's secretary of state. During her campaign, Brunner criticized Blackwell as an "umpire who wore a jersey of one of the teams" in 2004. Referring to the chaotic 2004 election in Ohio, she added, "It pains me to see this kind of turmoil in our state. I want to be a part of fundamental change. I want people to be able to trust the process."

At last, there was a glimmer of hope that investigators might finally get to the bottom of what actually happened in 2004. Judge Marbley's ruling and Brunner's election meant that now it might be possible to resolve the questions that were not answered by the flawed recount.

In addition to the documentation he sought, Arnebeck had brought on as an expert witness cyber security expert Stephen Spoonamore to testify as to whether SmarTech could have seized control of the election results. Spoonamore had met Mike Connell about a year after the Bush-Kerry election and developed an interesting relationship with him. By this time, Connell had established himself as a major figure in technology on the right. New Media's clients had included the Bush-Cheney campaigns and presidential transition websites, sites for the RNC, the Republican Governors Association, for Republican Party organs in at least thirty-one states, and for half a dozen up-and-coming presidential hopefuls, including John Thune, Mike Huckabee, and Rick Santorum. He represented dozens of political action committees and huge lobbyists. Clients for GovTech Solutions, Connell's "nonpartisan" spinoff from New Media Communications, included twenty-seven members of Congress, from House Majority Leader Tom DeLay on down.

For his part, Spoonamore, who defended corporate giants against hackers, had already come to see technology as a growing threat to democracy. He was not shy about touting his achievements and sounding the cry against electronic voting. "I am very accomplished at finding you out if you want to defraud a bank, MasterCard, or an ATM," Spoonamore said. "And a voting machine is a very stupid, badly designed version of a bank credit card machine. It is the worst of the worst. It is stupid, unsecured code, junk. It's so fricking easy to hack."

According to Spoonamore, the two men hit it off immediately. When it came to technical expertise, their skills were complementary. "He was a front-end guy," said Spoonamore, meaning that Connell dealt more with the user interface than he did, "and I'm a back-end guy. We respected each other and liked each other.

"I knew him better than a lot of people around him. I was doing quite a bit of work on democracy advocacy in Southeast Asia. Mike had become interested because of his religious missionary work. We were part of a team that created tools to enable the democratic opposition to get their message out."

Ultimately, Spoonamore, a lifelong Republican who had worked for Rudy Giuliani's presidential campaign, found Connell was both more partisan than he and more intimate with the dark side of politics. "He had been behind the Swift Boat website and had close personal relationships in the White House," Spoonamore said.

By contrast, Spoonamore thought Republicans had begun hacking electronic voting machines to steal elections, notably with the 2002 election of Georgia senator Saxby Chambliss over Max Cleland, the incumbent Democrat. Brash and outspoken, Spoonamore became a controversial figure among some voter-reform activists—one leading activist described him as "a fraudulent poseur"—but he also became known as an expert on cyber security issues, including electronic voting, for ABC News, CNN, NPR, and the BBC.

And given Connell's connections to Rove and the GOP hierarchy, Spoonamore was curious about how much Connell knew. "He was a funny breed, a stolid Midwestern businessman guy combined with someone who had the perpetual wariness of a political operator. It was a funny mix. He was more of a political operative than an IT guy, that's for sure."

At the time the two men met, there had been minimal fallout from the Ohio election controversy. Nevertheless, according to Spoonamore, Connell was increasingly wary of his colleagues. "By the time I met Mike, he had grown to significantly distrust the people he was working with," said Spoonamore. "He strongly felt that people were misusing the IT systems he built."

One of them, according to Spoonamore, was Karl Rove.

At one of their early meetings, Spoonamore tried to address the issue head-on. "About the third or fourth time we met, I said, 'Actually, I have a concern. There are some people that are stealing elections,' and I said, 'Are you involved?'

"And Mike, who had been an open and forthright guy, with that

Midwestern straightforwardness, was really uncomfortable, really fast. He looked at his shoes, looked at the floor, and he basically said, 'I am also concerned some of the systems I have been involved with are being misused.'"

And that was not the end of it. On October 11, 2006, Spoonamore met Connell in Washington, and suddenly, out of the blue, Connell asked a sensitive question. "How easy is it to destroy all records of email?'" he inquired. "Because I have clients down the street who are working on that problem." Connell pointed toward a nearby window in the White House to show whom he was talking about.

According to Spoonamore's contemporaneous notes of the meeting, "Mike specifically stated this included some systems impacting the White House email." Spoonamore replied that he wanted nothing to do with it.

Meanwhile, in late 2006 the *King Lincoln* suit was just getting started. Before taking office as Ohio's secretary of state, Jennifer Brunner discussed the 2004 elections with a civil servant in the Secretary of State's Office who had been aware that the netroot websites were still buzzing about fraud in that election.

"He brought the SmarTech situation to my attention, and the fact that this was looked on as suspect," said Brunner. She added that she "was personally concerned with what had happened," and intended to look into it as soon as she took office.

About a week before her term began, the employee invited Brunner into the Secretary of State's Office even though she had not yet been sworn in. To Brunner's astonishment, Blackwell's staff was in the midst of shredding thousands of documents. "I walked by one room of the elections, and it was filled with shredded paper," she says.

Another staffer in the Secretary of State's Office also witnessed masses of documents being destroyed. "What that was all about is anybody's guess," the employee said. "It is very unusual."

What were they shredding?

"I wish I knew," said Brunner, who was never able to determine the contents of the shredded material.

* * *

The *King Lincoln* lawsuit was under way, and there was ample reason to believe that examination of the ballots would answer, once and for all, the key questions about the extent of fraud in the 2004 presidential election in Ohio.

For months, self-appointed election sleuth Richard Hayes Phillips had been inspecting the ballots in conjunction with Arnebeck's team. He had started almost immediately after the election, first by examining the results in eight counties where the results seemed suspicious, then by analyzing the precinct results in those counties, and finally the ballots themselves.

As Phillips saw it, given the possibility that the exit polls might be flawed, the discrepancy between them and the official results sent up a red flag but did not alone prove that the election had been stolen. One could obtain proof only via the laborious process of actually examining the ballots one at a time at each of thousands of precincts.

As Triad's Brett Rapp pointed out, if the ballots had been tabulated by the wrong precinct setting, if the wrong page frame had been used, if the wrong header card had been used—if any such methods were used to manipulate the vote—all of that would be evident in an examination of the ballots. Likewise, there were precincts in which the official tally outnumbered the registered voters. There were precincts in which there were highly suspicious numbers of "undervotes"—that is, ballots in which voters picked candidates for every office except the presidency. Once again, the answers to these anomalies, no doubt, would come forth once the ballots were examined.

Ultimately, over many months, assisted by a team of citizen volunteers, Phillips analyzed 126,000 ballots from 18 counties in Ohio and compiled 30,000 images of forensic documents. He found voting machines and tabulators that were rigged, ballot boxes that were stuffed, ballots that were altered, and countless irregularities. His work was vital in persuading Judge Marbley to rule in favor of protecting the ballots.

The question now was whether official authorities would find the same thing.

Finally, the moment of truth was near.

* * *

In April 2007, Judge Marbley issued an order requiring all eighty-eight county boards of elections to transfer the ballots from the 2004 presidential election to a secure location. Marbley's ruling specifically called on the election boards to preserve "all ballots prepared and provided by it for use in an election, whether used or unused."

Unused ballots? Why bother with them?

Because, according to Phillips, "Failure to preserve the unused ballots makes it impossible for any board of election to verify the authenticity of the voted ballots."

Without the unused ballots, there is no way to prove that ballots in selected precincts were not punched in advance for independent and third-party presidential candidates. Without the unused ballots there is no way to prove that some counties didn't substitute fake ballots for real ones. In addition, in heavily Democratic areas Arnebeck suspected that unused ballots may have been pre-punched for third-party candidates so as to invalidate votes for John Kerry. Finally, they were necessary if one was to verify whether the statewide results for each county really jibed with the results at the local level or if cross-voting or other forms of vote manipulation had taken place.

Because the ballots were the subject matter of a lawsuit, Judge Marbley had specified that "the duty to preserve the ballots began when each county board of elections received a letter from the Plaintiffs" on August 31, 2006, notifying them of the filing of the lawsuit. Under the provisions of the lawsuit, Secretary of State Brunner was to take custody of the ballots in the spring of 2007.

Unfortunately, as Phillips put it, critics who claimed that there was not "a shred of evidence" to substantiate his charges were wrong because, "to the contrary, there are millions of shreds of evidence."

In other words, the vast majority of ballots and other election records had been shredded or otherwise destroyed.

What had gone wrong? The answer varied from one county to the next. Hancock County officials said they "received verbal instructions" from former secretary of state Blackwell's office that unused ballots "did not have to be retained, and these items were destroyed." Thirteen counties (Columbiana, Coshocton, Darke, Lawrence, Licking, Lorain, Madison, Morgan, Noble, Summit, Tuscarawas, Wayne, and Wood) failed to produce unused ballots, giving no explanation whatsoever. Five counties (Athens, Guernsey, Hamilton, Mercer, and Van Wert) expressed surprise that they couldn't find the unused ballots. Guernsey officials said they were destroyed in error when the county maintenance worker who was collecting trash picked them up by mistake.

According to Matthew Damschroder, Republican director of the Franklin County Board of Elections, Montgomery County's Board of Elections destroyed its ballots because they "just plumb ran out of (storage) room."

All in all, fifty-six out of Ohio's eighty-eight counties destroyed the unused ballots, or in one way or another did not comply with the order. Arnebeck was outraged. "The extent of the destruction of records is consistent with the covering up of the fraud that we believe occurred in the presidential election," he told a reporter. "The missing records reveal where the fraud occurred. You take as an example Warren County. It is well documented that there was a phony Homeland Security alert and that was the excuse for excluding the public and the press from observing what was going on during election day. So the missing unused ballots would suggest that ballots were remade to fit the desired result."

Later, in December 2007, Brunner issued a report on the electronic machines used in the 2004 presidential election in Ohio, which were made by Diebold, ES&S, and Hart Intercivic, concluding that all of them were vulnerable to being hacked, altered, or having their tabulations rejiggered. She recommended that Ohio eliminate the use of touch-screen voting machines.

Even though crucial evidence was now missing, Arnebeck tried to put a good face on the obstacles he faced. "On the one hand, people will now say you can't prove the fraud," he said, "but the rule of law says that when evidence is destroyed it creates a presumption that the people who destroyed evidence did so because it would have proved the contention of the other side."

It is an axiom among public relations professionals, particularly those who are expert in damage control, that if you want to bury a story that might harm your client's reputation you should release it on Friday afternoon. That way, it will be too late to make the evening newscasts and will be relegated to the Saturday papers, which are not widely read.

It is another axiom among PR professionals that if you can pick which weekend to release the story it is best to do so on a three-day holiday weekend. That way, by the time everyone gets back to work on Tuesday the story will be old news.

It is yet another axiom among PR professionals that if you can pick the month when you want to bury a story the best month is August, the slowest news month of the year.

On the afternoon of Friday, August 31, 2007, Labor Day weekend, Karl Rove left the White House.

Rove's last six months or so at the White House were not among his most newsworthy. In March, he caused a stir at the White House Correspondents Dinner, cavorting with reporters during an evening in which, as Jon Stewart put it on *The Daily Show,* "The media gets a chance, for one night, to put aside its cozy relationship with the government for one that is, instead, nauseatingly sycophantic." The highlight of the evening featured Rove rap singing and dancing as MC Rove, with NBC White House correspondent David Gregory, among others.

Among his remaining commitments was attending the Aspen Ideas Festival in July. "Nothing like spending a few days in the cool mountain air with rich liberals to remind me how nutty they can be," he mused, before driving on to nearby Kokomo, Colorado, where he had lived briefly as an infant.

Then, in August, he leaked his intentions to leave to *Wall Street Journal* columnist Paul Gigot, a loyal friend of the administration. He gave the same reason for leaving the Bush administration that hundreds of public servants have given for resigning. "Much as I'd like to be here," Rove said, "I've got to do this for the sake of my family." At the time, however, his son, Andrew, was in college in San Antonio, while Karl and Darby were on the road to a divorce.

On his last day of work, Rove signed several hundred thank-you letters to people who had been helpful to him at the White House. As a parting gift, he gave his staff and colleagues paperweights—a plaster cast of an elaborate Eisenhower Executive Office Building doorknob mounted on a wooden base.

In view of Rove's symbiotic relationship with George W. Bush, most observers saw him as a creature of Texas's most powerful political dynasty. But it was left to the *Washington Post*'s David Broder, a friend of Rove's, to remind America that even though Rove was leaving, he was likely to return to the game. "It would be a mistake for Democrats—or other Republicans—to think that 'Rovism' has run its course and that the last chapter in this story has been written," he wrote. "His game has always been long term, and he plays it with an intensity and attention to detail that few others can match. That kind of manager can always find candidates who will welcome his help. No one should let down his guard just because Rove is temporarily in eclipse."

Of course, some of Rove's legacy still awaited judgment, particularly when it came to allegations about the Ohio election fraud. Now that so much evidence had vanished, the *King Lincoln* case depended more than ever on star witnesses.

Sometime in 2007, Stephen Spoonamore unexpectedly ran into Connell while the two men were attending a conference in London. Increasingly, Spoonamore felt it was his mission to get Connell to open up. At an earlier meeting, he had confronted Connell about the possibility that his colleagues were stealing elections, and Mike had expressed his misgivings.

This time, the two men went out to dinner together. They talked about religion. Connell told Spoonamore about traveling to Burma to help religious dissidents. Spoonamore says he finally decided to confront Connell about his work with SmarTech. "Mike doesn't normally drink but that evening he had a cocktail. And I said: 'Mike, I have to get this out on the table because I like you and like working with you.'

"I actually took Mike's hand and I said: 'I've got to be frank with you, if these things are being built to hack then it is only a matter of time until you and I don't live in a democracy, like the very places we are trying to help.'"

Finally, according to Spoonamore, Connell told him he was fed up. "He said he got involved in politics in his zeal to protect the unborn, but now he felt he had been misguided," recalled Spoonamore. "He said the people around him didn't care, that all they cared about was political power. And he included the whole gang in Tennessee in that category—SmarTech, all of them."

"He said, 'I have to thank you. You're the only guy out there who knows how bad it is.' He was really a babe in the fricking woods. I can't tell you how odd a character he was. . . . He was a very weird, unique guy. Mike was the ultimate Pollyanna. . . . I saw him going through an awakening."

Meanwhile, the *King Lincoln* case proceeded apace. Significantly, on September 17, 2008, Spoonamore submitted an affidavit for the case, saying that SmarTech "had the correct placement, connectivity, and computer experts necessary to change the election in any manner desired by the controllers of the SmarTech computers."

In his affidavit, Spoonamore spoke about his friendship with Mike Connell. "While he has not admitted to wrongdoing, and in my opinion he is not involved in voting theft, Mike clearly agrees that the electronic voting systems in the U.S. are not secure. He further made a statement that he is afraid that some of the more ruthless partisans of the GOP may have exploited systems he in part worked on for this purpose. Mr. Connell builds front-end applications, user interfaces and web sites. Knowing his team and their skills I find it unlikely they would be the vote thieves directly. I believe however he knows who is doing that work, and has likely turned a blind eye to this activity."

But getting Connell to testify was more crucial. "Spoonamore made it his mission," said Bob Fitrakis. "He saw Connell as a salt of the earth guy, highly principled, who wants to spread democracy throughout the world and save unborn babies from the Holocaust, but someone who had been betrayed."

But just how much of an awakening was Connell going through? Spoonamore was not the only one who was concerned Connell had gotten too close to Rove's team. Connell's sister, Shannon, a liberal, had long been disappointed about her brother's ties to the Bushes. "He believed in good and evil very much, but I think he was too close to the evil to actually see it. As fabulous as he was, he was brought up as a country kid, so there was always that trust."

As a result, Shannon said, "He could have justified rigging elections because of his right-to-life upbringing. Saving unborn babies is paramount. I'm sure the people around him knew that. That is the one thing they could have played upon."

Connell's wife, Heather, saw it very differently. "He would never interfere with the democratic process," she said. "That's just ridiculous."

Sometime that summer, possibly around July, Connell saw Shannon, even though he was in the thick of a busy election season, and told her he planned on getting out of politics. "I was amazed at how at peace he seemed when he had not been before," she said. "He was getting out. He looked at politics as a dirty game."

As for any role Spoonamore might have played in changing Connell's perspective, Shannon had no firsthand knowledge. But she said, "It rings true. I think Spoonamore's words might have changed Mike's mind."

To make things more complicated, there was a presidential election coming. Having deeply alienated the prospective Republican nominee, Arizona senator John McCain, during the 2000 primaries, Rove would not have a presidential campaign to run for the first time since 1996. Nevertheless, he played the long game. That meant writing columns, appearing on television, working on his memoir, giving speeches, and raising money for political action groups.

At the same time, Mike Connell's New Media was working for John McCain as he battled through the primaries in early 2008. As the presidential race between McCain and Barack Obama, the presumptive Democratic nominee, took shape, suddenly the prospect of Connell's testimony took on a larger significance, even potentially affecting the 2008 election.

Now Arnebeck and Fitrakis undertook a new strategy that, they hoped, would eventually lead to filing racketeering charges against Karl Rove.* In July 2008, Arnebeck filed an Ohio Corrupt Practices Act/RICO claim designating Rove "as principal perpetrator." At the same time, in a related filing, Arnebeck sent U.S. Attorney General Michael Mukasey a "document hold notice" requesting the complete

---

* At this writing, June 2012, no such charges have been filed.

records of emails "sent to and from the White House, and federal agencies with which Mr. Rove was communicating."

According to Arnebeck, the purpose of the "document hold" was to protect such electronic records from destruction.

Meanwhile, Arnebeck subpoenaed Mike Connell. "We believe there is clear evidence of a coordinated campaign in which Mr. Rove is involved, in which Mr. Connell is an instrument," he said. "And this emphasizes his value as a witness in bringing some of this together. We're not saying that he [Connell] did anything wrong in the sense of his conduct, but we're saying that these conflicting roles raise some issues."

If Connell's testimony was what Arnebeck hoped it might be, it had the potential to be politically explosive if it came out before the November elections. Arnebeck talked to Connell's attorney Jim Ervin about it.

"I know the game and you know the game," Arnebeck said. "We'd like to take his deposition before the election. Will you cooperate?"

"No," Ervin said. "We will vigorously oppose that. But if you do it after there will be no problem."

A waiting game began. Arnebeck was dubious. "We were not pressing full tilt to get [Connell's deposition] before the election because I had concluded we would not win against their determined opposition," he said.

Meanwhile, as Arnebeck waited to find out when Connell would move forward, there was another turn of the screw. Through a third party, Arnebeck got a tip that concerned Connell's safety. As Arnebeck recalled, the message was "Connell will talk and he's in danger. He's in danger from Rove."

But there were serious questions concerning the reliability of the tip. One reason for questioning its authenticity was that the tipster's message was being relayed by a well-known con man named Brett Kimberlin, who first won notoriety during the 1992 presidential campaign when Mark Singer, a staff writer for *The New Yorker*, wrote a 22,000-word article about Kimberlin, his allegations that he once sold marijuana to Vice President Dan Quayle, and his imprisonment. It concluded with the assertion of Erwin Griswold, the distinguished attorney who had been dean of Harvard Law School and solicitor general of the United States, that Kimberlin was "a political prisoner."

When he expanded the article into a book, *Citizen K: The Deeply Weird American Journey of Brett Kimberlin,* Singer ended up writing about how he had been conned in what the *Los Angeles Times* called "the longest correction of a magazine article ever produced." Ultimately, it turned out that Kimberlin really was just a convicted drug smuggler, perjurer, and bomber who had served time for a series of bombings in 1978 at the Indianapolis Speedway—and a terrific con man.

"Originally, I took the bait because the most salient elements of Kimberlin's story seemed irrefutable—powerful evidence of political hypocrisy," wrote Singer. "But then I did what any reporter instinctively does: pulled on a piece of string, trying to discover where it would end. In this instance, it turned out that the string was grafted to a tangled mass of yarn—of a different color and texture than I'd imagined."

The more Singer inspected Kimberlin's life, the more he saw Kimberlin as a master manipulator whose claim to fame, that he allegedly sold drugs to Dan Quayle, forced Quayle to do what was impossible, to prove a negative—that he had never met Kimberlin.

This was Arnebeck's source?

At the time, Arnebeck's only experience with Kimberlin was benign. As Arnebeck saw it, Kimberlin genuinely wanted to uncover the truth. But then Arnebeck got on the phone with Mark Singer, who warned him away from Kimberlin.

"It came as a surprise," said Arnebeck. "I asked, 'Don't you believe in the possibility of redemption? Couldn't it be that Kimberlin has turned over a new leaf?'"

As Arnebeck recalled, Singer said, "No. His character is very set. No, I don't believe he can turn over a new leaf. And if you don't listen to me, you'll be sorry. If you don't recognize what you are dealing with. . . . He's a fundamentally flawed character." Arnebeck had "great qualms" about Kimberlin, and saw him as someone who could easily be discredited.

At the time, Arnebeck added, Spoonamore had similar information about threats to Connell. As Spoonamore saw it, Connell was being told, "Mike, if [the 2004 Ohio election results are] exposed as a fraud, you're going to take the fall, so it's up to you."

But was Kimberlin telling the truth? Or was he trying to insert himself into a presidential campaign by being the conduit for a phony tipster just as he had tried to insert himself into the 1992 presidential campaign with his stories about Dan Quayle? Were the threats against Connell real or not? Was there a tipster after all? Or was he once again taking facts and embroidering them with falsehoods?

And if Kimberlin was tainted, what about other figures in the case? Spoonamore was not above making explosive allegations about politicians having people "whacked." Was Spoonamore exaggerating his accounts of his talks with Connell? Was it possible he and Kimberlin had made Connell into something he wasn't, that Connell really wasn't the man who knew too much?

After his talk with Singer, Arnebeck did indeed have doubts about Kimberlin. But he had only the highest regard for Spoonamore. More to the point, Arnebeck had a witness whose life might be in danger. Protecting Connell was his highest priority. "I now had a reason to believe that there was a threat against a key witness in an important piece of litigation. So that's when I reported it."

On July 24, Arnebeck wrote U.S. Attorney General Michael Mukasey, "We have been confidentially informed by a source we believe to be credible that Karl Rove has threatened Michael Connell, a principal witness we have identified in our King Lincoln case . . . that if he does not agree to 'take the fall' for election fraud in Ohio, his wife Heather will be prosecuted for supposed lobby law violations. This appears to be in response to our designation of Rove as the principal perpetrator in the Ohio Corrupt Practices Act/RICO."

Arnebeck added that the reasons for the reported threats were unclear: "One possibility is that they were trying to pressure him to take the fall. The other is that they were trying to get him to shut up."

The next day, July 25, Spoonamore wrote an email to Connell, saying Arnebeck and the judge would do everything they could to make sure he was protected:

191

From: Stephen Spoonamore <stephen.spoonamore@gmail.com>
Date: Fri, Jul 25, 2008 at 9:04 AM
Subject: Fwd: Cliff and Immunity for you and yours.
To: Mike Connell <mlconnell@technomania.com>
Cc: arnebeck <Arnebeck@aol.com>

Mike.

Cliff [Arnebeck] said that he would walk you and your wife into
the chambers of the Federal Judge. . . . If the threats extend to other
members of your family or circle, he needs to know. That's how it
works. Cliff and this judge will not allow you, or any witness or
potential witness to be blackmailed, or intimidated.

Again, my best to my friend.
—Spoon.

By this time, Connell's wife, Heather, was concerned about what
was going on. "I point-blank asked, 'Was your life threatened?' And
he told me 'No.'"

It was unclear whether Connell was simply minimizing the danger so as not to upset his wife or the threats were merely fabrications.

Up to this point, the media had ignored the Connell story. But as the
elections approached, netroot websites finally took interest. In October, Rebecca Abrahams, a former ABC News producer, wrote about
Connell on the Huffington Post, characterizing him as the missing
link when it came to discovering the lost emails in the U.S. attorneys
scandal. Abrahams cited Stephen Spoonamore as saying, "While he
doesn't know whether Connell had a role in the White House email
purge, he's vital to uncovering the truth about the missing communications." Likewise, at Raw Story, a left-wing blog, Larisa Alexan-
drovna, a reporter who had been covering the Don Siegelman story,
reported on the ongoing legal battle to force Connell to testify. Others, such as ePluribus Media, the Free Press, Brad Blog, and Brett
Kimberlin's site, Velvet Revolution, went at it as well.

As the election approached, Arnebeck got another call from Kimberlin. This time, the message was: if Connell talked he would be "in danger from Rove."

On Friday, October 31, 2008, four days before the presidential election, Arnebeck met Mike Connell in court for the first time at a hearing in an attempt to finally get Connell deposed. Arnebeck introduced himself to Connell. "I told him of the high regard Spoonamore held him [in]. His reputation, as I understood it, he was said to be preeminent in his field. Spoonamore said no one has anyone else like Connell; he was in a league of his own."

Arnebeck regarded the exchange as "a positive interaction." Connell was relaxed and cordial.

U.S. District Judge Solomon Oliver was less so, however. "He really put me through the hoops in terms of why do you need this deposition, what is it that I intend to ask, how long will it take," said Arnebeck.

The judge then retired to his chambers. When he returned, to widespread astonishment, he ruled that the deposition would take place on Monday, November 3, 2008, the day before the election.

As they left, Arnebeck told Connell that he looked forward to seeing him on Monday. His hope was that the deposition would effectively continue the conversations Connell had been having with Spoonamore.

The deposition began a few minutes after noon on Monday, November 3, 2008, in the law offices of Benesch, Friedlander, Coplan & Aronoff in Cleveland. It was effectively too late to have any possible bearing on the presidential election the next day.

Arnebeck began by asking Connell about his professional credentials, work experience, and his work for various Republican candidates. Then he asked Connell if he was aware of any threats with regard to his testifying.

"No," Connell replied.

Arnebeck then asked Connell to describe his work for Blackwell's office in 2004. "There had been a problem in the past . . ." he testified, "in previous elections where they had crushing traffic, the system failed, which means that Web pages were not available. . . . So they needed to have a failover facility."

Asked how SmarTech was chosen to serve as the secondary location, Connell explained, "I was not involved in the selection; I can't recall how they entered into the picture. But an independent decision was made to go with SmarTech."

This was surprising to Arnebeck. Dozens of sites developed by Connell at New Media and GovTech were hosted at SmarTech. Arnebeck had assumed the decision to use SmarTech was Connell's. But now Connell seemed to be saying Ken Blackwell's office had made the decision.

Finally, Arnebeck got to the most crucial question of all, regarding whether a man-in-the-middle attack had been set up. He showed Connell the schematic diagram of the computer setup between the Secretary of State's Office and SmarTech on election night.

"It is the understanding of our expert that the SmarTech computer shown in this configuration would be capable of sending instructions, receiving instructions and receiving information from both the county-level tabulators and the computers at the Secretary of State's Office. Is that your understanding of this system as well?" Arnebeck asked.

"No," Connell replied. "Again, so you guys are clear, this is not connected to the tabulators in any way."

When the deposition ended, Connell cordially said good-bye. "He's a helluva nice guy," said Arnebeck.

To anyone who hoped for breakthrough revelations, the Connell testimony was anticlimactic and disappointing. "Computer Expert Denies Knowledge of '04 Vote Rigging in Ohio," McClatchy Newspapers headlined the story.

Interrupted, as it was, by dozens of objections from his attorneys, Connell's testimony was also a study in obfuscation and noncommunication. And on several occasions Connell explicitly rejected the premises behind Arnebeck's case. He said he had no direct knowledge about Karl Rove's emails.

Ultimately, even the ever-hopeful Arnebeck conceded that during his two hours of testimony Connell "denied any knowledge of the altering of votes."

Nevertheless, to Arnebeck and Fitrakis a close reading of the transcript yielded glimmers of hope. "As I reflect on what he said, he gave us a lot of important stuff," said Arnebeck. "He was not denying that there was an obvious security problem [that allowed hacking the vote]. He was shifting the responsibility."

As Arnebeck saw it, Connell made it clear that security was not his focus, that security was built into the Secretary of State's data processing system. He had built a low-cost method to interact with that system, without alternative security protocols. "That cross system communications protocol was backed up/mirrored on the SmarTech servers in Chattanooga," said Arnebeck. "Therefore, SmarTech could utilize that communications protocol to interact with the ORACLE data system—bypassing the expensive and resource intensive audit protocols of the OSOS data system."

In other words, Arnebeck and Fitrakis said, Connell had set it up so the secretary of state's system could be hacked at SmarTech in Chattanooga. "I interpreted it as him saying he designed the gun, but didn't pull the trigger," said Bob Fitrakis.

Arnebeck intended to depose Connell again. There were many unanswered questions. How close was Connell to Karl Rove? What did they talk about? How did they interact? Or did Rove use intermediaries? Barry Jackson, Connell's close friend from college days, had been Rove's right hand in the White House. Had he played a role?

Both Arnebeck and Fitrakis still took the threats against Connell seriously, and saw him as someone who was not in a position to talk candidly. "I saw Connell as a dead man walking," said Fitrakis. "I even told him not to fly his private plane."

The day after the deposition, Tuesday, November 4, 2008, Americans went to the polls to decide between Barack Obama and John McCain. On Fox News, Karl Rove predicted a landslide victory for Obama. He was right, of course, but he neglected to mention that this historic election was in many ways a verdict on his legacy.

What had he and George Bush wrought? Unfettered deregulation had left the nation's banking system teetering on a precipice, and had led to a Wall Street collapse and the worst economic crisis since the Great Depression. Overseas, American troops were stuck in two seemingly endless quagmires in Afghanistan and Iraq that were enormously costly in terms of blood and treasure. On social issues, evangelicals were at war with science. Instruments of government were being wielded as political weapons.

Rove's great dream, of course, had been that, like Mark Hanna, he would forge a historic electoral realignment that would create an enduring Republican majority. Instead, pundits on both the right and left agreed that he had done the opposite. In a *New York Times* op-ed piece, "Building a Coalition, Forgetting to Rule," Bush speechwriter David Frum wrote, "We were so mesmerized by the specious analogies between 1996 and 1896 that we forgot that analogies are literary devices, not evidence." Frum added that Rove's approach of all politics and no policy "has created a lethal political environment for Republican candidates."

And in *The Guardian*, Sidney Blumenthal asserted that Rove and Bush had effectively ended "the Republican era in American politics, an era that began in reaction to Lyndon Johnson's Great Society, the Vietnam war and the civil rights revolution, was pioneered by Richard Nixon, consolidated by Ronald Reagan, and wrecked by George W. Bush."

Bush's approval ratings were in the twenties—abysmally low, meaning that he was winning recognition as one of the worst presidents in the history of the United States. Instead of luring new constituencies to the party, Rove had instituted "voter fraud" initiatives to disenfranchise millions of voters, largely minorities and immigrants who leaned heavily Democratic.

But even that wasn't enough. The Democrats had won the White House and both houses of Congress. Change had come. Now Rove's vision was in ashes.

Arnebeck and Fitrakis were elated by the results of the election. "In our minds the good guys had won," said Arnebeck. "There would be a new administration. The FBI and the Department of Justice would deal with election theft." The two lawyers wondered if they might even drop the suit, presuming it would be preempted by federal action.

Six weeks later, on December 18, 2008, a month before Obama moved into the White House, Connell flew his Piper Saratoga, N9299N, to

Washington, D.C., where he met with the Knights of Columbus to discuss rebuilding their website. He spent the night at a hotel and prepared to fly home to Ohio the next day. His company, New Media Communications, was having its office Christmas party that evening. His wife, Heather, and the rest of the staff would be there, and it was important that he attend.

Connell went to College Park Airport in Prince George's County, Maryland, outside Washington, and at 2:27 p.m., he called the Raleigh Automated Flight Service Station to figure out when he could return to Akron. The weather was not great. He was concerned about icing, but he hoped to leave right away.

"Would you like a standard briefing and just cover everything or do you need just to kinda hit the highlights?" asked the briefer.

"I don't want to waste your time," Connell replied. "Let's figure out if this sounds like a suicide mission or not, and then we'll go from there."

Connell provided the briefer with a proposed route of flight with an altitude of 6,000 feet. He asked about icing conditions and whether he could arrive in Akron before the weather worsened. The briefer told him that the freezing level in Akron, Ohio, was "close" to about 3,000 to 4,000 feet but it might drop as the day went on.

After about twenty minutes, Connell hung up and filed a flight plan. At 3:30, he finally called his wife, Heather, to say he had been cleared.

One minute later, he took off in his Piper Saratoga, keeping in contact with Potomac Terminal Radar Approach Control for the initial part of the flight. At first, the flight was uneventful, but at 4:42 Connell reported encountering "moderate chop."

By 5:30, Connell was nearing Akron and the Canton-Akron Air Traffic Control Tower began giving him instructions for his final approach course. At 5:42, the local controller told him to descend and maintain an altitude of 3,200 feet. Connell acknowledged the clearance, and asked if there were any pilot reports of icing below 6,000 feet.

There were none. Seven minutes later, at 5:49, the controller told Connell to fly at a heading of 250 degrees and maintain 3,200 feet.

Two minutes later, Connell contacted the control tower and was

cleared to land on runway 23. He made a gradual left turn to inter-
cept the localizer, a component of the instrument landing system that
provides runway guidance.

It was now 5:51, but something was wrong. He was descending as
if on approach at an airspeed of just over 100 knots, but his plane was
to the left of the localizer.

The controller informed Connell that he was off course, and Connell replied, "Correcting."

But according to a report by the National Traffic Safety Board,
recorded radar track information showed that Connell did not correct to the right. Instead, he continued to fly a course to the left of,
and almost parallel to, the approach course centerline.

Another minute later, at 5:52:31, the tower controller transmitted
a warning to Connell: "You're still well to the left of the localizer, sir.
Would you like to go back around for the approach?"

Six seconds later, Connell replied, "Please repeat."

The tower repeated.

Connell responded, ". . . nine nine November we'd like to correct."

The tower controller responded, "Roger . . . two and a half miles
from the field cleared to land runway twenty-three for nine nine."

Connell acknowledged the landing clearance. Then, at 5:53:02, he
transmitted, "Uh, can we do a three sixty and, uh, reestablish ourselves?"

But the controller was unable to approve the request. Instead,
he told Connell to climb and maintain 3,000 feet. Connell was now
heading "due north and climbing."

The controller replied, "No delay in the climb, climb and maintain
three thousand."

Connell didn't respond.

At 5:53:47, the controller transmitted, "Nine two nine nine
November, did you copy?"

Three seconds passed.

"Nine nine November declaring an emergency!" Connell
screamed. Then, "Oh, fuck!"

The plane was in a spiral dive. A few seconds later, the cockpit burst
open. In nearby Canton, residents said they heard what sounded like
an engine sputtering.

The controller continued to try to communicate: "November nine nine November, maintain altitude. The airport is two miles west of you."

But Connell did not respond.

On the ground, an eyewitness saw two bright lights coming almost nose first toward the ground, with the engine "roaring."

"I was standing in the kitchen and I looked out the window and all I saw was fire," Taylor Fano told the *Akron Beacon Journal*. "It took out the flagpole and the cement blocks surrounding the flagpole. . . . It skidded across the driveway and right in between a line of pine trees and a small fence around an in-ground pool."

Mike Connell, forty-five, was killed instantly.

No credible evidence has emerged suggesting Connell's plane crash was due to foul play. According to a report released by the National Transportation Safety Board in January 2010, more than a year later, Connell's plane was not equipped with an anti-ice/deice system and was not approved for operations in icing conditions. Officially, the NTSB ruled that the probable cause of the accident was "the pilot's inappropriate control inputs as a result of spatial disorientation, which led to an aerodynamic stall and loss of control." Contributing factors, the report said, included ice accumulation that reduced the plane's aerodynamic performance, and Connell's inability "to establish the airplane on the proper approach course."

The NTSB report noted further that there was "a high likelihood of encountering supercooled large droplet (SLD) icing in the area" at the time of Connell's flight. Other pilots going into and out of the Akron airport at the time of the accident all reported icing conditions, and, the report said, "[t]hree of the pilots reported a rapid accumulation of between 1 and 2 inches of ice within a 15-minute period prior to and after the accident. One pilot reported that he required a significant amount of engine power to maintain airspeed and had a hard landing due to ice accumulation on his airplane."

About nine months after Connell's death, Cliff Arnebeck received an unusual letter that claimed to provide information about the crash. The envelope contained a cover letter, signed with the pseudonym

Mark Felt, the name of the late FBI official who was Bob Woodward's real-life Deep Throat for Watergate, that had a brief message: "Enclosed is a document that is not supposed to exist."

The document in question was what was purported to be an "after-action" report written by a covert operative who claimed to have sabotaged Mike Connell's plane. In the report, the unnamed operative claims that he arrived at College Park Airport at 4:26 a.m. on December 19, 2008, early in the morning on the day of Connell's fatal flight. The operative claims he proceeded to RW33 (Runway 33), and, detecting no surveillance, found the plane, unlocked the door, and "installed AMD [a microprocessor] on the static port system."

Arnebeck said he believed the document was legitimate and was likely an account by a private operative who had been hired to sabotage the plane.

However, two intelligence analysts examined the documents on behalf of the author and assessed them as highly suspect. In addition, according to the NTSB report, an examination of the plane after the accident "revealed no anomalies that would have precluded normal operation."

But many people suspected that Connell's plane had been sabotaged intentionally, because, as Rove's cyberguru, he knew too much about what happened to the election in Ohio in 2004. Cliff Arnebeck described Connell's death as "an assassination." Spoonamore said Karl Rove had murdered Connell. Connell's sister, Shannon, believed it was murder. Project Censored called for a federal investigation. Robert F. Kennedy Jr. called the case "more serious than Watergate." More than half a dozen netroot sites pursued the story for years. In February 2010, British author Simon Worrall's "The Mysterious Death of Bush's Cyber-Guru" appeared in *Maxim,* and was subsequently expanded into an ebook, *Cybergate: Was the White House Stolen by Cyberfraud?*

None of which was surprising, because the events involving Rove and SmarTech and the many tantalizing unanswered questions they raised added up to a provocative and frustrating whodunit that had all the elements of both the story of the century and an unsolvable, conspiracy-laden black hole. Nearly a decade earlier, Rove's backers had put together a company in Chattanooga, Tennessee, that later evolved, under different ownership, into a powerful high-tech weapon for Republicans that provided legitimate websites for conservatives, but also hosted sensitive material for nonpartisan government agencies and committees. Rove and more than eighty of his colleagues in the Bush administration had used it to host millions of their emails, off-site from the White House servers, seemingly so that their official communications—which, by law, should have been subject to the Presidential Records Act—would be free from scrutiny. Rove had been deeply involved in the Plame Wilson affair and U.S. attorneys scandal, and in both cases, when Rove's emails were sought by investigators, they were no longer available.

Likewise, when it came to investigating allegations of electoral fraud in Ohio in 2004, the vanishing continued. Even though the actual ballots had been protected by a court order, they too had been destroyed. All of which meant that the best source left to answer questions raised by these scandals was Mike Connell. And now, after his life had allegedly been threatened, Connell, the man who potentially knew too much, had been killed in a mysterious plane crash.

In the end, however, there were only two possibilities: Either Mike Connell had been murdered or he had been the victim of an accident. As for the first, the evidence simply wasn't there.

That left only one inescapable conclusion: If it was an accident, Karl Rove was one of the luckiest men on the planet. Mike Connell's sister, Shannon, put it best. "His death would have been a really nice Christmas present for Rove," she said.

FOURTEEN

Back from the Dead

For all his many strokes of luck, Rove's departure from the White House was ignominious at best. The presidency he had built was widely regarded as a historic disaster. He was depleted physically, emotionally, and financially. He was still hounded by the press. And his marriage was in tatters.

More to the point, now that he was out of the White House, what next? He had become known as Bush's Brain. But what did that mean without George W. Bush?

The answer was that Rove's entire life had been about politics, and that was not about to change. Even though he had not achieved a permanent Republican majority in George W. Bush's two administrations, he had by no means relinquished its pursuit. The scandals that Rove had survived had tarnished his reputation, but they were also evidence of his willingness to use the power of the state to pursue his goals. He was willing, it appeared, to do whatever was necessary.

Rebuilding would not be easy. The brand he had created for the Republican Party had meager value. "Nobody who's come of age during the Bush era will stand up and say, 'I'm a Bush Republican,'" GOP consultant Ed Rollins told journalist Paul Alexander at the end of Bush's second term. "'I'm going to spend the rest of my life being a Bush Republican.'"

Moreover, Rove had so deeply alienated rivals in the party—John McCain, for example—that he had no horse to ride. There was no one to serve as his George Bush this time around.

Nonetheless, as early as April 2008, even before Bush's term had ended, Rove was hard at it—writing columns, appearing on television, giving speeches, writing his memoir, and becoming an analyst for Fox News, *Newsweek,* and the *Wall Street Journal.* "I enjoyed a new experience: being a spectator at a presidential campaign rather than a participant," Rove wrote in *Courage and Consequence.* "Among other things, I learned that it is much easier to pontificate on campaigns than it is to run them."

But that is not all he was doing. Rove eagerly set about building independent political action groups, just as he had in Texas years before. According to a report by journalist Peter Stone in the *National Journal,* that spring Rove was working round the clock meeting with Republican operatives and GOP donors, including billionaires, hoping to raise about $100 million. "Karl is up to his eyeballs in this," said one prominent GOP consultant. "They're trying to figure out who is going to do the presidential, who is going to do the Senate and who is going to do the House. They're trying to assign resources to maximize the dollars and minimize duplication. Karl has taken it over."

Sources told the *National Journal* that Rove had been hitting up friends like Texas oilman T. Boone Pickens and Las Vegas casino mogul Sheldon Adelson.

In 2008, Obama's sweeping victory left the GOP with a power vacuum that Rove eyed covetously. His relationships with Fox and the *Wall Street Journal* gave him an income and a pulpit. And he had begun to build an independent base within the party in which he would have autonomy and be able to control the purse strings when the right candidate surfaced.

Rove still had to wrap up the loose ends from the Bush years. In July 2009, he testified before the House Judiciary Committee about the U.S. attorneys scandal and the prosecution of Don Siegelman. The Committee concluded that Rove had played a significant role in the firings of the U.S. attorneys, but it did not make public any conclusions about his alleged role in Siegelman's prosecution.

For years the Internet had been abuzz about Rove's relationship with a lobbyist from Texas named Karen Johnson. In December, he and Darby were finally granted a divorce and Karen Johnson soon publicly surfaced as his girlfriend. "It's always sad to see a marriage end," said Rove's colleague Ed Gillespie. (In June 2012, Rove married

Johnson in a ceremony attended by George W. Bush and casino mogul Steve Wynn, a former Democrat who loaned the couple his jet for their honeymoon and quietly donated millions to Crossroads GPS.)

On the other hand, at roughly the same time, Rove became the beneficiary of another piece of luck. In 2007, Citizens United, a conservative group known for making right-wing political documentaries, had made a film called *Hillary: The Movie* about presumptive Democratic nominee Hillary Clinton. Citizens United had intended to offer the movie via Video on Demand before the Democratic primaries in the 2008 election season, but had been thwarted when the Federal Election Commission ruled that the documentary was nothing more than an "electioneering communication." That meant it violated the McCain-Feingold Act, the 2002 federal campaign-finance-reform law, and could not be broadcast before the election.

The FEC decision was subsequently upheld by a three-judge panel that ruled the movie "is susceptible of no other interpretation than to inform the electorate that Senator Clinton is unfit for office, that the United States would be a dangerous place in a President Hillary Clinton world, and that viewers should vote against her."

Citizens United appealed, and the case made its way up the legal system. When it was first argued before the U.S. Supreme Court, on March 24, 2009, the case appeared to be, as Jeffrey Toobin put it in *The New Yorker,* one of "modest importance" that addressed a relatively narrow issue of campaign finance law.

But as it was being argued something happened. Deputy Solicitor General Malcolm Stewart rose to represent the U.S. government, and his unexpected answer to just one question dramatically changed the American electoral process. Stewart, a graduate of Princeton and Yale Law School, like most lawyers who won a sought-after position in the Solicitor General's Office, had impeccable credentials and a sterling reputation. But in this case, as Toobin put it, his appearance was "an epic disaster."

The problem began when Justice Samuel Alito, a conservative appointee of George W. Bush, spotted a weak point in Stewart's argument and went to work.

McCain-Feingold prohibited the broadcast of electioneering via electronic communications, in this case Video on Demand. But Justice Alito wanted to know if that was also the case with other media. "Do you think the Constitution required Congress to draw the line where it did, limiting this to broadcast and cable and so forth?" Alito asked. "Could the law prohibit a corporation from providing the same thing in a book?"

Yes, Stewart said.

If Karl Rove had been listening in, this is the point at which his ears would have perked up and the wide, wide grin of a Cheshire cat would have spread across his face.

"That's pretty incredible," replied Alito. "You think that if a book was published, a campaign biography that was the functional equivalent of express advocacy, that could be banned?"

Stewart tried to backtrack, but it was too late. The damage had been done. The government had taken a stand suggesting it should be able to regulate the contents of books. The issue that had initially come before the Court had to do with campaign finance. But now the *Citizens United* decision could be framed instead as an issue that was about freedom of speech, the First Amendment, and government censorship.

Ultimately, it was left to Justice Anthony Kennedy to write the decision for the majority, and he hewed closely to that template. "Speech is an essential mechanism of democracy, for it is the means to hold officials accountable to the people," he wrote. "The right of citizens to inquire, to hear, to speak, and to use information to reach consensus is a precondition to enlightened self-government and a necessary means to protect it."

To Kennedy, prohibiting individuals or corporations from funding political commercials, or restraining in any way, even for a brief time was censorship pure and simple, "By taking the right to speak from some and giving it to others, the Government deprives the disadvantaged person or class of the right to use speech to strive to establish worth, standing, and respect for the speaker's voice. The Government may not by these means deprive the public of the right and privilege to determine for itself what speech and speakers are worthy of consideration. The First Amendment protects speech and speaker, and the ideas that flow from each."

Kennedy insisted corporations had the same rights to free speech that individuals have. "The Court has recognized that First Amendment protection extends to corporations . . ." he wrote. "By suppressing the speech of manifold corporations, both for-profit and nonprofit, the Government prevents their voices and viewpoints from reaching the public and advising voters on which persons or entities are hostile to their interests."

The McCain-Feingold Act, which had limited the use of soft money, was now dead. Moreover, for all the talk about freedom of speech and the First Amendment, the Court had overturned a century of law and had eliminated virtually all constraints on funding by corporations, unions, and the wealthy with regard to federal elections. The political implications were staggering, and the new opportunities to use money to leverage both the primaries and general election were virtually limitless. The Supreme Court had brought American politics back to the time before the Progressive Era—to the time of William McKinley and Mark Hanna. It was everything Rove had dreamed of.

The *Citizens United* decision was handed down on January 21, 2010, at a time when the Republican Party was going through an epic transformation. Two days earlier, Republican Scott Brown had won the Massachusetts Senate seat vacated by the death of Ted Kennedy. This was not merely a traditionally Democratic seat. Kennedy had first won the seat in 1962, and held it until he died in 2009. His brother John F. Kennedy had won it ten years earlier. Thanks to support from the powerful new insurgency known as the Tea Party, Brown had taken the seat of a great liberal icon in one of the most liberal states in the Union. The message came through loud and clear: The Tea Party was transforming the Republican Party.

Two weeks later, on February 4, the first Tea Party Convention was held in Nashville, Tennessee, with Sarah Palin cementing her position as de facto leader by giving the keynote address. Suddenly, Karl Rove had a new problem to deal with: an angry, defiant, right-wing libertarian populist insurgency funded by arch-reactionary multibillionaires Charles and David Koch was becoming a powerful force within the Republican Party.

Rove didn't particularly like it. "He dislikes party elements he can't control," said Roger Stone. "He can't control Sarah Palin. These are the people he calls kooks. He likes establishment, inside the Beltway types."

At the same time, he could not ignore these powerful forces. Having anticipated these developments, Rove had sat down several weeks earlier for lunch at the Mayflower Hotel in Washington, five blocks from the White House, with two close colleagues, Ed Gillespie, who served as counselor to the president in the Bush White House, and Steven Law, general counsel to the U.S. Chamber of Commerce, the most powerful lobbying group in the country and a key supporter of Republican causes.

Their agenda was to figure out how to harness the voter anger they had seen erupt at town hall meetings all over the country the previous summer. "Clearly there was a tremendous amount of grass-roots energy building—a grass-roots prairie fire that was building in intensity," Law told Jim Kuhnhenn of the Huffington Post. "We felt that one of the things we could do was pour gasoline on that."

That meant money—and lots of it.

Meanwhile, Rove's ascent as party boss was fueled by an unwitting accomplice. A former lieutenant governor of Maryland, Michael Steele had been elected the RNC's first African-American chairman immediately after Obama had become America's first black president. Steele had launched his chairmanship with the pledge that the Republicans could become competitive again in areas such as the Northeast. The GOP, he said, was now going after the younger voters, Hispanics, and blacks.

"Get ready, baby," Steele said. "It's time to turn it on."

He added, "We need to uptick our image with everyone, including one-armed midgets."

What followed was so mortifying that even satirists were at a loss for words.

Ham-fistedly wielding the lingo of a clueless middle-aged dad trying to impress his tattooed, hipster kids, Steele launched an "off-the-hook" PR effort to recast a shattered party dominated by suburban white men with what he called "a hip-hop makeover."

When he was asked if the makeover would be cutting-edge, Steele replied, "I don't do 'cutting-edge.' That's what Democrats are doing.

We're going beyond cutting-edge." And as for Obama's stimulus package, Steele said that was just "bling bling."

Whatever problems the Republicans had—and they were many—putting a middle-aged black man on the podium trying to master the hip-hop idiom was not going to get young voters, blacks, or Hispanics to abandon Barack Obama. Nor did it endear Steele to a party dominated by Southern white men, Christian evangelicals, Tea Partiers, country club Republicans, and corporate interests.

Style was not Steele's only problem. He came in for another round of criticism when he published a book that, critics said, appeared to promote himself at the expense of the party. Three former RNC chairmen—Frank J. Fahrenkopf Jr., Jim Nicholson, and Rich Bond—lashed out at Steele after it was revealed he was delivering paid speeches across the country. To which he replied, "I'm the chairman. Deal with it."

Donors were irate at his extravagant expenditures. Fees for charter flights doubled. Wolfgang Puck catered the RNC's Christmas party. Outlays for flowers and limousines soared. And when Karl Rove joined the chorus of critics, Steele had a ready reply. "Stuff it," he said.

The coup de grâce came on March 29, 2010, when Jonathan Strong at the Daily Caller, a conservative website, broke the story about Steele's lavish travels. A trip to Hawaii cost the RNC $43,828—plus airfare. On other trips, there were chic hotels such as the Venetian and the M Resort in Las Vegas and the W in Washington. But Steele's February trip for the RNC to California was the kicker. It included a $9,099 stop at the Beverly Hills Hotel, $6,596 at the nearby Four Seasons, and $1,946.25 at Voyeur West Hollywood, a bondage-themed nightclub featuring topless women dancers imitating lesbian sex.

Steele did not go to the Voyeur himself—an RNC aide was the culprit—but the damage was done. This was the party of family values after all, and nearly $2,000 was being spent to entertain campaign contributors at a lesbian stripper joint. Comedy Central's website put it succinctly: "Michael Steele Is Winning Back America, One Lesbian Stripper at a Time."

To make matters worse, the following Thursday, which just happened to be April Fool's Day, RNC officials confessed that a fundraising letter had mistakenly used an 800 number instead of the

Washington, D.C., area code, 202. As a result, instead of reaching the Republican Party, prospective donors were offered the opportunity to engage in phone sex with a "nasty girl" for $2.99 a minute.

Even without such indignities, the bottom line was that Steele was not bringing in the money. In early 2010, the *National Journal* reported, the RNC's coffers had only $8.4 million compared with nearly three times as much the previous year, when Steele was elected chairman.

GOP loyalists rebelled. "I've hinted at this before, but now I am saying it—don't give money to the RNC," said Tony Perkins, president of the Family Research Council, the conservative Christian family values group. "If you want to put money into the political process, and I encourage you to do so, give directly to candidates who you know reflect your values."

On MSNBC, talk-show host Joe Scarborough, a former Republican congressman from Florida, said, "Michael Steele should resign or be fired." Headliners including Sarah Palin, former Speaker of the House Newt Gingrich, and Mississippi governor Haley Barbour all declined invitations by Steele to address his fund-raising events.

Rove had been holding his fire, but even an operative as disciplined as he could not resist commenting on whether the lesbian stripper episode reflected on Steele. "Sure it does," he said. "The chairman of the Republican National Committee, for good or for ill, is the steward of the party's money. . . . The question is not Michael Steele. The question is the management of the building and whether the procedures are in place to spend money on elections—and not to spend money on jets and bondage clubs."

For Rove, the timing of Steele's implosion could not have been better. On April 21, less than a month after the lesbian stripper revelations, Rove formalized his alliance with American Crossroads and other SuperPACs by inviting two dozen high-level Republican operatives to his Weaver Terrace home for a summit conference at which he effectively replaced the RNC with his shadow operation.

For the most part, Rove's new operation was intended to be under the radar. At one point, a Crossroads spokesman emailed attendees a YouTube link to a clip from the movie *Fight Club*, in which Brad

Pitt's character says, "The first rule of Fight Club is: You do not talk about Fight Club. The second rule of Fight Club is: You do not talk about Fight Club."

Nevertheless, it wasn't long before Politico's Kenneth P. Vogel and Mike Allen caught on. "The Republican Party's best-connected political operatives have quietly built a massive fundraising, organizing and advertising machine," they wrote in a piece titled "Rove, GOP Plot Vast Network to Reclaim Power."

What Rove was doing was low-profile, but for him it was nothing new. Wayne Slater, the co-author of *Bush's Brain* and *The Architect*, pointed out that Rove had done the same thing in Texas years earlier when he was at odds with the powers that be in the Texas Republican Party. "When Karl didn't feel that the party chairman was a sufficient ally, then he just discouraged people from giving to the Republican Party," said Slater, "and instead had them contribute to a separate entity. It was his own deal. He had a lot of influence over the money, who would contribute to whom, and when."

Now, thanks to *Citizens United,* similar mechanisms could be amped up a hundredfold. Donations could be unlimited. In addition, the *Citizens United* decision allowed incorporated 501(c)(4) public advocacy groups such as the National Rifle Association, or Citizens United itself, to make expenditures in political races. Unlike SuperPACs, they did not have to disclose the names of their donors. "Disadvantaged" persons and classes, such as the Koch brothers and Rove's billionaire backers, were, as Supreme Court Justice Anthony Kennedy put it, no longer "deprived" by the government from making their voices heard.

Characterizing the decision as "a neutron bomb" dropped in the middle of the midterm election season,* Michael Waldman, director

---

* It is worth noting that a number of legal scholars believe that the significance of the *Citizens United* decision has been overstated and that the basic principle that has allowed the vast influx of private money into elections had already been established by the Supreme Court in 1976 in *Buckley v. Valeo.* "The key principal is that *Buckley v. Valeo* already had established that independent spending was constitutionally protected speech," said Richard H. Pildes, professor of law at NYU School of Law. "You saw the results of that with the Swift Boat Veterans for Truth and the George Soros money in 2004.

"The unique thing about *Citizens United* is that it opened the same PACs to cor-

of the Brennan Center for Justice at NYU School of Law, wrote in the *New York Times*:

> It is breathtaking in its scope: it overturns doctrine dating back a century and laws upheld in 1990 that banned corporate managers from directly spending shareholder money in elections. . . .
>
> This matches or exceeds *Bush v. Gore* in ideological or partisan overreaching by the court. In that case, the court reached into the political process to hand the election to one candidate. Today it reached into the political process to hand unprecedented power to corporations. . . .
>
> Why will this matter? Isn't there a lot of money sloshing around in politics already? Consider Exxon-Mobil. In 2008, its political action committee (PAC) raised about $1 million from its employees and offices. Its profits that year—which it was legally barred from pouring into politics—were $45 billion. It was illegal for Exxon to spend that money on elections; now with this decision, it will be legal. Exxon or any other firm could spend Bloomberg-level sums in any congressional district in the country against, say, any congressman who supports climate change legislation, or health care, etc.

The *Citizens United* decision, of course, allowed Democratic-leaning groups the same latitude, but multibillionaires and major corporations leaned heavily toward the Republicans. The U.S. Chamber of Commerce alone represented Goldman Sachs, Chevron, Texaco, and hundreds of other corporations. More than 93 percent of the money it spent supporting electoral campaigns went to Republicans.

Hundreds of millions of dollars poured in from corporate America, which was angry at Obama because of his health care program and initiatives to regulate the financial community and the environment. American Crossroads, and its sister group, Crossroads GPS, raised

porations and union spending. That was one thing that Buckley had not addressed. *Citizens United* said there was no constitutional reason to treat them differently." Even if the Citizens United decision had not taken place, Pildes said, American Crossroads and other SuperPACs still would have been able to collect most of their contributions because most of the money came from individuals, not corporations.

more than $65 million, the Huffington Post reported. The American Action Network, which shares office space with Crossroads, spent $22.7 million. The U.S. Chamber of Commerce's goal was $75 million.

But Rove still had a major political problem. The Tea Party was the most vital new force in the GOP, and Rove personified the GOP establishment it detested. Tea Partiers were the ultimate deficit hawks, but, under Bush, the national debt had nearly doubled, to more than $10 trillion. Moreover, Rove himself had pushed for some of Bush's most expensive programs, such as his Medicare drug bill and the 2008 bank bailout.

How could Rove harness the power of this new movement when he was in some measure the object of its anger? How could he make the best use of the largesse of their billionaire backers?

At times, he did it by attacking views espoused by Tea Partiers— the "birther" charge that President Obama was born in Kenya and therefore was not eligible to be president—without attacking the Tea Party itself. "The right-wing base of the Republican party," Rove said, "and I'm part of that right-wing base, is not in love with the issue of birthers. I mean, there is an element inside the Republican Party, and outside the Republican party, that's fallen in love with this but the majority of Republicans and the vast majority of Americans accept he is a U.S. citizen capable of being president."

No single force represented a bigger challenge to Rove than David and Charles Koch. As the multibillionaire owners of Koch Industries, the second-largest private company in the country, with annual revenues of $100 billion, the brothers counted huge oil refineries, Georgia-Pacific lumber, Dixie cups, Brawny paper towels, and many other companies among their holdings. Deeply conservative Libertarians, they had founded Americans for Prosperity as a political advocacy group in 2004.

With the advent of the Tea Party, the Koch brothers and Americans for Prosperity became the chief backers of the so-called grassroots movement. Its website, Americans for Prosperity, claimed to have 2 million activists, but as recently as 2009 it boasted only eight thousand registered members.

One Tea Party–related ad paid for by Americans for Prosperity said,

"Today, the voices of average Americans are being drowned out by lobbyists and special interests. But you can do something about it." As Jane Mayer pointed out in a *New Yorker* profile of the Koch brothers, the ad did not mention its corporate funders. Obama adviser David Axelrod explained, "What they don't say is that, in part, this is a grassroots citizens' movement brought to you by a bunch of oil billionaires."

In the fall of 2009, as Obama's approval ratings fell and the Tea Party took to the streets, David Koch took heart that his vision might finally be realized. And later, in the wake of the *Citizens United* ruling, as the 2010 midterm election season got under way, he also decided that Americans for Prosperity, Americans for Limited Government, and other conservative groups could donate millions of dollars to Tea Party candidates.

Of course, just as the Tea Partiers saw Rove as the architect of spendthrift policies that all but destroyed fiscal conservatism. In turn, Rove and his associates—effectively what was left of the Republican establishment—saw the Tea Partiers as rabid zealots whose policies could easily backfire on the Republicans.

Nevertheless, Rove came up with a win-win strategy that involved working with Koch brothers' operatives to make sure that Rove's PACs and the Kochs' were not stepping on each other's feet. First, Rove put together biweekly meetings between operatives from his groups and the Kochs', including Americans for Prosperity, Americans for Limited Government, and the 60 Plus Association. "It was very coordinated," said a strategist who participated in some of the meetings. "There wasn't one race in which there were multiple groups airing ads at the same time."

In addition, as Joe Hagan pointed out in *New York* magazine, Rove got American Crossroads to support a Tea Party candidate in a race that would get national attention. If the candidate won, Rove could claim credit for knocking out a big-name Democrat. If the candidate lost, Rove's doubts about the electoral viability of the Tea Party's more marginal, fringy tendencies would be proved correct.

He picked Sharron Angle, a senatorial candidate running against Senate Majority Leader Harry Reid in Nevada.

A Southern Baptist from Reno, Nevada, Angle, as a state legislator, had voted "no" so often in the forty-two member state assembly that the votes were often called "forty-one to Angle." Among her many extreme positions, Angle called for the withdrawal of the United States from the United Nations and the dismantling of the U.S. Department of Education; she also asserted that Sharia law was about to be instituted in two American cities, Dearborn, Michigan, and Frankford, Texas.

In early June 2010, American Crossroads put in $120,000 for an ad buy blasting Harry Reid for pushing through the $787 million stimulus package. Later, also in June, came another $120,000 buy. By September, American Crossroads and Crossroads GPS had poured $900,000 into attack ads against Reid in Nevada.

At the same time, other far-right Tea Partiers—such as Christine O'Donnell in Delaware, Ovide Lamontagne in New Hampshire, and Carl Paladino in New York—were beating Old Guard GOP candidates in primaries all over the country.

Not all of these candidates were to Rove's liking—most notably, O'Donnell, a Delaware senatorial candidate who had trouble keeping a job and holding on to her home, lied on her résumé, waged a political war against masturbation, announced she "dabbled in witchcraft," went to a "satanic altar," and then launched a campaign alerting the electorate that she "was not a witch."

All of which was a broomstick too far for Rove. "There were a lot of nutty things she has been saying that just simply don't add up," he said on Fox News in September. "This is not a race we're going to be able to win. . . . We also can't make progress if we have candidates who've got serious character problems."

But Rove's critique was mild next to the response it triggered from the newly ascendant far right. The headline on the website of right-wing blogger Michelle Malkin put it succinctly: "War." "I just finished watching Karl Rove trashing GOP Senate primary winner Christine O'Donnell . . ." wrote Malkin. "Might as well have been Olbermann on MSNBC."

More important, former vice presidential candidate Sarah Palin, also a regular on Fox, joined the battle, backing O'Donnell and attacking "the hierarchy of the political machine" that believed O'Donnell couldn't win in the general election. On September 18, she singled

out Rove by name and delivered what she called "a quick woodshed moment" to Rove for failing to back O'Donnell and other far-right candidates.

Normally, such internal squabbles were kept out of public view. The Tea Party was damaging the Republican brand, and Rove had struck back, but the Republican Party could not afford a full-scale civil war. As if to compensate for having slammed one O'Donnell, Rove doubled down with Sharron Angle. By September, Crossroads GPS and American Crossroads had spent $1.7 million in Nevada on ads attacking Reid. Then, in one week in October alone, the two Rove groups ponied up another $1.4 million in TV ads for Angle.

But the Angle race was just a microcosm of the hundreds of state and federal races going on across the country. Early on in the 2010 midterm campaign, the Democrats had thought they had the fund-raising advantage over the Republicans—but that was before the *Citizens United* decision became a factor. In late September, Senator John Kerry wrote a fund-raising solicitation for Democrats being attacked by American Crossroads: "Karl Rove is back—like an even worse sequel to a movie panned by the critics."

As election day neared, it was reported that the Rove-Gillespie groups were spending $14 million on Senate races alone. According to Politico's Ken Vogel, the buy erased "any doubts that the groups . . . have the cash to be major players in next month's election. And with nearly 75 percent of the buy paid for by undisclosed donors, the expenditure highlights . . . the shift to anonymous political activity."

By mid-October, the White House finally began to respond, with Obama, Vice President Joe Biden, and White House adviser David Axelrod all attacking Karl Rove and the U.S. Chamber of Commerce. "It's a two-fer," said former Clinton aide James Carville. "You hit the Chamber for outsourcing jobs, and then you attack Rove, the person most identified with the most unpopular Republican president.

In all, $3.5 billion was spent on campaigning—and these were mid terms, not presidential, elections. "We knew this election could make spending history, but the rate of growth is stunning," said Sheila Krumholz, executive director of the Center for Responsive Politics and its website, OpenSecrets.org. "This kind of money in 20

makes the 2000 presidential election—hardly a distant memory
look like a bargain at $3.1 billion. And tens of millions of dollars ⸝
it is now coming from organizations who, by law, need not disclose
their donors."

As a result of *Citizens United*, at least $264 million in spending by
outside groups was reported to the Federal Election Commission for
2010—four times as much as was spent in the 2006 midterms.

What was also striking was how many of the heavy hitters were
longtime Rove donors. Texas homebuilder Bob Perry, who had been
with Rove in the eighties, gave $7 million. Harold Simmons, another
Texas billionaire Rove loyalist, gave $2.7 million. Texas natural gas
billionaire Trevor Rees-Jones donated $2.3 million. And so forth.
Moreover, according to Politico, through mid-October more than 57
percent of the money raised by Rove's groups came as anonymous
donations through Crossroads GPS.

On November 2, 2010, 82.5 million Americans went to the polls
and dealt Barack Obama's policies and the Democratic Party a devastating defeat. The Republicans recaptured the House of Representatives by gaining sixty-three seats, the biggest swing in a midterm in
seventy-two years. In the Senate, the GOP picked up six seats that
had been held by Democrats, leaving the Democrats with a 53–47
edge.

Ultimately, Tea Partiers Christine O'Donnell and Sharron Angle
both lost their bids for the Senate. But, overall, the Tea Party had
indisputably asserted itself as an astonishingly powerful force in the
midterms. When the dust settled, the Tea Party Caucus boasted sixty-
two members in the House of Representatives and four in the Senate.

As for Rove, he had managed to stay above the fray just enough
to avoid bloodshed with his Tea Party rivals, as he consolidated his
power within the GOP. The bottom line? According to Bloomberg
News, "Rove's American Crossroads and Crossroads GPS backed
the victor in 23 of the 36 House and Senate races where a winner was
declared. American Action Network, which shared space with the
Crossroads groups, won 14 races and lost 10. The nation's biggest
business lobby, the U.S. Chamber of Commerce, supported the winning candidate in 38 of 59 contests in a year dominated by voter concerns about the economy and joblessness."

There was no doubt about it: The Republicans had taken one big step toward regaining power, and Karl Rove had come back from the dead. Once again, he had his sights on the presidency and he needed only one thing: a candidate.

FIFTEEN

Last Man Standing

Even before Rove left the White House in 2007, pundits began to speculate about what his next move would be. "It's hard to imagine that he won't end up profitably pontificating about the 2008 race for Fox News," reporter Tim Grieve wrote in Salon.

Grieve was right, but that didn't mean Karl Rove had become just another talking head. Millions of people who saw him on Fox may have *thought* they were just watching a savvy analyst give his take on the events of the day. But that was naïve. Rove's goals remained unchanged. Now that he controlled the purse strings to hundreds of millions of dollars, Rove was a kingmaker, a puppet master, not merely a political analyst. His new journalistic venues were potent platforms from which to advance his political ambitions.

In that regard, Fox News and the *Wall Street Journal,* both of which were owned by Rupert Murdoch, were perfect for him. The two most influential and strategic outlets in the conservative media, they served as ideal perches from which he could dispense the Rovian narrative as he played a long, deep, and subtle political chess game through the media. That became apparent in 2011 as the GOP presidential field began to take shape.

Fox was an especially interesting case in point. For years, Fox chairman Roger Ailes had been playing an unusual double game. Through his work as media strategist for Richard Nixon, Ronald Reagan, and George H.W. Bush, Ailes had discovered that there was a substantial audience that was hungry for a conservative take on the news, and he knew exactly how to reach them. In fact, when he worked in the Nixon White House in 1970, he had even put together the initial plans for what became Fox News and wrote a 318-page draft titled "A Plan for Putting the GOP on TV News."*

Now that these plans had been fully realized, Ailes played two roles. On the one hand, he was a spectacularly successful TV executive who ran a "fair and balanced" 24/7 news network. On the other, he was the media czar of the Republican Party—meaning that Fox was a political organization as much as it was a news organization, and its influence was so great, it was often the tail wagging the dog of the Republican Party.

This duality was especially true in 2011, when for the first time Fox News's ratings topped those of CNN and MSNBC combined, and, at the same time, the network employed no fewer than five prospective GOP presidential candidates: former ambassador to the United Nations John Bolton, former Speaker of the House Newt Gingrich, former Arkansas governor Mike Huckabee, former Alaska governor and vice presidential candidate Sarah Palin, and former Pennsylvania senator Rick Santorum. "Republicans originally thought that Fox worked for us," said former Bush speechwriter David Frum. "Now we're discovering that we work for Fox."

All of which meant that Ailes was such a powerful force that no GOP politician seriously considered running for president without consulting him. "You can't run for the Republican nomination without talking to Roger," one Republican told *New York* magazine. "Every single candidate has consulted with Roger."

But, since Ailes's talent pool included the superstars of both the Republican establishment and the Tea Party, the latter of which now enjoyed Sarah Palin as its poster girl, it was inevitable that ultimately the two poles of the party would come to a head and that some of the contradictions inherent in party politics would manifest themselves on the air. Sarah Palin was a case in point.

Even though John McCain's choice of Palin as his running mate was widely regarded as disastrous, immediately after the 2008 election the hockey mom politician from Alaska quit her job as governor

---

* The story behind how the network came to be and the plan itself were both published by Gawker and can be read at http://edge-cache.gawker.com/gawker/ailesfiles/ailes1.html.

219

and transformed herself into a celebrity who provided an unremitting stream of fodder for supermarket tabloids. Outdoorsy and mediagenic, Palin fused Hollywood-caliber charisma with a defiant right-wing populism that vowed "to take back our country" for the plain-speaking, hardworking, patriotic, regular folks next door.

Palin's saga was an endless series of tabloid tropes. She *was* her very own reality show: There was Palin's Down syndrome baby, Trig. There was her daughter Bristol's out-of-wedlock pregnancy and subsequent appearance on *Dancing with the Stars*. There was Levi Johnston, Bristol's estranged fiancé, who posed nude for *Playgirl* and later named his daughter (by a different mother than Bristol), Breeze Beretta, after his favorite gun.

All of which enhanced, rather than dampened, Palin's fame. In late 2009, her book *Going Rogue* shot to number one on the *New York Times* bestseller list, and became a massive bestseller. In early 2010, she agreed to be the keynote speaker at the Tea Party's first convention in Nashville.

Spectacularly inexperienced, the gaffe-prone Palin had at various times said that North Korea was a U.S. ally, that the U.S. Constitution was based on the Bible, and that Paul Revere warned the *British*. It was later revealed that she did not even know who Margaret Thatcher was. But none of that seemed to matter. In November 2010, she asserted that she could easily beat Obama when he came up for reelection, and gave every indication she was seriously considering a run.

Because Fox's candidate-commentators, including Palin, all had contracts that bound them exclusively to Fox, that meant when producers from C-SPAN, NBC, ABC, CBS, CNN, and MSNBC all tried to interview Palin, they were told they had to first get Fox's permission.

But Palin was having it both ways: winning constant national attention as a presidential contender but declining to officially announce her candidacy. As Politico reporters Jonathan Martin and Keach Hagey framed the dilemma, Fox is "such a lucrative and powerful pulpit that Palin, Gingrich, Santorum and Huckabee have every reason to delay formal announcements and stay on contract for as long as they can." They added that Fox "indicated that once any of the candidates declares for the presidency he or she will have to sever the deal with the network."

Then, in March 2011, Fox announced it was suspending the contracts of Newt Gingrich and Rick Santorum for sixty days while they mulled their presidential prospects. But, the conservative *National Review* noted, Palin got a free ride even though Fox's flagship news program, *Special Report,* covered her as if she were a presidential candidate and gave her 5–1 odds of winning the GOP nomination.

From a ratings point of view, of course, it made sense for Roger Ailes to keep Sarah Palin on the air as talent. He had hired her because she was hot. "People are attracted to Fox News in part because that's where they can see Sarah Palin," said Pat Buchanan, who had once played a dual role as a candidate-commentator. "So I would think he would want to keep them there."

But politics was a different matter. After a January 2011 shooting rampage by a lunatic gunman in Tucson, Arizona, killed six and severely wounded Democratic congresswoman Gabrielle Giffords, Ailes had advised Palin to lie low. Having just published an electoral map that identified vulnerable Democratic congressional districts, including Giffords's, with rifle crosshairs, Palin was under fire for heated rhetoric that, some said, helped fuel the violence. But instead of following Ailes's advice, Palin responded by saying in a nationally televised speech that blaming her was a "blood libel," a reference to a heinous anti-Semitic accusation. After that, Ailes made no secret that he thought she "was an idiot" who was damaging the conservative movement. But in opting to go for profits and high ratings, Ailes risked losing something much more important: namely, the next presidential election.

Enter Karl Rove, who had never had any real fondness for Palin. During the previous election cycle, Rove had aggressively touted Mitt Romney as a stronger choice than Palin for the GOP vice presidential slot. In October 2010, just before the midterms, Rove had taken his first real shot at her, telling the London *Telegraph* that American voters would not regard Palin, who was about to launch a cable TV show exploring the Alaskan wilderness, as presidential material.

"With all due candor," Rove said, "appearing on your own reality show . . . I am not certain how that fits in the American calculus of 'that helps me see you in the Oval Office.'"

Later, Rove proceeded to mock Palin by imitating her fishing.

"Did you see that?" he asked an interviewer when the show began. "Holy crap! That fish bit my thigh. It hurts!"

Palin struck back. "Karl has planted a few other political seeds out there that are quite negative and unnecessary . . ." she said. "I kind of feel like, why did he feel so threatened and so paranoid? I'm here to help the cause."

Such banter would have been innocuous enough coming from two ordinary talking heads. But that's not what was going on. Palin was a leading contender for the 2012 Republican nomination. Now she was in battle with Rove, who, with two White House wins under his belt and his hands on hundreds of millions dollars in SuperPAC lucre, was effectively the party boss. In generations past, such intramural political conflicts took place in smoke-filled rooms, but now Fox's two biggest stars grappled on air before a gaping audience. Behind the cameras, Ailes was rooting for Rove.

Palin was not the only prospective president for whom Rove had undisguised distaste. This was a time of chaos in the Republican Party—in large measure because Rove and Bush had not left much behind. As a result, uncontrollable rogue elements were in ascent and an outlandish ensemble of pretenders were vying for the Republican throne. In May 2011, Herman Cain, an African-American pizza magnate and radio talk-show host from Atlanta, entered the race, as did Libertarian Ron Paul, a former congressman, and Newt Gingrich. In June, Minnesota congresswoman Michelle Bachmann, former ambassador to China Jon Huntsman, and former Pennsylvania senator Rick Santorum entered. Donald Trump, the real estate mogul and self-proclaimed reality show king, dipped his toe and carefully coiffed hair in the waters.

But as soon as each pretender to the throne came on the scene Rove moved in to safeguard the Republican brand, and, like a laser-sharp sniper, carefully picked off the candidates one at a time. By espousing his "birther" theories about Obama's legitimacy as president, Donald Trump, Rove asserted, was discrediting the entire Republican Party. "He's a joke candidate," said Rove. "Let him go ahead and announce for election on 'The Apprentice.' The American people aren't going to be hiring him, and certainly, the Republicans are not going to be hiring him in the Republican primary."

"He's off there in the nutty right," Rove added.

Likewise, in May, when Cain announced his candidacy, Rove dismissed him as a political lightweight, as that "talk radio guy in Atlanta." "It's not just your own personal narrative," Rove said. "It is what have you done in your life that gives us confidence that the vision you're laying out is something that you can actually do?"

The Republican lineup of would-be presidents was, Rove knew, a motley crew. And from the Republican point of view that was particularly frustrating, given that, over the summer, with the economy still sputtering and the White House flailing in its attempts to resolve the debt-ceiling crisis, Obama's numbers had sunk into the low forties. The Republicans had a real shot—if they could get their act together.

By this time, Wall Street insiders knew that Rove secretly, quietly supported former Massachusetts governor Mitt Romney. In 2008, he had touted Romney as having "strong executive experience both in business and in government, . . . an interesting story to tell with saving the U.S. Olympics," and a résumé in dealing with the economy.

An endless series of televised debates—twenty-seven in all—had begun in May 2011 between the various GOP contenders. Week after week, Romney performed creditably and led the pack in the polls, with more than 20 percent of Republican voters. He was clearly the front-runner, the presumptive nominee. Republican voters never really liked or trusted him and he quickly reached his ceiling. Palin was still undecided, and had just enough clout that she could possibly win the nomination—and lose the general election for the Republicans.

Then, on August 13, 2011, Texas governor Rick Perry officially declared his candidacy and suddenly surged ahead of Romney.

Now Rove had to deal with a slightly different dilemma. Back in 1990, he had actually launched Perry's career by guiding his client to victory as agriculture commissioner in Texas. But eight years later, when Perry was in a tight race for lieutenant governor, Rove wanted him to curtail negative ads against his Democratic opponent in order to protect Governor George W. Bush's standing among Hispanics. Perry continued to hold that against Rove and Bush, and, when he became governor he turned into a hostile critic of President Bush's programs from the right. In 2010, Rove had tried to stop Perry—and failed—by running Senator Kay Bailey Hutchison against him for reelection.

But this time, the stakes were much higher. By August, Perry's numbers were soaring. A Huffington Post headline breathlessly declared, "Rick Perry Looks to Leave Mitt Romney and Karl Rove in the Dust."

On August 16, Rove entered the fray, declaring Perry's position on Social Security "toxic" and asserting that Perry's attack on Federal Reserve chairman Ben Bernanke was "not presidential." Two former Bush aides, Tony Fratto and Pete Wehner, joined in, echoing Rove's sentiments. The *Washington Post*'s Chris Cillizza and Aaron Blake wrote about Rick Perry's "Karl Rove problem." Perry's numbers continued to climb. But Rove had just begun.

Meanwhile, Palin remained the great question mark in the Republican field. She had been sitting out all the debates because she had not formally declared. On the other hand, she was spending an enormous amount of time in Iowa, site of the Iowa caucus that launches the presidential primary season, and there was no plausible reason for being there if she had no presidential ambitions.

Finally, on Sunday, August 21, with Palin's bus tour making a round of stops in Iowa, Rove called her bluff. "I'm not much of a gambler," he said on Fox, "but I'd put a little more money that she gets in than if she doesn't, because of the schedule she's got next week in Iowa—it looks like that of a candidate, not a celebrity. . . . [I]f she doesn't get in shortly after next week, then I think people are going to basically say she's not in, she won't be in, if she gets in, I'm not going to be for her."

Palin did not take kindly to Rove's comments. Two days later, on Tuesday, August 23, she struck back via an unsigned blogpost on SarahPAC, her political action committee:

Three years ago DC pundits predicted with glee the demise of Sarah Palin's political career. This past weekend their tune changed, citing false information that she has made a decision and set a date regarding a future campaign. Any professional pundit claiming to have "inside information" regarding Governor Palin's personal decision is not only wrong but their comments are specifically intended to mislead the American public. These are the same tired establishment political games that fuel the 24 hour news cycle and that all Americans will hopefully reject in 2012, and this is more of the "politics-as-usual" that Sarah Palin has fought against throughout her career.

Rove was appalled. "It is a sign of enormous thin skin if we speculate about her, she gets upset," he said. "And I suspect if we didn't speculate about her, she'd be upset and trying to find a way to get us to speculate about her." If she was unhappy with all the speculation, he added, she should "simply say 'I'm not running.'"

By September, with the primaries only five months away, Rove had fired salvos at Palin, Cain, Trump, Bachmann, and Perry. Of them, only Perry stood firm. On September 12, polls showed Perry with 31.8 percent of the Republican voters—a 12-point lead over Romney.

It took a Democrat, Howard Dean, who ran for president in 2004, to put things in perspective: "The Bush people don't fool around, as you know. . . . You can say a lot of things about Bush's presidency and his failures as president, but one thing nobody should say [anything] bad about [is] his political team. They know what they're doing, and they are ruthless, and they are going to take Perry out."

On October 1, the *Washington Post* ran a major three-thousand-word feature on Rick Perry's West Texas roots in an attempt to give readers insight into the background of a man who was being taken seriously as a contender to become the next president of the United States. The headline, on the Internet edition, told a large part of the story: "At Rick Perry's Texas Hunting Spot, Camp's Old Racially Charged Name Lingered."

The lead to the story told the rest:

In the early years of his political career, Rick Perry began hosting fellow lawmakers, friends and supporters at his family's secluded West Texas hunting camp, a place known by the name painted in block letters across a large, flat rock standing upright at its gated entrance.

"Niggerhead," it read.

There was more, of course. Perry and his father had begun hunting there in the eighties. In 1997, after his father had initially leased the property, Perry added his name to the lease. No one seemed to know when or how the rock appeared on the property. When asked about it, Perry said the word on the rock is an "offensive name that has no place in the modern world."

But the details didn't really matter. The media pounced, and soon Perry was finished. On October 3, his poll numbers dropped to 25 percent, down nearly seven points from his high. On October 4, he lost another 3 points. On October 5, down another 1.4 points.

If Perry had not gotten the message by this time, Sarah Palin had. As a celebrity noncandidate, she had an estimated income of $5 million. If she were to run, presumably she would have to give up much of it, including her $1 million-a-year contract with Fox. By this time, an ABC News poll showed that just 31 percent of GOP primary voters said Palin should run, while 66 percent said she shouldn't get into the race.

Moreover, two GOP icons who were essential to any Republican presidential candidate, Roger Ailes and Karl Rove, had made it very clear they were not on her side. On October 5, 2011, Palin made her announcement. "After much prayer and serious consideration, I have decided that I will not be seeking the 2012 GOP nomination for president of the United States," she said in a prepared statement. "As always, my family comes first."

Meanwhile, Rick Perry was still in free fall. By October 15, two weeks after the Camp Niggerhead story broke, he was down to 12.8 points, in third place, a drop of nearly 20 points and still falling.

And who was behind leaking the story? All over the Internet, on both left- and right-wing sites, bloggers asserted that the story has "Karl Rove's fingerprints all over it."

But in fact there were no fingerprints. It was impossible to trace who dug up that damaging piece of information about a small town in Texas and who might have channeled it through go-betweens to a certain reporter—and who happened to have a well-funded operation to perform precisely such opposition research. The only thing that was clear was that no one benefited from the story more than Rove's anointed candidate, Mitt Romney—and that John McCain, among others, could have testified that many times in the past such moments had taken place in Rove's campaign.

In late October, Herman Cain, the new favorite and the new anti-Romney, soared to first place in Perry's wake, ahead of Romney, with 26 percent of the vote. But before long Rove pulled out a whiteboard on Fox and wrote down all of Cain's failings.

In response to which Cain claimed that Rove was trying to destroy him. "It's a good thing the voters are not looking at Karl Rove's little whiteboard, Cain replied. "I believe it is a deliberate attempt to damage me because I am not, quote unquote, the establishment choice," he told a reporter. "But why not go with the choice that the people seem to like?

"What has Karl Rove done?" Cain continued. "If I become the nominee, he has given Democrats talking points for a commercial."

But beginning on November 1, Cain was hit with a barrage of sexual harassment allegations. "It is suspicious to this Republican Party observer that former Bush political adviser Karl Rove is pumping the story for all it's worth," blogged one former Capitol Hill staffer. "Given the presumption in Republican circles that Rove was responsible for the anti–Rick Perry data dump, it is not unreasonable to wonder if he is behind this latest sneak attack—all the while playing the 'independent' commentator declaring Cain's doom on various news outlets."

Even in London, pundits blogged: "The Cain Uproar—Did Rove Do It?" Again, no fingerprints. And, like Perry, Cain began his inexorable decline. Within two weeks, his ratings had dropped by six points. By December 1, 2011, he was down to fourteen points—a twelve-point drop from his peak. Three days later, he abandoned the race.

And yet, even after all the misfortune his rivals had encountered, Mitt Romney had yet to distinguish himself. But that was to be expected, Rove said. "Nobody breaks out of the pack, at this point. . . . There's no consolidation of the field in a race like this until people actually start voting."

And that would not be long. The Iowa caucus was slated for January 3, 2012.

* * *

Now that Palin, Perry, and Cain were history, only two potentially serious contenders were left—Gingrich and Santorum. With Cain's demise, the pattern soon repeated itself. First, Gingrich filled the slot as the anti-Romney, and Rove hammered away at him, asserting that he would not even get on the ballot in several key states and it's "embarrassing to be so poorly organized."

And, once again, Rove's ferocious attacks worked their magic, bringing Gingrich down from a thirteen-point lead over Romney on December 13 to a dead heat by the time Iowans went to the polls. This time, however, there was an additional factor: The airwaves in Iowa were flooded with anti-Gingrich ads funded by SuperPACs. As GOP strategist Ed Rollins put it, the day before the Iowa caucus, "The master, obviously, is my friend Mr. Rove, who has basically put together a better campaign of SuperPACs than anybody's ever done in history for a Presidential campaign."

The numbers told the story. As attack ads hit the air in Iowa, Newt Gingrich, who had been leading the national polls, tumbled to fourth place, with a mere 13 percent of the vote.

All of which left the unlikely figure of former senator Rick Santorum, who had lost his bid for reelection in his home state of Pennsylvania in 2006 by eighteen points, to carry the banner as the anyone-but-Romney candidate. For much of his campaign, Santorum's popularity had been hovering in the 5 percent range, putting him, at times, sixth in an eight-person race. But now, to everyone's amazement, as Iowans went to the polls on January 3, Santorum was neck and neck with Romney.

In fact, at two a.m. on January 4, 2012, as the returns were coming in on Fox News, Santorum was actually leading by a few dozen votes. It had been a long, exciting night.

But then, just a few minutes after two, Fox anchor Chris Wallace brought Karl Rove on Fox with a special news break:

CHRIS WALLACE: Yeah, Karl, you've just gotten some word from
    a source in the Republican National Committee. Tell us what
    it is.
KARL ROVE: First that they made the correction in Story County,

which moved it from an eighteen-point margin for Santorum
to a four-point, four-vote margin for Santorum. . . In Clinton
County, the one outstanding precinct in the state . . . will show
an eighteen-vote victory in that precinct for—for Mitt Romney, which will give him a statewide victory of fourteen votes
over—over Rick Santorum.

WALLACE: Now, I— You know, this is obviously pretty big news.
You're saying that Romney is going to win the Iowa Caucuses
by fourteen votes.

ROVE: By fourteen votes.

WALLACE: How solid is your evidence for your . . .

ROVE: From a pretty good, reliable source.

The next day, the *Wall Street Journal*'s coverage of the primary was
headlined, "A Big Win for Romney in Iowa," by Karl Rove:

Not long ago few thought Mitt Romney could win both the very conservative Iowa caucuses and then the quirky, slightly contrarian New
Hampshire primary. If he did, most assumed he would have a lock
on the Republican nomination. For understandable reasons: No other
GOP presidential candidate in an open race has achieved back-to-back
victories in these first two contests.

By this time next week, we'll know if Mr. Romney is 2–0. If so, he
becomes the prohibitive favorite.

Two weeks later, however, the Daily Beast reported that incorrect
precinct numbers from one Iowa town had misallocated twenty extra
votes to Romney. In other words, Rick Santorum had actually won
the Iowa primary.

But it was too late. Rove's narrative had already become the consensus.

The flip side of the surprising strength shown by Santorum and Gingrich was that Romney was a weak candidate. That meant both Santorum and Gingrich had to be stopped at all costs. As a result, the
SuperPAC money began flowing like water.

There were fifty-seven primaries and caucuses scheduled over the next six months—one for every state in the Union, plus U.S. territories such as Puerto Rico, American Samoa, and Guam. But three key dates would determine Romney's strength as a candidate. On January 21, 2012, there was the South Carolina primary, a deeply conservative Southern state in which Romney hoped to show surprising strength. On January 31, there was Florida, in which it was crucial that Romney deal a blow to Gingrich. And March 6 was Super Tuesday, with ten states holding their primaries, including Ohio, the big prize.

The Romney-Rove axis was not the only team with SuperPACs. Newt Gingrich had found his own billionaire, Las Vegas casino mogul Sheldon Adelson. And Santorum had the backing of Foster Friess, a right-wing billionaire from Wyoming.

And so the war of the SuperPACs began. Some Old Guard establishment Republicans had been dubious about Rove, about whether he had a real identity beyond his ties to the Bush family, but now they saw him and his operatives go into action.

A key Rove surrogate operating under the radar was Carl Forti, a GOP strategist whom Politico dubbed "Karl Rove's Karl Rove." Rove himself had called Forti "one of the smartest people in politics you've never heard of." In 2008, Forti had served as political director for Mitt Romney during his first stab at winning the GOP nomination. And, in the 2010 midterms, Politico deemed him "the figure most intricately involved in the outside groups transforming the 2010 election season with a deluge of hard-hitting ads."

In 2012, Forti wore two hats. On the one hand, he was political director of Rove's SuperPAC, American Crossroads, and on the other he was head of Romney's enigmatically named SuperPAC, Restore Our Future. To reporters who suggested Forti may have violated American Crossroads' promise to remain neutral during the primaries, Crossroads said, "Carl is a contract employee with American Crossroads. He has other clients. We knew that he had other clients. But clearly, none of us are gonna be involved personally in the presidential campaign."

Crossroads president Steven Law added, "The work that Carl does for us is work that every contender for the Republican nomination would be supportive of, which is that he is helping find ways to make sure President Obama doesn't return to office."

But the work Forti did for Romney's PAC was another story. On January 12, Restore Our Future allocated $1,218,097 for attack ads against Gingrich in the January 21 South Carolina primary. Similarly, it raised more than $1.7 million for anti-Gingrich ads in the Florida primary to take place ten days later. By January 13, Restore had amassed a total of $7,683,140 for anti-Gingrich ads in primaries across the country.

Gingrich fought back. Four days later, with ample help from Sheldon Adelson, he had more than $3.2 million for anti-Romney ads.

South Carolina, of course, had been the site of George W. Bush's decisive 2000 primary victory over John McCain, the one that had been achieved with the help of push polls suggesting that McCain had fathered an illegitimate child with a black woman. As January 21 approached, Gingrich's poll numbers soared, seemingly impervious to Rove's attacks.

The week before voting in South Carolina, ABC News appeared to offer a late-breaking gift for Romney when it interviewed Gingrich's second wife, Marianne, who said that the former Speaker of the House had sought an "open marriage." But in the Republican debate on the Thursday before the primary, Gingrich artfully turned the question against the moderator, and the media, for daring to pry into his personal life.

On the Friday before voting, South Carolina Republicans received a phony email made up to look like a Gingrich campaign press release saying that "Newt Gingrich released the following statement regarding reports that he forced ex-wife Marianne Gingrich to terminate a pregnancy."

Similarly, thousands of bogus CNN Breaking News Alerts asserted that Gingrich had pressured Marianne to have an abortion.

Who was behind it? As usual, there were no fingerprints.

But whoever was behind it, the ruse didn't work. When the votes were counted in South Carolina on January 21, Gingrich polled a strong 40 percent of the vote, with Romney in second place, thirteen points behind. Santorum was still alive. It was now a three-man race.

Florida, ten days, later, would be crucial. This was Gingrich territory, neighboring as it did his home state of Georgia, and Romney needed to prove he could score well in the Deep South among voters who might not be disposed toward a former governor of Massachusetts.

Forti and Rove opened the spigots full bore. One after another, Romney attack ads tore into Gingrich. In "Desperate," the SuperPAC hit Gingrich for his work at Freddie Mac. In "Unreliable Leader," Gingrich's chaotic tenure as Speaker of the House was attacked as "erratic," "outrageous," and "a political problem." There was "Mr. Washington Insider" attacking his ethics problems in the nineties.

Gingrich fought back as best he could, raising more than $4.4 million for attack ads against Romney. But in the end he was no match for Rove's forces. Ultimately, Restore Our Future put in more than $18 million in attack ads against Gingrich in the primaries.

When the votes were counted on January 31, Romney had won 46 percent—a decisive fifteen-point victory over Gingrich, who was now mortally wounded.

Then, on February 6, Rick Santorum astonished observers by sweeping Missouri, Minnesota, and Colorado. As Rove saw, "It gives him the upper hand and the battle with Newt for the, you know, not-Romney slot. Here, before, Newt has been saying, my junior partner ought to get out. That ain't going to work any longer. And then finally, it gives him an opportunity to do something that he hasn't done before, which is get an organization and get money. He is running on fumes. And his organization has been sort of thrown together, sort of like making an airplane while you fly."

Now the emergence of Santorum, a long shot with little funding, underscored how weak a candidate Romney had been. Super Tuesday, March 6, was not far away. On that day, ten states—Arkansas, Georgia, Idaho, Massachusetts, North Dakota, Ohio, Oklahoma, Tennessee, Vermont, Virginia—staged their primaries. Theoretically, by then a strong candidate should be able to wrap up the nomination, if not mathematically, at least in the mind of the party. It was important that Romney do well—particularly in Ohio.

Technically, Ron Paul was still in the race, but, effectively, the Republican primaries had become a two-man, maybe a three-man, race. Rove's goal was to drive a stake through the heart of a faltering Newt Gingrich and then take care of Santorum.

According to one Romney adviser, Santorum was a blank slate, "so everyone's projecting onto him what they want because he's the last anti-Romney." Attack ads would define him on two fronts: as someone who has never run anything, and as someone whose experience in Washington rendered him vulnerable. "The biggest thing he ever ran is his Senate office," said the aide. "They're going to hit him very hard on earmarks, lobbying, voting to raise the federal debt limit five times. The story of Santorum is going to be told over the next few weeks in a big way."

Once again, the ad buys began. "Arlen and Rick" made Santorum out to be a faux conservative who had supported moderate Republican senator Arlen Specter, Santorum's colleague from Pennsylvania. "Never" asserted that "Rick Santorum has never run a business or state. Instead, he is a Washington politician who voted for the Bridge to Nowhere, [Obama Supreme Court nominee] Judge Sotomayor, and opposed creating E-Verify, the conservative illegal immigration reform." "Not Electable" pointed out Santorum's failure to win reelection.

The money poured in and the ads aired—again and again. On February 16, there was $885,986 to oppose Santorum in Michigan alone. Funds for attack ads poured into Arizona and Ohio as well. By February 22, Romney forces had put together nearly $3 million to attack Santorum. Two days later, the figure was $6,472,823 in Santorum attack ads. Money poured in to go after Santorum in Oklahoma, Mississippi, Ohio, and Alabama. By March 2, four days before Super Tuesday, the figure topped $11 million. Ultimately, a total of $21 million in attack ads against Rick Santorum was spent in the spring primaries.

Then, instead of training his fire on Romney, Santorum suddenly declared that President John F. Kennedy's position on the separation of church and state was "nauseating" and that President Obama's belief that every American should have the opportunity to attend college made him "a snob." The pundits reeled. Romney and Rove were blessed to have such tone-deaf opposition.

On February 28, Romney squeaked by with a three-point victory over Santorum in Michigan, where he had grown up and his father had been governor. Given that he had spoken out against the auto industry bailout, the state's lack of enthusiasm was not surprising.

Nevertheless, Romney's inability to close the deal was giving way to loose talk of a brokered convention. But as Rove saw it, Santorum had just squandered one of his last chances to deal Romney a lethal blow.

Super Tuesday could be the end. "Mr. Santorum is focused on Ohio, Tuesday's key battleground with 66 delegates," Rove wrote in his *Wall Street Journal* column, where he proceeded to lower expectations for his favorite candidate. "Mr. Romney can afford a narrow loss there as long as he wins a solid plurality of all the Super Tuesday delegates. Mr. Santorum's candidacy will realistically be at an end if he loses the Buckeye State, though he could linger for weeks. Even a win leaves him on life support unless he can also best Mr. Romney in Tuesday's Southern contests, coming in first or second with Mr. Romney trailing in second or third place."

When the results came in, Romney had won six out of ten states—squeaking by in Ohio 37.9 to 37.1 percent. There were many more primaries to come, but in fact it was all over but the shouting. That was because it was nearly mathematically impossible for any of Romney's competitors to outstrip him in the delegate count. Immediately after Super Tuesday, Sarah Palin proffered her once-sought-after endorsement to Newt Gingrich, whose campaign was all but dead. Rove carefully assessed its value. "It's not worth snot," he said.

Afterward, in an interview with CNBC, Romney said, "I must admit that after last night I feel pretty darn good." Thanks to Rove and the SuperPACS, he was well on his way to becoming the Republican nominee.

But if the country was just beginning to understand that Romney was the Republican nominee, Rove had already moved on to the next phase. It was one thing for Romney to walk over a weak field of Republican challengers—after Rove took them down. It was quite another for him to go up against President Barack Obama, he of the silver tongue, a powerful organization, and all the advantages (and disadvantages) of incumbency.

Facing Obama, Romney would have to overcome his image as an uncaring plutocrat, to win over centrist voters, after tacking hard to the right during the primaries, and to reshape the political narrative in a completely different direction. As one Romney aide put it, it was time for an Etch A Sketch, in which what had been drawn out before could, with a quick shake, be made to miraculously disappear and be replaced with a completely different drawing. And that just happened to be one of Karl Rove's greatest talents.

SIXTEEN

Mitt Romney's Last Buyout

Tall and slender at sixty-five, Mitt Romney looked presidential. With his Hollywood good looks, a chiseled jaw, and a helmet of charcoal hair flecked with gray, he was almost Reaganesque but for a stiffness in his bearing, an inescapable sense of detachment suggesting that he did *not* connect, and the absence of the common touch.

Indeed, the critique about Romney that stung most, especially in the context of high unemployment, was Mike Huckabee's 2008 quip that, far from being the common man, Romney *"looks like the guy who fired you."* All of which raised questions about Romney's wealth, how he earned it, and how that would play with the American electorate. In the midst of uncertain and volatile economic times, was a patrician investment banker what the American voter was looking for?

At Bain Capital, the Boston-based private equity firm at which he'd made his name, Romney had mastered the art of the leveraged buyout, taking over a company, making an offer, putting down a tiny fraction of the sale price, financing the rest, and, then, as soon as the company had turned around, cashing out—often at a huge profit.

His success was undeniable. A wheel-rim maker called Accuride was his first hit. Then Romney had done it again and again—with a medical equipment company, with a credit services company, with Domino's Pizza, and the list goes on; among them were firms that succeeded as well as those that failed, costing hundreds of workers their jobs, while Bain took the profits. He had even saved Bain itself from bankruptcy, made it rich, and, over the years, earned a personal fortune of more than $200 million.

Given the sputtering state of the economy, the question was whether Romney would be seen as someone whose fiscal prowess could cure America's economic ills. Or would he be seen as a remorseless corporate raider who took home millions while rapaciously cutting jobs?

Then, in the spring of 2012, after Super Tuesday, as the focus of his campaign shifted from his GOP challengers to beating President Barack Obama in November, Mitt Romney unwittingly became involved in what was likely his last leveraged buyout.

This time around, the money being put down—over $1 billion—was huge, but then again, the stakes were astronomically high. This was a highly leveraged buyout in which the targeted acquisition would end up overseeing an annual budget of more than $3.8 *trillion*.

The parties involved were unusual as well. The buyer was the Republican establishment, led by Karl Rove. The deal was to be funded by the SuperPACs Rove had created and coordinated. The final twist: The acquisition was Mitt Romney himself.

Unlike a normal LBO, there was no formal signing of documents. But on April 5, former Republican National Committee chairman Ed Gillespie left American Crossroads and joined the Romney campaign as a senior adviser. Technically, Romney had not locked up the nomination yet, but, Politico reported, Gillespie would serve as a strategist "without portfolio to the likely GOP presidential nominee, offering counsel on planning for the Tampa convention, the candidate's message, and a general election strategy for a campaign."

Romney's training and experience as a businessman lent itself to the idea of politics as being merely a question of solving managerial problems, of finding the right business plan, and the right personnel. From his point of view, he was acquiring funding for a presidential campaign, a strategic plan to win the White House, and an experienced management team to implement it. "I am pleased that Ed is joining my team," Romney said in a statement. "He brings a wealth of experience that will prove invaluable in the political battle that lies ahead. Barack Obama is building a $1 billion campaign war machine, and Ed will play an important role in countering it."

What was unsaid, however, was more important. Gillespie had

been a trusted ally of Rove's for years—at the RNC, on George W. Bush's campaigns, in the Bush White House, and, of course, as Rove's partner in forming American Crossroads. Gillespie would not have made the move unless the nomination was in the bag. All of which meant that, through Gillespie, Rove now had strategic oversight of Romney's campaign.

In large measure, that was because the protracted and difficult battle against two utterly implausible candidates, Santorum and Gingrich, had left Romney weakened, significantly behind Barack Obama both in fund-raising for the general election and building ground operations in key swing states.

"The only way Romney can get back into the race quickly will be through the expenditure of substantial SuperPAC dollars," political strategist Doug Schoen wrote in *Forbes,* explaining how Romney's weakness had rendered him a tempting takeover target. "Specifically, the key actors in this process will be Karl Rove, whose SuperPAC American Crossroads has raised $200 million, as well as the pro-Romney SuperPAC, Restore Our Future. . . . But make no mistake about it— the 2012 campaign now is not Obama vs. Romney. It is Obama vs. Karl Rove, American Crossroads, and Restore Our Future."

Officially, in joining Romney, Gillespie had cut ties with American Crossroads because of restrictions that prohibited "coordination" between SuperPACs and specific candidates. "SuperPACs have to be entirely separate from a campaign and a candidate," Romney explained. "I'm not allowed to communicate with a SuperPAC in any way, shape, or form. My goodness, if we coordinate in any way whatsoever, we go to the big house."

But in reality, such constraints were literally a joke—fodder for satirists Jon Stewart and Stephen Colbert, the latter even setting up his own SuperPAC to call attention to "a loopchasm" in the law: namely, that candidates could speak out as citizens publicly—on television, on the Internet, in the press—and make their needs and desires known. "I can't tell you," Colbert explained to Jon Stewart, "but I can tell everyone through television. And if you happen to be watching, well, I can't prevent that, Jon."

* * *

And so the great coming together began between Rove's SuperPACs and Romney's operation. Up until this point, talent and money had been divided among the many disparate GOP contenders. But now it would all serve the same end of electing Mitt Romney as president and helping other Republicans take over the Senate and retain Congress.

Meanwhile, Rove's surrogates took over the command posts of the Romney operation to ensure professional management of the campaign. Some key pieces of the puzzle were already in place. Romney's chief of staff since 2002, Beth Myers, was so close to her boss that the *Washington Post* deemed her his "office wife." She had also been a loyal protégé of Rove's when the two of them worked on the Reagan-Bush campaign in Texas in 1980. "We were great friends then and we're great friends now," said Rove. "She's really smart, incredibly meticulous. Very well organized, a lot of integrity.... Works well with other people, and incredibly discreet—all of which are traits that will serve her well in this job."

"She and Karl still remain friends," said Romney aide Doug Gross. "Karl has been through these wars and can provide her with sound advice."

On April 16, Romney announced that Myers would be in charge of the selection process to choose his vice presidential running mate. "Having played a role in this process," Rove wrote in his *Wall Street Journal* column, "I know that if done well this will be a political proctology exam for each individual considered. Ms. Myers and an army of lawyers, researchers and accountants will examine the person's every public statement, vote or executive decision.... Team Romney will discover that every prospect has strengths and warts. There is no perfect candidate."

Another powerful but low-profile figure was none other than Carl Forti, a Rove acolyte, who, as noted earlier, had been Romney's political director in 2008, and simultaneously occupied key positions in both American Crossroads and Restore Our Future. Having managed an $80 million budget for the National Republican Congressional Committee in 2006, at the time, the GOP's largest-ever independent expenditure campaign, Forti had the ideal credentials for the post–*Citizens United* era in which SuperPACs played an even bigger role than the party itself.

Working very much under the radar, Forti, according to GOP operative Bradley Blakeman, was "a strategic political warrior" whose knowledge of issues, polling, and implementation of complicated strategies made him "the Alexander the Great of the Republican independent expenditure world."

Meanwhile, Stuart Stevens, a media specialist who had worked with Rove on George W. Bush's campaigns, had taken over the job of shaping Romney's image and running his media operation. Likewise, former Mississippi governor Haley Barbour, a longtime friend of Stevens's from their home state and an immensely powerful former head of the RNC, announced that he would help Romney through his work with American Crossroads. And Barbour's nephew, Austin Barbour, moved up from Mississippi to Boston to become a finance chairman of the Romney campaign.

As for his uncle, Haley Barbour, whom Politico had deemed "the most powerful Republican in politics" just two years earlier, joining Team Romney was certain to have an impact on the bottom line. "He is without peer when he is raising money," said Congressman Tom Cole (R-Okla.), a former RNC chief of staff.

Now that Rove's colleagues occupied key strategic posts in the Romney campaign, the money started rolling in. The disparate groups of billionaires and SuperPACs that had been behind Rick Perry, Newt Gingrich, Rick Santorum, and other insurgent candidates quickly consolidated behind Romney.

On April 10, Foster Friess, the billionaire who supported Rick Santorum, announced he was supporting Romney. "I'm obviously going to be of help in whatever way I can," Friess told Politico.

He added that it might come in the form of supporting Rove's Crossroads groups, though, like many people, he was bewildered by the array of new SuperPACs. "I'm not sure if I have already," Friess said. "I know that I have contributed to some other groups, but I can't remember which ones. There are so many of them. They're all over the place."

Next into the fold came Sheldon Adelson, the eighth-richest man in America, with $24.9 billion, who, according to the *Las Vegas Sun*, had already given $21.5 million to Newt Gingrich's campaign and is the single biggest contributor to Israeli prime minister Benjamin Netanyahu. As recently as March, Adelson had expressed reservations about Romney. "He's not the bold decision-maker like Newt Gingrich is. . . . Every time I talk to him, he says, 'Well, let me think about it,'" Adelson told JewishJournal.com.

On April 15, Adelson, who sometimes wore a button reading "Obama . . . Oy vey," contributed $5 million to the Congressional Leadership Fund, which supports establishment GOP candidates vying for targeted House seats—a positive sign for Romney. Then, at the end of April, the *Sun* reported, Adelson was openly expressing "gushing admiration for Karl Rove."

"I'm going to give one more small donation—you might not think it's that small—to a SuperPAC," he said, apparently referring to American Crossroads. "And then if I give, it will be to a c-four," a reference to 501(c)(4) nonprofits, which are exempt from disclosures.

On May 29, Romney, whose Mormon credo forbids gambling, met Adelson, the wealthiest gaming executive in the world, at a reception at the Venetian Hotel in Las Vegas, where the executive offices are located, and came away a winner. "[Adelson] is very focused on defeating Barack Obama," one friend told CNN. "He is going to be the Republican Party's 800-pound gorilla in defeating Barack Obama."

Soon, the Adelson payoff began. On June 6, it was announced that Adelson would give at least $1 million to Restore Our Future, the Romney SuperPAC. A week later, the casino billionaire upped the ante to $10 million, in the process becoming the biggest single donor to Romney's efforts.

And that appeared to be just the beginning. According to *Forbes*, a source close to Adelson said the gaming magnate believes that "no price is too high" to protect the country from Obama's "socialization" of America, as well as to secure the safety of Israel, and that as a result Adelson's contributions would be "limitless." Adelson himself had said he might contribute a total of $100 million to conservative causes during the 2012 election cycle.

But the biggest donors of all were the Koch brothers, who had initially budgeted roughly $200 million for conservative candidates and causes in 2012. Though never a Tea Party favorite, in the past Romney had enjoyed financial support from its biggest patrons. In 2008, both David and Charles Koch had endorsed his presidential campaign, and in 2012 William Koch, a third, less prominent brother, gave $1 million to Romney's Restore Our Future, and added another $1 million later on.

Moreover, the Kochs' various campaigns had already started attacking Obama. In March, a $3.6 million ad campaign sponsored by the American Energy Alliance, the political arm of the Koch brothers–funded Institute for Energy Research, slammed Obama's policies for causing high gas prices. In response to the ads, a spokesman for the Democratic National Committee charged the Kochs with "funding yet another shadowy outside group to defend the interests of Big Oil and protect their own tax breaks and profits with Mitt Romney being the ultimate beneficiary."

Meanwhile, the meetings at Rove's Weaver Terrace home in Washington continued, with an eye to coordinating the various SuperPACs. Increasingly, in the wake of Romney's Super Tuesday victory, their success depended on differing factions putting aside their reservations about Romney. At times, the Koch brothers had positioned themselves as rivals, but by early spring Koch operative Marc Short had begun attending the Weaver Terrace gatherings again.

The Kochs, of course, were so powerful that they were not merely a subset of Rove's empire. Over the spring, the Koch brothers had doubled their fund-raising target to $400 million and, according to a report by Peter Stone in Huffington Post, they strategized about how to put it all together by flying in a few dozen wealthy conservatives to a conference they organized at the PGA National Resort & Spa in Palm Beach one weekend.

George W. Bush consultant Mark McKinnon put the $400 million figure in context with a tweet: "Think the $$ political system is screwed up? Koch brothers alone are planning to spend more $$ than McCain's entire 2008 presidential budget."

The new strategy they came away with was one that mirrored exactly what Rove had already begun to do with Crossroad GPS. Rather than funnel everything through Americans for Prosperity, their SuperPAC that had been widely criticized as a vehicle for "astroturfing," the Kochs decided to distribute tens of millions of dollars to a network of conservative organizations, including the National Rifle Association, Grover Norquist's Americans for Tax Reform, the National Right to Life Committee, Ralph Reed's Faith and Freedom Coalition, the 60 Plus Association, and the American Future Fund. "By spreading their wealth throughout the conservative ecosystem," wrote Stone, "the Kochs can exploit trusted brands with passionate followings that reach beyond the Tea Party base."

Money went to the NRA's Trigger the Vote campaign to reach millions of gun owners who had not yet registered to vote. It went to help Wisconsin governor Scott Walker, a Koch brothers favorite, in his June 5 recall battle, in which, buoyed by more than $30 million in contributions, much of it from out-of-state SuperPACs, Walker became the first governor in history to survive a recall election. Millions were earmarked for ten battleground states, especially Florida, Ohio, and Virginia, as well as key senate races to help the Republicans regain the upper house.

The *Citizens United* decision was not the only way in which the Supreme Court was serving Rove's interests. On June 4, 2012, the conservative majority on the court refused to hear Don Siegelman's appeal, even though 113 former state attorneys general asked the court to review the case. As this book went to press, he awaited sentencing by Judge Mark Fuller. Siegelman's case is one of many that suggest the 2007 U.S. attorneys scandal was a far deeper and more complex scandal than original reports indicated, and is more than just another entry on the mind-numbing ledger of indignities wrought by Karl Rove. For starters, the real disgrace is *not* that the Bush Justice Department fired ten U.S. attorneys for failing to toe the party line. Rather, it is about those U.S. attorneys who remained—the hard-line Republican U.S. attorneys who were not fired—and how they used the judiciary as a political weapon to such an extent that for more than three hundred Democrats, Don Siegelman among them, winning high office carried with it not just the threat but the reality of a federal investigation or indictment.

The Koch brothers were not the only ones on the right to raise their sights, and by the end of May Rove's SuperPAC network, including the Koch brothers and the U.S. Chamber of Commerce, had a new target: $1 billion.

The $1 billion figure, Politico reminded its readers, was in addition to funds brought in by the Romney campaign and the Republican National Committee, which intended to bring in another $800 billion, giving Romney a total of $1.8 billion to spend. By contrast, just four years earlier, in 2008, John McCain spent $370 million for his entire campaign. Romney would have nearly five times as much.

Having created an entity far more powerful than the RNC itself, Rove sought to solidify his power by gaining access to the Voter Vault, the RNC's prized database, which was housed on SmarTech servers in Chattanooga. According to *Roll Call*, RNC staffers described the database as the RNC's "'greatest asset' and argued that by giving up control of the file, which the RNC shares with state parties, the committee would be agreeing to diminish its power dramatically."

Rove's eyes were on more than simply capturing the White House. He wanted to keep the House of Representatives and win back the Senate as well. As early as November, a full year before the election, Rove's Crossroads GPS group had begun airing attack ads targeting Elizabeth Warren in Massachusetts as a bailout queen, Tim Kaine in Virginia, Senator Claire McCaskill in Missouri, Senator Ben Nelson* in Nebraska, and Senator Jon Tester in Montana. "Instead of focusing on jobs, Elizabeth Warren sides with extreme left protests," one ad said. "At Occupy Wall Street, protesters attack police, do drugs, and TRASH public parks!"

Similarly, a U.S. Chamber of Commerce ad campaign against Senator Sherrod Brown of Ohio asked if he was "running from his tax-raising, job-killing record?" and portrayed the fifty-nine-year-old Democrat as looking exceptionally haggard and disheveled because a scraggly beard had been Photoshopped onto his likeness.

More to the point, thanks to Rove's SuperPACs, Senator Brown and Tim Kaine, the former Virginia governor who was running for the Senate, were being outspent by more than three to one. In Kaine's case, as of late May, he had run 380 ads compared with 1,980 attack

---

* Nelson subsequently decided not to run for reelection.

ads aired by Crossroads GPS and the Chamber of Commerce against him, *Bloomberg BusinessWeek* reported.

And accuracy wasn't one of Crossroads' strong points. In June, American Crossroads attacked Kaine by claiming that he had urged $500 billion in Medicare cuts. But PolitiFact, a fact-checking project run by the *Tampa Bay Times*, found that assertion to be false. Noting that the $500 billion claim has become a familiar Republican talking point in the context of Obamacare, PolitiFact explained that the new health care law "does not cut $500 billion from current Medicare spending."

Likewise, in Florida, Republican congressman Connie Mack, who was facing a primary before challenging Bill Nelson, the incumbent Democratic senator, had run 6,464 ad spots by late May, compared with zero for Nelson. One ad asserted that Nelson advocated spending federal funds to see how monkeys reacted under the influence of cocaine. But again, PolitiFact took issue with the ad's accuracy, and reported, "Mack's claim is pretty bananas. Yes, Nelson was among senators to approve the stimulus package, which directed large sums of money to scientific research. But Nelson didn't pick out the monkey project. A federal agency did. Even a critic who calls the project wasteful says you can't blame Nelson."

And, thanks to Rove's friends at Fox News, when it came to national ads attacking Obama, he could get enormous amounts of extra mileage—unpaid—for his advertising dollar. On April 26, American Crossroads released an ad attacking Obama as a "celebrity president." The next day, according to Media Matters, the progressive watchdog site, Republican strategist Brad Blakeman went on Fox to proclaim the ad a huge success because "Karl has gotten more earned media than the amount he invested in the ad."

But that was largely because Fox News promoted it on no fewer than seven separate news shows in a twenty-four-hour period. It started at 8:30 a.m. the day the ad was released, when Fox Nation promoted the ad with the headline "Celebrity Obama Crushed by Rove Ad."

While the website rotated its story about the ad throughout the day, in late afternoon on Fox News's *The Five*, Fox contributor Dana Perino, Rove's colleague in the Bush White House, was calling the ad "effective," "funny," and "fabulous." At six p.m., Fox's *Special Report* ran two segments mentioning the ad. And so it went—on *The O'Reilly Factor, Hannity, Fox & Friends,* and *America's Newsroom*—again and again. Ailes was giving Rove almost unlimited play.

The *Citizens United* ruling gave Democrats the same latitude to raise money from billionaires, but, thanks to new regulatory measures, Wall Street had effectively deserted Obama. Moreover, having criticized the *Citizens United* decision, many Democrats did not have the stomach to play by the new rules to meet Rove's challenge. Most rich liberals felt they would be acting unethically.

"The inability of Democrats to play in the same league as Karl Rove financially is a humiliating debacle that might be unprecedented, measured by comparing wealthy donors of one party to wealthy donors of the other, in the history of presidential politics," wrote Brent Budowsky in *The Hill*. "The president and Democrats seem befuddled by how to react to the *Citizens United* decision, while Karl Rove understands with crystal clarity. Rove mobilizes his army, rallies his wealthy, organizes his venture and puts his money in the bank."

In contrast, in late spring, the Democratic Party sent out an email to its constituents signed by Barack Obama. In the subject line, it said, "Hey." The text read, "I need your help today.... Please donate $3 or more before midnight. Thank you, Barack."

But the response, initially at least, to Obama's entreaties was weak. In 2008, more than 550,000 people gave more than $200 to Obama, in the process creating the longest list of individual donors in American politics. But according to BuzzFeed's Ben Smith and Rebecca Elliott, at the same time in 2012, nearly 90 percent of those people had not reupped.

Likewise, compared with their GOP counterparts, the Democratic SuperPACs were feeble. By mid-April, the four biggest Democratic SuperPACs and two allied nonprofits had a mere $8.3 million on hand, thanks in part to $1 million each from its two largest contributors, comedian Bill Maher and hedge fund billionaire James H. Simon.

Obama had started off the year with a six-point lead over Romney in the polls, but Romney began to close the gap. In April, it narrowed to two points, but Obama still had a solid lead in the Electoral College. On his website, Rove posted an Electoral College map showing 284 votes either solidly for Obama or "leaning Obama," and, similarly, 172 either solidly for or leaning toward Romney. Even if all 82 votes that were toss-ups went for Romney, Obama would win.

But the campaign had barely begun, of course. And other Rove initiatives that had been long in the works might help close the gap. In thirty states across the country, Republicans had amped up fears of voter fraud and passed legislation that would restrict the voter rights of college students, immigrants, senior citizens, the disabled, and the homeless. The laws included new rules about where and how new voters could register, as well as tougher voter identification requirements.

In many states, the bills faced legislative and judicial battles. But aides to President Obama said the Obama-Biden campaign had to act as if all the laws were in force for the next election. "We have to assume that these laws will be in effect in November," Obama field director Jeremy Bird told the *New York Times*. "We are not allowing laws that are challenging and put in our way to stop us from doing what we need to do."

Meanwhile, the Republican ad barrage continued apace against Obama in the battleground states of Ohio, Pennsylvania, and West Virginia. By mid-April, Rove's groups alone had already spent more than $11 million on ads against Obama.

By early May, Obama's lead was down to just one point—a dead heat. Finally, after months on the sideline, major liberal donors, led by financier George Soros, put together a strategy of sorts to combat Rove's onslaught, preparing to invest $100 million in SuperPACs by focusing on grassroots organizing, voter registration, and turnout instead of on negative advertising.

"Culturally, the left doesn't do Swift Boat," Soros adviser Michael Vachon explained. "It's not what we do well."

A month earlier, Rove's electoral map had forecast an Obama victory, but in his *Wall Street Journal* column on May 24, "Romney's Roads to the White House," Rove took another look at what might happen on the first Tuesday in November.

Mapping out a "3–2–1" strategy for Romney, Rove itemized what was necessary for Romney to win. All he had to do was take three states that McCain narrowly lost in 2008—Indiana, North Carolina, and Virginia; take back two big battleground states that Bush had won—Florida and Ohio; and, finally, win one—just one—additional state in the Union. Anywhere. It was more than just possible, Rove concluded. Now, it was probable. "Mr. Obama long ago lost his chance to duplicate his 2008 performance . . ." he wrote. "He's now forced to fight for states he easily won in 2008. The odds now narrowly favor a Romney win."

Rove further hinted that an effective line of attack would be to paint Obama as a weak, ineffective leader, especially in terms of the economy, a hostage to events rather than a master of them. "When asked 'Which candidate do you trust to do a better job handling the economy?' Mr. Romney polls as high or higher than Mr. Obama . . ." Rove wrote. "The self-portrait the president has painted is of a weak liberal, buffeted by events. That will make this election more like 1980—when Ronald Reagan defeated an ineffectual Jimmy Carter—than 2004."

Of course, there were still five months to go before the election—an eternity in politics, during which there were certain to be surprises. As of late spring, the Democrats seemed poised to gain several House seats, but were unlikely to regain control. There was a strong possibility, even a probability, that the Republicans would win the Senate as well. Even if the Democrats held, without the votes to stop the Republicans' constant filibusters, they would be powerless to pass significant legislation. The White House, meanwhile, had become a toss-up.

But in early June, global events conspired to aid Rove's cause. On June 1, in the wake of weak numbers on the jobs front, and fears of an economic collapse in the Eurozone, the stock market got jittery. In response, the GOP-leaning Rasmussen tracking poll gave Romney a four-point lead. It looked to be a tight race.

Obama wasn't competitive with the Republicans when it came to SuperPACs, but he had other resources. In May, the president raised nearly $15 million in one night at George Clooney's Los Angeles home. In June there was a $40,000-a-plate dinner at Sarah Jessica

Parker's New York home, cohosted by *Vogue* editor Anna Wintour, that drew Meryl Streep, designer Michael Kors, and other celebrities, and, that same evening, Mariah Carey headlined another Obama fund-raiser in New York. Julia Roberts, Reese Witherspoon, Spike Lee, Will Smith, Oprah Winfrey, Ellen DeGeneres, and Cher joined the Obama bandwagon.

Then, on June 19, Bob Bauer, chief counsel for the Obama campaign, struck out at Rove in a complaint to the Federal Election Commission demanding that Crossroads GPS disclose its donors because, he said, the group was clearly a "political committee." Bauer also wrote Rove and Steven Law, the president of Crossroads, urging them to disclose their donors.

Normally, Rove was rigorously disciplined when it came to being on message. But suddenly, in an interview on Fox News by Greta Van Susteren the next day, with no provocation whatsoever, he veered wildly off message and attacked Bauer. In addition to claiming that GPS was a "social welfare" group, not a political committee, Rove attempted to discredit Bauer by falsely asserting that he was the lawyer for Jill Simpson, Rove's nemesis in the Siegelman affair, and declaring, again falsely, that Simpson had not testified under oath. "This is, frankly, thuggish behavior," Rove said. "You know, earlier, we were talking about the time that I went up to the Congress to testify. One of the accusers was Bob Bauer, who was the attorney for a woman named Dana Jill Simpson, who alleged that I had encouraged her to investigate—a woman I've never met in my entire life—and that I asked her to investigate the sexual shenanigans of Democratic governor Siegelman of Alabama.

"And you know, Bob Bauer was an attorney, got her on *60 Minutes*. Big hoo-ha about it. And when I—when I was in—when I went before the hearing on the—before the Congress after all this hoo-ha on her, it turned out they considered—the Democratic staffers told me she was an unreliable witness and they weren't going to call her. And she refused to cooperate with the Justice Department investigation of the charges that she and Governor Siegelman made."

Simpson later provided a sworn affidavit asserting that she had never met Bauer and that he had never represented her. And, of course, Rove's statements to the contrary, she had testified under oath before the Judiciary Committee, and it was Rove who had refused to do so. Longtime observers of Rove were stunned by his uncharacteristic loss of composure and could only speculate why Simpson rankled Rove so completely.

Four days later, however, Rove was in his element as never before, serving as a featured attraction at a Republicanpalooza of sorts, more formally the "Romney Victory Leadership Retreat" at the Chateaux at Silver Lake in Park City, Utah. The occasion was a meeting bringing together the presumptive Republican nominee, his senior advisers, the billionaires who were funding him, and, of course, Karl Rove, around whom, the *Atlantic Wire* reported, wealthy bankers "behaved like schoolgirls after a cute boy walks by in the hall."

In addition to rubbing elbows with Romney himself, wealthy donors—admission was restricted to those who had already given $50,000 or raised $100,000—could schmooze or attend seminars with Condoleezza Rice, James Baker III, John McCain, Beth Myers, Bobby Jindal, Paul Ryan, former Homeland Security secretary Michael Chertoff, and Jeb Bush.

But Rove was the big hit—sending the audience into stitches by mimicking the Cajun accent of Democratic strategist James Carville, recounting how Dick Cheney accidentally shot his friend in the face while hunting, and teasing a Wall Street banker about his casual attire.

"You're the most underdressed banker I've ever met," Rove teased.

Then, the *New York Times* reported, after Rove was out of earshot, the men breathlessly narrated the play-by-play of the conversation that had just taken place, exulting in their proximity to the great Karl Rove.

"That's the price of admission right there," one donor said. "Your six minutes with Rove."

All joking aside, if Romney won the White House, the consequences would be monumental. With at least one liberal likely to leave the Supreme Court during the next administration, a Republican victory meant the right would probably control the court for a generation to come. Neoconservative advisers to Romney would regain control of American foreign policy. And the austerity budget measures Republicans demanded would risk plunging the economy into depression.

Whatever the outcome of the elections, Rove had come a long way. Just a few years earlier, as a brand in politics, his name had been toxic. He had been the brains behind one of the most discredited presidents in U.S. history, who had started two horribly costly wars and, having inherited a booming economy, left the nation near economic collapse. He was the bull's-eye on the targets in some of the biggest political scandals of the decade—the outing of Valerie Plame Wilson as a covert operative, the use of the judiciary as a political weapon to attack Don Siegelman and scores of Democratic foes, and the firing of the U.S. attorneys who did not play partisan hardball with him. After all that, Rove had narrowly escaped indictment, and resigned from the White House in disgrace, leaving his party in disrepair and allowing the Democrats to take the White House and both houses of Congress.

Even now, Rove remained surrounded by unsolved mysteries. What had happened to the millions of White House emails that went missing? What was his real role, if any, with SmarTech and with other players in the 2004 election, and how far had it really gone? There were many unanswered questions about the massive 2004 electoral fraud in Ohio, the destruction of evidence relating to it, and more.

It remained to be seen whether Romney would actually win, and, if so, whether he would be as pliant as Rove hoped. Likewise, it was too early to say whether Rove really would build his permanent Republican majority.

Regardless of the answers, on some level Rove had already won. Undeniably, he was back. He had changed the game. He had reinvented himself. He was no longer merely Bush's Brain. Instead, he was the man who stood at the podium, baton in hand, orchestrating the various movements within the Republican Party. As the maestro, he motioned where the big money from the billionaires would flow. He dictated which candidates would succeed and which would fail. Nobody had elected him. And he had no term limit. Even rival operatives in the party who loathed him evinced a grudging respect. "He's playing a very long game," said GOP operative Roger Stone. "He's playing for control of the party. That's where the power is. That's where the money is. Even if Romney loses, that's good for

Karl, because he will still be in control. And there's always Jeb Bush in 2016."

Drawing in the cantankerous Koch brothers and Sheldon Adelson, Rove had even consolidated the money under his power. He had co-opted the Tea Party, defanging the uncontrollable elements in it, marginalizing their leaders and seizing their resources. Sarah Palin, Donald Trump, Herman Cain, and Rick Perry had been consigned to the dustbin of history. Mitt Romney was forever indebted to Rove. He had built his new machine into a ruthlessly efficient political operation outside, above, and, finally subsuming the party structure, beholden to no one but himself. "No one else," said Stone, "can construct a power center like he can."

Since he was a young man battling for office within the College Republicans, "ratfucking" for Nixon, smearing Democrat after Democrat, and after laying eyes on the cowboy figure of George W. Bush, promising to build him a permanent Republican majority, Rove had long envisioned playing a historic role the Republican Party. But only now, at last, had Karl Rove become the party boss.

ACKNOWLEDGMENTS

This book would not have been possible without the help of many people. For the third time, I have had the privilege of being edited by Colin Harrison at Scribner, and, as always, his editorial judgment has been superb. I am also grateful to Susan Moldow and Nan Graham, who oversaw a terrific team at Scribner that treated the book with the highest level of professionalism. They include Kelsey Smith, Katie Rizzo, Brian Belfiglio, Kate Lloyd, and Erich Hobbing. My thanks also go to Elisa Rivlin for her comprehensive legal review.

My agent, Sloan Harris of International Creative Management, has been enormously supportive throughout and has always been there with valuable advice. At *Vanity Fair,* I'm also indebted to Graydon Carter and Dana Brown.

I am especially grateful to Sidney Blumenthal, whose friendship and insight have been invaluable. I am equally indebted to Marji and Don Mendelsohn for their generous support and wise counsel. Sidney, Don and Marji, and Phyllis Roome all read the manuscript prior to publication, and I thank them for helping me avoid embarrassing mistakes. Any that may remain are my responsibility alone.

Thanks also to Tim Voell for providing such hospitable and congenial working conditions in Rhinecliff, New York.

Among the many people who were either interview subjects or gave me assistance with the book, or with my work for *Vanity Fair* that later appeared in the book, I'd like to thank John Aaron, Joe Abate, Richard Armitage, Cliff Arnebeck, Jeff Averbeck, John Batchelor, Mark Bollinger, Mark Brabant, Jennifer Brunner, Vince Cannistraro, Bert Coleman, Heather Connell, Michael Cunnyngham, Robert Destro, Priscilla Duncan, Bob Fitrakis, Brad Friedman, Jim Frierson, Thomas Gallion, Philip Giraldi, Melvin Goodman, Bev Harris, Scott Horton, Harri Hursti, Larry C. Johnson, Doug Jones, Pat Lang, Michael Ledeen, Craig Mac-Donald, Bob Mangan, Mary Mapes, Ray McGovern, James Moore, Tom Pauken, Richard Hayes Phillips, Brett Rapp, Rebecca Sacks, Don Siegelman, Dana Jill Simpson, Wayne Slater, Steven Spoonamore, Roger Stone, Shannon Walton, Michael Weissman, Larry Wilkerson, and Joe Wilson.

Karl Rove gave me a few minutes of his time when I met him in Cedarville, Ohio. I thank him for that, and I regret that he was unable to schedule a more extensive interview later.

And I would also like to thank the many sources who helped me on a background or not-for-attribution basis. Helpful as such sources have been, this book also relies extensively on government documents, congressional investigations, and news accounts from hundreds of newspapers and journals from all over the world. It would have been impossible to research this book without the Internet, and I am especially grateful to the people and institutions that have built the Internet research tools that enabled me to search through such vast amounts of material from all over the world so quickly. Wherever possible, I have cited relevant websites in the endnotes. The reader should be advised, however, that Internet links are not eternal and some web addresses may be out of date.

Because I made a practice of citing original sources, a number of extraordinarily useful resources do not appear in my endnotes nearly as often as they should. Among them, I'm particularly grateful to History Commons, whose timelines on the U.S. attorneys scandal, the Valerie Plame Wilson affair, and other issues are invaluable resources.

Many other friends and colleagues helped either by contributing in one way or another to the book itself with their professional expertise or through much-needed moral support. They include John Anderson, Richard Barrett, Len Belzer and Emily Squires, Patti Bosworth, Charlie Bresler, Peter Carey, Robin and Susan Madden, Liam O'Sullivan and Patricia Maugain, Jamie Robins, Cody Shearer. My gratitude goes to my family—my father, Roger; Chris, Shanti, Thomas, Marley, and Miles; Jimmy, Marie-Claude, Adam, and Matthew; and Harlow and Richard Unger; and my warmest to Lionel, Penelope, and Olivier.

And finally, thanks and love to Phyllis, who has had the dubious privilege of putting up with me on deadline, for her love and support.

NOTES

Chapter 1: The Man Who Swallowed the Republican Party

1 *Karl Rove's five-bedroom:* "Is Karl Rove Leaving Washington D.C.?" The Real Estalker, July 30, 2009, http://realestalker.blogspot.com/2009/07/is-karl-rove -leaving-washington-dc.html.

1 *Six years earlier, he held:* Karl Rove, *Courage and Consequence* (New York: Simon & Schuster, 2010), p. 362.

1 *"Karl Rove will be a name":* Scott Horton, "Six Questions for Paul Alexan- der, Author of *Machiavelli's Shadow,*" *Harper's,* July 2008, http://harpers.org/ archive/2008/07/hbc-90003167.

2 *"I had to worry":* Joe Hagan, "Goddangit, Baby, We're Making Good Time," *New York,* February 27, 2011, http://nymag.com/news/politics/karl-rove -2011-3/index1.html.

3 *This last decision was also:* James Moore and Wayne Slater, *The Architect* (New York: Three Rivers Press, 2007), p. 91.

5 *"Ed's got the better rap":* Peter H. Stone, "Bush's Brains, Rove + Gillespie Raise GOP Bucks," *National Journal,* March 31, 2010, http://undertheinfluence .nationaljournal.com/2010/03/big-time-donors-not-so.php?print=true&print comment=2081092.

5 *As Al Kamen reported:* Al Kamen, "There's a PAC for That," *Washington Post,* March 22, 2012, www.washingtonpost.com/politics/theres-a-pac-for -that/2012/03/22/gIQAOOIJUS_story.html.

6 *On March 8, 2010, Gillespie:* Stone, "Bush's Brains, Rove + Gillespie Raise GOP Bucks."

6 *Meanwhile, Rove's list included:* Jim Rutenberg, "Rove Returns, with Team, Planning G.O.P. Push," *New York Times,* September 25, 2010, www.nytimes .com/2010/09/26/us/26rove.html?pagewanted=all.

6 *In just one month:* Stone, "Bush's Brains, Rove + Gillespie Raise GOP Bucks."

6 *"Karl has always said":* Mike Allen and Kenneth P. Vogel, "Karl Rove, Repub- lican Party Plot Vast Network to Reclaim Power," Politico, May 6, 2010, www .politico.com/news/stories/0510/36841.html.

6 *"an informal discussion of the 2010":* Stone, "Bush's Brains, Rove + Gillespie Raise GOP Bucks."

6 *over chicken pot pie:* Rutenberg, "Rove Returns, with Team, Planning G.O.P. Push."

7 *Meanwhile, Rove and Gillespie:* Peter H. Stone, "Inside the Shadow GOP," *National Review,* October 27, 2010, www.nationaljournal.com/njonline/no_20101004_4486.php.

7 *Altogether, according to the* National Journal: Peter Stone, "Campaign Cash: The Independent Fundraising Gold Rush Since 'Citizens United' Ruling," iWatch News, Center for Public Integrity, October 4, 2010, updated May 24, 2011, www.iwatchnews.org/2010/10/04/2470/campaign-cash-independent-fundraising-gold-rush-citizens-united-ruling.

7 *That was enough money:* Ibid.

8 *"Where they have a chess piece":* Allen and Vogel, "Karl Rove, Republican Party Plot Vast Network to Reclaim Power."

8 *"America is a two-party state":* Author interview with John Batchelor.

8 *In the early sixties, as a young boy:* Rove, *Courage and Consequence,* p. 7.

8 *"My mother [thought about]":* Party Hardy, "Karl Rove's Juggernaut," *New Republic,* September 25, 2006, www.tnr.com/article/karl-roves-juggernaut.

9 *"It was like she was trying":* Ibid.

9 *"the classic fuck-you gesture":* Ibid.

9 *"There are two important things":* David D. Kirkpatrick, "Does Corporate Money Lead to Political Corruption?" *New York Times,* January 23, 2010, www.nytimes.com/2010/01/24/weekinreview/24kirkpatrick.html.

10 *"Karl Rove would be able to teach":* Author interview with Larry Johnson.

10 *"I'm a myth":* Paul Gigot, "The Mark of Rove," *Wall Street Journal,* August 13, 2007, http://online.wsj.com/article/SB118697458949295744.html.

Chapter 2: A Nixonian Education

17 *"just like* Pride and Prejudice*":* "Stephen Colbert Hams It up with Jane Austen and Karl Rove," Left Bank of the Charles, March 13, 2010, www.leftbankofthecharles.com/2010/03/stephen-colbert-hams-it-up-with-jane.html.

18 *"massive and unprecedented":* "Preserving Democracy: What Went Wrong in Ohio, Status Report of the House Judiciary Committee Democratic Staff," January 5, 2005.

19 *"free beer, free food":* Rove, *Courage and Consequence,* p. 24.

19 *Rove became a master:* Ibid.

19 *"I think he is exactly":* Author interview with Joe Abate.

19 *A man of dubious culinary tastes:* Rove, *Courage and Consequence,* p. 34.

21 *"You could play the hardest":* "Boogie Man: The Lee Atwater Story," *Frontline,* November 11, 2008, www.pbs.org/wgbh/pages/frontline/atwater/etc/script.html.

21 *"With Lee, you could have a battle":* Author interview with Tom Pauken.

22 *"Atwater put up with Rove":* Paul Alexander, *Machiavelli's Shadow* (New York: Rodale Press, 2008), p. 9.

22 *"He came into the business":* Author interview with Wayne Slater.

23 *"He controlled the mechanism":* Ibid.

23 *"Given that the Republican business guys"*: Ibid.

23 *"It was the poster-child case"*: Joshua Green, "The Brutal Genius of Karl Rove," *Australian Financial Review,* October 29, 2004, p. 5.

24 *"You had insurance companies"*: Author interview with Doug Jones.

24 *"Rove was smart enough to understand"*: Author interview with Craig McDonald.

24 *"Raising money from the high-rolling"*: Ibid.

25 these *"citizens" committees: Hot Coffee,* Susan Saladoff, director, June 2011.

25 *"to get the Texas Legislature"*: Lynn Tran and Andrew Wheat, "Tort Dodgers," Texans for Public Justice, April 1997.

26 *"He did exactly what he's doing"*: Author interview with Tom Pauken.

26 *In addition, there were no fewer:* Tran and Wheat, "Tort Dodgers."

27 *"ruthless," "Ollie North in civilian clothes"*: Ed Rollins, *Bare Knuckles and Back Rooms* (New York: Broadway Books, 1996), p. 125.

27 *"You start out in 1954"*: Alexander P. Lamis, *The Two-Party South* (New York: Oxford University Press, 1990).

27 *It began before the Democratic National:* Sidney Blumenthal, *Pledging Allegiance* (New York: Harper, 1991), p. 264.

28 *"God, this guy's ugly"*: Jane Mayer, "Attack Dog," *New Yorker,* January 13, 2012, www.newyorker.com/reporting/2012/02/13/120213fa_fact_mayer#ixzz1m0Sj6yDz.

28 *"strip the bark off"*: "The Boogie Man: The Lee Atwater Story."

28 *"Y'all a pussy"*: Ibid.

29 *"I do not know who did this"*: James Moore and Wayne Slater, *Bush's Brain* (Hoboken, NJ: Wiley, 2003), p. 38.

29 *"Karl all but came out"*: Ibid., p. 56.

30 *"I can literally remember"*: Nicholas Lemann, "The Controller: Karl Rove Is Working to Get George Bush Reelected, but He Has Bigger Plans," *New Yorker,* May 12, 2003, p. 68.

30 *But soon, thanks to Rove:* Moore and Slater, *Bush's Brain.*

31 *"If there's any single thing"*: Rove, *Courage and Consequence.*

31 *His adoptive father:* Moore and Slater, *The Architect,* p. 132.

31 *thanks to his thirty-seven piercings:* Xeni Jardin, "Karl Robe's Pierced Family Jewels, part 2," Boingboing, August 21, 2007, www.boingboing.net/2007/08/21/karl-roves-pierced-f.html.

31 *"refused to say why"*: Rove, *Courage and Consequence,* p. 16.

32 *"The first few questions are routine"*: "The Boogie Man: The Lee Atwater Story."

32 *Famously, in a South Carolina congressional race:* Ibid.

32 *"the practice is inexpensive"*: Rove, *Courage and Consequence,* p. 150.

32 *"more or less likely to vote for"*: www.hnn.us/articles/13026.html

32 *"This is not an issue"*: Moore and Slater, *Bush's Brain.*

32 *"avowed homosexual activists"*: Ibid.

32 *"[homosexuality] is not something"*: Stuart Eskenazi, "Rogue Elephant," *Houston Press,* September 3, 1998, www.houstonpress.com/content/prontVersion/220157.

33 *"This Is What Ann Richards Wants"*: Moore and Slater, *The Architect,* p. 37.

33 *"I thought it was a joke"*: Ibid.

33 *"There was clearly an organized"*: Moore and Slater, *Bush's Brain*, p. 208.

33 *"puts a layer of operatives"*: Moore and Slater, *Bush's Brain*, Kindle edition, location 51.

Chapter 3: Chattanooga Choo Choo

34 *A rare boomtown in recession-racked America:* Chattanooga Chamber of Commerce, www.yellowpages.com/business/site?link=http%3A%2F%2Fwww .chattanoogachamber.com.

35 *"the first top-tier networks"*: "Enterprising Networking News: Fiber Blaster," eWeek, April 23, 2001, www.eweek.com/c/a/Enterprise-Networking/Fiber -Blaster/.

35 *Enter Mercer Reynolds and Bill DeWitt:* Author interview with Mike Cunnyngham.

35 *The two men had first met Bush:* Anne Michaud, "George W. Bush," *Cincinnati*, November 1999. See also George Lardner Jr. and Lois Romano, "Bush Name Helps Fuel Oil Dealings," *Washington Post*, July 30, 1999, www.washington post.com/wp-srv/politics/campaigns/wh2000/stories/bush073099.htm.

35 *He partied with Bush:* David Aikman, *A Man of Faith: The Spiritual Journey of George W. Bush* (Nashville: Thomas Nelson, 2005), p. 63.

35 *As for Bill DeWitt:* Helen Thorpe, "Hail the Conquering Hero," *New York*, September 1999, http://nymag.com/nymetro/news/politics/national/ features/1462/index1.html.

35 *"It's crazy"*: Cliff Peale, "Friends of Bush Drawn Into Spotlight," *Cincinnati Enquirer*, January 18, 2001, www.enquirer.com/editions/2001/01/18/loc_ friends_of_bush.html.

36 *It was the perfect site:* "Powerful Portal: Airnet Technology Featured in Business Publication," Airnet News, January 2007, www.airnetgroup.com/index .php?s=news&n=6.

36 *Long before YouTube:* "Enterprising Networking: Fiber Blaster," eWeek, April 23, 2001, http://mobile.eweek.com/c/a/Enterprise-Networking/Fiber -Blaster/.

36 *stream films and other video content:* Craig Havighurst, "Online Feature Films Just Got Better," *Tennessean*, November 22, 2000, p. 1E.

36 *In 1999, NextLec/st3:* Judy Sarles, "Firm Ramps Up for IPO," *Nashville Business Journal*, April 2, 2000, www.bizjournals.com/nashville/stories/2000/04/03/ story8.html?page=all.

36 *In 2001, the company acquired rights*: Barry Courter, "Lights, Camera, Chattanooga Sitcom: Pilot Links Local Talent, First, Restaurant," *Chattanooga Times Free Press*, April 8, 2001, p. A1.

36 *Then it partnered with Apple's:* "st3 to Stream Twangfest," June 8, 2001, www.thefreelibrary.com/st3+to+Stream+Twangfest%3B+st3's+Dedicated +New+Media+Network+to+Stream . . . -a075396261.

36 *other investors put in a total*: Author interview with Michael Cunnyngham.

36 *"Everything you know about William McKinley"*: Joshua Green, "The Rove

Presidency," *Atlantic,* September 2000, www.theatlantic.com/magazine/archive/2007/09/the-rove-presidency/6132/.

37 *But the larger point:* William Horner, *Ohio's Kingmaker: Mark Hanna, Man and Myth* (Athens: Ohio University Press, 2010), p. 296.

37 *the permanent majority:* Green, "The Rove Presidency."

37 *Even though the company was located in Chattanooga:* "Today's Bush Campaign News," *Bulletin's Frontrunner,* August 28, 2000.

37 *Reynolds's relationship with Bush:* Author interview with Michael Cunnyngham.

37 *One of Cunnyngham's most important:* Ibid.

37 *That meant that on a day-to-day basis:* Ibid.

38 *"that dot-com bubble crap":* Author interview with Jeff Averbeck.

38 *"the best piece of spamming software":* Author interview with Michael Cunnyngham.

38 *"the single greatest advancement":* "Voter Vault," Filpac, www.filpac.com/votervault.htm.

38 *"When they hooked up with us":* Author interview with Michael Cunnyngham.

38 *The person behind New Media:* Author interview with Shannon Walton, Mike Connell's sister.

39 *"He was extremely intelligent":* Author interview with Heather Connell.

39 *"I'm not proud of that":* Author interview with Shannon Walton.

39 *More than just roommates:* Author interview with Heather Connell.

39 *"Barry was trying to start up Republicanism":* Author interview with Larry Lassiter.

40 *In 1994, Connell:* "Political Bug Leads to the Web," *Crain's Cleveland Business,* November 3, 2001.

40 *"He was a very self-motivated guy":* Author interview with Mark Brabant.

40 *He developed databases and web services:* Bob Fitrakis, "Behind the Firewall: Bush Loyalist Mike Connell Controls Congressional Secrets as His Email Sites Serve Karl Rove," *Free Press,* July 29, 2008, www.freepress.org/columns/display/3/2008/1665.

41 *"the first real statewide site":* Steve Gleydura, "CyberScene: Spinning the Web," IB Mag.com, November 1999, http://ibmag.com/Main/Archive/CyberScene_Spinning_the_Web_10702.aspx.

41 *Then, New Media joined forces with the DCI Group:* Fitrakis, "Behind the Firewall."

41 *By late 1998, New Media put together:* http://web.archive.org/web/19980712011025/http://newmedia.technomania.com/politics.html. NB: Many web addresses for defunct websites, such as Mike Connell's Technomania site, can be found by using the Wayback Machine, which archives millions of pages for sites that have been discontinued.

41 *"He was the best in the business":* Author interview with Bert Coleman.

41 *Whether they were senators or governors:* http://web.archive.org/web/20020806150907/http://www.technomania.com/featuredsite.asp.

42 *In late 2001, the original company:* "st3 Technology Firm Goes Bankrupt and Closes Doors," *Chattanoogan,* January 9, 2002, www.chattanoogan.com/2002/1/9/16604/st3-Technology-Firm-Goes-Bankrupt-And.aspx.

42 *In addition to hosting George W. Bush's sites:* Based on computer research using Domain Tools.

43 *"I wouldn't be where I am today":* Interview with Mike Connell, *Inside Business,* November 2, 1999.

44 *To make matters worse:* Ron Suskind, "Why Are These Men Laughing?" *Esquire,* January 2003, www.ronsuskind.com/newsite/articles/archives/000032.html.

44 *"It's gotten to where you have to actually destroy":* Moore and Slater, *The Architect,* p. 257.

44 *According to Bush forces:* "McCain Charges Bush Is Push Polling; Bush Denies It," *Bulletin's Frontrunner,* February 11, 2000.

44 *"promiscuously homosexual father":* Benjamin Wallace-Wells, "Getting Ahead in the GOP," *Washington Monthly,* October/November 2005, www.washingtonmonthly.com/features/2005/0510.wallace-wells.html.

44 *"They became partners":* "Feather Larson & Synhorst DCI," SourceWatch, www.sourcewatch.org/index.php?title=Feather_Larson_%26_Synhorst_DCI.

45 *"Karl Rove Central":* Josh Gerstein, "Avalanche of Cash Is Set to Descend on Election Battle," *New York Sun,* October 12, 2006.

45 *"on your behalf":* Laura Miller, "Powers Behind the Throne," Center for Media and Democracy's PR Watch, 2004, www.prwatch.org/prwissues/2004Q4/powers.html.

45 *The campaigns got into trouble:* Ibid.

45 *"the perfect guide to winning":* http://townhall.com/columnists/davidhorowitz/.

45 *"In political warfare you do not fight":* Akiva Gottlieb, "David Horowitz Is Homeless," *Tablet,* May 2, 2012, www.tabletmag.com/jewish-news-and-politics/98401/david-horowitz/.

46 *In June, it was hailed:* "Two Websites Designed by New Media Communications Receive National Recognition," June 22, 2000, http://web.archive.org/web/200101050302/http://www.technomania.com/news.asp?FormMode=Release&ID=22.

46 *In July, New Media announced:* http://web.archive.org/web/20001017234221/http://www.technomania.com/.

46 *On July 31, New Media began live:* http://web.archive.org/web/20001017234221/http://www.technomania.com/.

46 *Meanwhile, Connell's old friend Barry:* Daily Kos, February 12, 2006, www.dailykos.com/story/2006/02/12/186621/-Setting-up-Eastern-Europe-to-support-the-Iraq-War.

46 *"Barry has never been out in the forefront":* Author interview with Bert Coleman.

46 *in the midst of the bitterly contentious:* Ibid.

46 *"Hey, hey, yo, yo":* Evan Thomas and Michael Isikoff, "War of the Weary," *Newsweek,* December 4, 2000, p. 30.

46 *On December 4, well before the contested election:* http://web.archive.org/web/200102020810/http://technomania.com/.

46 *Tasked with running the portentously named:* Dengre, "Setting up Eastern

Europe to Support the Iraq War," Daily Kos, February 12, 2006, www.dailykos
.com/story/2006/02/12/186621/-Setting-up-Eastern-Europe-to-support-the
-Iraq-War.

47 *Even at this point, to the business world:* Sarles, "Firm Ramps Up for IPO."

48 *"When [GovTech Solutions] emerges":* Mike Connell interview with *Crain's
Cleveland Business,* April 18, 2001.

48 *In early April 2001, GovTech had:* http://web.archive.org/web/20010404051157/
http://govtechsolutions.com/.

48 *Then GovTech won contracts:* http://web.archive.org/web/20011021121309/
http://govtechsolutions.com/portfolio.asp.

48 *GovTech's contracts included the House Financial Services:* http://web.archive
.org/web/20020604075936/http://govtechsolutions.com/clients/index.html.

48 *"SmarTech and GovTech data":* Background interview, source at SmarTech.

Chapter 4: Sweet Home Alabama

50 *"We will fuck him":* Sidney Blumenthal, "Upending the Mayberry Machiavellis," Salon, April 12, 2007, www.salon.com/2007/04/12/bush_destruction/.

51 *"I heard many, many staff discussions":* Ron Suskind, *The Price of Loyalty*
(New York: Simon & Schuster, 2004), pp. 170–71.

52 *"It is breathtaking":* Janet Hook, "GOP Seeks Lasting Majority," *Los Angeles
Times,* July 21, 2003, p. 1.

52 *His roots there went back:* Joshua Green, "Karl Rove in a Corner," *Atlantic,* November 2004, www.theatlantic.com/joshua-green/page/32.magazidoc
/200411/green.

53 *"We were trying to counter the positives":* Ibid.

53 *"If you control the court":* Author interview with Don Siegelman.

53 *"expert political paratrooper" and "someone you dropped":* Scott Horton, "The
Remarkable 'Recusal' of Leura Canary," *Harper's,* September 14, 2007, www
.harpers.org/archive/2007/09/hbc-90001209.

54 *"Rove had learned a couple of things":* Author interview with Don Siegelman.

55 *"I walk away and I think":* Ibid.

55 *"I don't care who else":* Ibid.

55 *"It was awful":* Ibid.

57 *In an interview on CBS's:* "Did the Ex-Alabama Governor Get a Raw Deal?"
60 Minutes, February 11, 2009, www.cbsnews.com/2100-18560_162-3859830
.html?pageNum=2&tag=contentMain;contentBody.

60 *"It was as if the voters went Democrat":* Author interview with Don Siegelman.

60 *"When Baldwin County reported two sets":* James H. Gundlach, "A Statistical Analysis of Possible Electronic Ballot Box Stuffing," paper presented at the
Annual Meeting of the Alabama Political Science Association, April 11, 2003,
www.auburn.edu/~gundljh/Baldwin.pdf.

62 *"She told me this stuff before":* Author interview with Mark Bollinger.

62 *"[B]ecause I never met the woman":* Rove, *Courage and Consequence,* p. 36.

62 *"hillbilly from hell," has been "horribly underestimated":* Author interview
with Priscilla Duncan.

62 *"I sure wouldn't want her":* Author interview with Tommy Gallion.

62 *In an interview he gave in 2008:* Lisa DePaulo, "Karl Rove Likes What He Sees," *GQ,* April 2, 2008, http://abcnews.go.com/Politics/Vote2008/story?id=4569091&page=8#.T6hNlr9SHgV.

63 *But in fact an electronic search:* U.S. House of Representatives, Committee on the Judiciary, September 14, 2007, Dana Jill Simpson interview with exhibits, pp. 49–51.

Chapter 5: Unintended Consequences

64 *In the aftermath of the worst:* Jennifer Agiesta, "Behind the Numbers," *Washington Post,* July 24, 2007, http://voices.washingtonpost.com/behind-the-numbers/2007/07/approval_highs_and_lows.html.

64 *America "must not only be":* Lawrence F. Kaplan and William Kristol, *The War Over Iraq* (New York: Encounter Books, 2003), p. 121.

64 *"Every ten years or so":* Jonah Goldberg, "Baghdad Delenda Est, Part Two," *National Review,* April 23, 2002, www.nationalreview.com/goldberg/goldberg042302.asp.

65 *"Karl is about power":* Author interview with Roger Stone.

65 *"We can go to the country on this issue":* Joe Conason, "Rove Waves Flag for G.O.P. Candidates," *New York Observer,* January 28, 2002, www.observer.com/2002/01/rove-waves-flag-for-gop-candidates/.

65 *"[Voters] will see the battle for Iraq":* Lemann, "The Controller: Karl Rove Is Working to Get George Bush Reelected."

66 *Rove "said that guys like me":* Ron Suskind, "Faith, Certainty and the Presidency of George W. Bush," *New York Times Magazine,* October 17, 2004, www.nytimes.com/2004/10/17/magazine/17BUSH.html.

68 *His incendiary rhetoric aside:* "Thomas B. Edsall and Dana Milbank, "White House's Roving Eye for Politics," *Washington Post,* March 10, 2003, Final Edition, p. A01. Also, author interview with Michael Ledeen.

69 *"The reports made no sense":* Author interview with Ray McGovern.

69 *"The whole idea of the Niger deal":* Author interview with Lawrence Wilkerson.

69 *A few hours later, Valerie Plame:* Valerie Plame Wilson, *Fair Game* (New York: Simon & Schuster, 2007), p. 108.

69 *"My husband has good relations":* "Report on the U.S. Intelligence Community's Prewar Intelligence Assessments on Iraq," July 9, 2004, www.globalsecurity.org/intell/library/congress/2004_rpt/iraq-wmd-intell_toc.htm.

70 *"They were just relentless":* Author interview with Lawrence Wilkerson.

70 *"A key piece of evidence linking Iraq":* "Debating the U.N.'s Relevance," CNN Politics, March 12, 2003, http://articles.cnn.com/2003-03-12/politics/cf.opinion.un.relevance_1_relevance-favor-of-military-action-chief-nuclear-inspector?_s=PM:ALLPOLITICS.

71 *"consistently underestimated or missed":* Craig Unger, *The Fall of the House of Bush* (New York: Simon & Schuster, 2007), p. 292.

72 *Further, the United States had alienated the Sunnis:* "Interview with Lt. Col.

Andrew Krepinevich (Ret.)," *Frontline,* www.pbs.org/wgbh/pages/frontline/endgame/interviews/krepinevich.html.

72 *"a former US ambassador":* Nicholas Kristof, "Missing in Action: Truth," *New York Times,* May 6, 2003, www.nytimes.com/2003/05/06/opinion/missing-in-action-truth.html.

72 *Vice President Cheney's office made inquiries:* Scott McClellan, *What Happened: Inside the Bush White House and Washington's Culture of Deception* (New York: Public Affairs, 2008), p. 8.

73 *"Step right up":* Michael Isikoff and David Corn, *Hubris: The Inside Story of Spin, Scandal, and the Selling of the Iraq War* (New York: Crown, 2006), p. 231.

73 *On Sunday, July 6, 2003:* Rove, *Courage and Consequence,* p. 318.

73 *that "it was highly doubtful":* Joseph C. Wilson IV, "What I Didn't Find in Africa," *New York Times,* July 6, 2003, www.nytimescom/2003/07/06/opinion/what-i-didn-t-find-in-africa.html.

73 *Rove had never even heard:* Rove, *Courage and Consequence,* p. 318.

73 *"Wilson's op-ed hit them":* Ibid, p. 319.

73 *"pompous and more than a little":* Ibid.

73 *"[I]t was clear to me he meant":* Ibid.

73 *Rove was told that Cheney:* Ibid.

74 *"effectively debunked the Niger arms":* James B. Stewart, *Tangled Webs: How False Statements Are Undermining America: From Martha Stewart to Bernie Madoff* (New York: Penguin Press, 2011), p. 138.

74 *"The White House press corps was ready":* Rove, *Courage and Consequence,* p. 320.

74 *Over the next two days, Rove:* Ibid.

74 *"Under the cloak of anonymity":* McClellan, *What Happened,* p. 8.

75 *"It is impossible for any of us":* Amy Goodman and Jeremy Scahill, "The Ashcroft-Rove Connection—The Ties That Blind," Common Dreams, October 2, 2003, www.commondreams.org/views03/1002-03.htm.

75 *the morning after Wilson's op-ed piece:* Grand Jury testimony, I. Lewis Libby, March 5, 2004, www.justice.gov/usao/iln/osc/exhibits/0207/GX1.pdf.

75 *"[N]ow they have accepted Joe":* Stewart, *Tangled Webs,* p.141.

75 *"Well, there is zero, nada":* "Press Gaggle by Ari Fleischer," July 7, 2003, http://georgewbush-whitehouse.archives.gov/news/releases/2003/07/20030707-5.html#9.

76 *"We couldn't prove it":* McClellan, *What Happened,* p. 169.

76 *"It was the first public acknowledgment":* Ibid.

76 *"the identity of Joe Wilson's wife":* Ibid., p. 9.

76 *"almost an afterthought":* Rove, *Courage and Consequence,* p. 320.

77 *"to discredit Wilson":* McClellan, *What Happened,* p. 9.

77 *"I didn't dig it out":* Timothy M. Phelps and Knut Royce, "Columnist Blows CIA Agent's Cover," *Newsday,* July 22, 2003, www.commondreams.org/headlines03/0722-04.htm.

77 *He and Rove had been close friends:* Rove, *Courage and Consequence,* p. 355.

77 *The two men occasionally socialized:* Stewart, *Tangled Webs,* Kindle location 3597.

77 *always off the record:* Isikoff and Corn, *Hubris,* Kindle location 4502.

78   *"a grade A-plus source"*: Robert D. Novak, *The Prince of Darkness: 50 Years Reporting in Washington* (New York: Crown, 2007), p. 571.

78   *"Rove obviously thought"*: Ibid., p. 7.

78   *"[w]hat you did not find in my columns"*: Ibid., p. 572.

78   *It was also clear that if Novak*: Stewart, *Tangled Webs*, Kindle location 3159–3160.

78   *"Wilson's an asshole"*: Wilson, *Fair Game*, p. 140.

78   *"It was pretty clear to me"*: Transcript, *Hardball with Chris Matthews*, MSNBC, July 3, 2007, updated: July 5, 2007, http://today.msnbc.msn.com/id/19618592/#.T8-6So5uEYU.

78   *"I think that you are going to be unhappy"*: Jeralyn, "Murray Waas: Rove's Latest Defense Strategy," Talk Left, December 16, 2005, www.talkleft.com/story/2005/12/16/778/55026.

79   *"worked at the CIA"*: Rove, *Courage and Consequence*, p. 329.

79   *The entire conversation*: Stewart, *Tangled Webs*, Kindle locations 3599–3601.

79   *"I didn't know or think"*: Rove, *Courage and Consequence*, p. 331.

79   *"All I had done"*: Ibid., p. 329.

79   *"You know that, too"*: Isikoff and Corn, *Hubris*, p. 265.

79   *"to this day, I have no recollection"*: Rove, *Courage and Consequence*, p. 330.

80   *"it was, KR said, Wilson's wife"*: Matthew Cooper, "What I Told the Grand Jury," *Time*, July 17, 2005, www.time.com/time/magazine/article/0,9171,1083899-3,00.html.

80   *"I've already said too much"*: Isikoff and Corn, *Hubris*, p. 274.

80   *"[Cooper] immediately launched into Niger?"*: Rove, *Courage and Consequence*, pp. 329–30.

81   *Later that day, Scooter Libby*: Isikoff and Corn, *Hubris*, p. 298.

81   *"Rove told me that Bob Novak"*: I. Lewis Libby, Grand Jury testimony.

81   *"[H]e thought it was a good thing"*: Ibid.

81   *"I was uneasy"*: Wilson, *Fair Game*, pp. 140–41.

81   *"Well, the SOB did it"*: Ibid., p. 142.

82   *Novak had finally published*: Robert Novak, "Mission to Niger," Townhall.com, July 14, 2003, http://townhall.com/columnists/robertnovak/2003/07/14/mission_to_niger.

82   *"Wilson never worked for the CIA"*: Ibid.

82   *"I felt like I had been sucker-punched"*: Wilson, *Fair Game*, p. 142.

82   *"What about the many people overseas"*: Ibid., pp. 142–43.

83   *"wrong and a huge miscalculation"*: Mike Allen and Dana Priest, "Bush Administration Is Focus of Inquiry," *Washington Post*, September 28, 2003, http://archive.truthout.org/article/bush-administration-is-focus-inquiry.

83   *"I like Karl Rove"*: David Broder, "Karl Rove's Trajectory: The Presidential Adviser, Famously Smart, Is Getting Too Much Attention," *Pittsburgh Post-Gazette*, May 15, 2003, p. A13.

83   *The article explained that the leak*: Isikoff and Corn, *Hubris*, p. 290.

84   *UPI's Nicholas Horrock compared*: Nicholas M. Horrock, "Shades of Watergate?" United Press International, July 14, 2003.

Chapter 6: The Turn of the Screw

85 *His wife, Heather:* Author interview with Heather Connell.
85 *"Good ideas will go as high":* Mike Lewis, "New Media Comm.—Have We Looked into These Guys Yet?" DemocraticUnderground.com, December 27, 2004, www.democraticunderground.com/discuss/duboard.php?az=view_all&address=203x201647.
86 *"Mike had a direct relationship":* Author interview with Stephen Spoonamore.
86 *As a conservative African-American:* "Ken Blackwell, King of Voter Fraud, Is Fox News's ACORN Hypeman," Daily Kos, October 17, 2008, www.daily kos.com/story/2008/10/17/633528/-Ken-Blackwell-King-of-Voter-Fraud-is -Fox-News-s-ACORN-Hypeman.
87 *On February 24, 2003:* Jonathan Riskind, "GOP Expects Presidential Race to Be Tight in Ohio," *Columbus Dispatch,* February 26, 2003.
87 *He added that the state's election results:* Ibid.
87 *Blackwell's office announced:* Mark Naymik and Julie Carr Smyth, "State to Buy Voting Machines," *Cleveland Plain Dealer,* February 26, 2003, p. B1.
87 *"Several county elections officials":* Ibid.
87 *"The people who developed that [software] code":* Alison Grant, "Diebold Defends Vote Machines: Company Says Critic Used Wrong Software, Faulty Testing Procedures," *Cleveland Plain Dealer,* July 26, 2003.
88 *The previous three years, Diebold had made:* "Donor Lookup," OpenSecrets. org, www.opensecrets.org/indivs/search.php?name=Diebold&state=&zip=& employ=&cand=&old=Y&sort=N&soft=Y&capcode=hjggz&submit=Submit +your+Donor+Query0000.
88 *he was "committed to helping Ohio":* Julie Carr Smyth, "Voting Machine Controversy," *Cleveland Plain Dealer,* August 28, 2003, www.commondreams.org/ headlines03/0828-08.htm.
88 *asked Blackwell to disqualify Diebold:* Ibid.
88 *forty out of Ohio's eighty-eight counties:* Erika D. Smith, "Ohio Counties Choose Diebold: 40 of 71 Select Green Company to Supply Voting Machines," *Beacon Journal,* January 16, 2004.
88 *During the rest of July 2003:* Unger, *The Fall of the House of Bush,* p. 312.
88 *"This may be the first time in recent history":* Dana Bash, "Democrats Want Uranium Claim Probed," CNN.com, July 9, 2003, http://edition.cnn.com/2003/ ALLPOLITICS/07/08/sprj.irq.bush.sotu/.
89 *In July, Senate Majority Leader Tom Daschle:* Fox News, July 9, 2003, www .foxnews.com/story/0,2933,91372,00.html; McClellan, *What Happened,* p. 170.
89 *"Scooter and Karl are out of control":* Isikoff and Corn, *Hubris,* p. 291.
89 *On July 17, Rove flew:* Rove, *Courage and Consequence,* p. 344.
89 *Rove, of course, had long been comfortable:* Craig Unger, *House of Bush, House of Saud: The Secret Relationship Between the World's Two Most Powerful Dynasties* (New York: Scribner, 2004), pp. 279–80.
90 *In an earlier visit there:* Rove, *Courage and Consequence,* p. 345.
90 *In short, Matthews appeared:* Ibid.
90 *In his memoir, Rove disavows:* Ibid.

90   *"[Joe] had a look on his face":* Wilson, *Fair Game*, p. 147.

90   *"war on two citizens":* Joseph Wilson, *The Politics of Truth* (New York: Carroll & Graf, 2004), p. 1.

90   *On August 8, for the first time:* Douglas Jehl, "After the War Weapons Intelligence: Iraq Arms Critic Reacts to Report on Wife," *New York Times,* August 8, 2003, p. 8.

91   *"At the end of the day":* "Karl Rove Again Linked to Outing of CIA Operative Valerie Plame," Democracy Now!, July 6, 2005, www.democracynow .org/2005/7/6/karl_rove_again_linked_to_outting.

91   *"People we knew claimed to have sources":* Author interview with Joe Wilson.

91   *On an unspecified date in late August:* Stewart, *Tangled Webs,* p. 201.

91   *"Are you the one behind":* Ibid., p. 164.

92   *"I explained to Bush":* Rove, *Courage and Consequence,* p. 347.

92   *"Novak hadn't asked me":* Ibid.

92   *"[I]t sounded to me like":* Ibid.

92   *Bush sounded annoyed:* Ibid.

92   *But "if Rove said he didn't do it":* Stewart, *Tangled Webs,* p. 202.

92   *The Justice Department's counterespionage section:* McClellan, *What Happened,* p. 179.

93   *"I haven't heard that":* Ibid.

93   *"You weren't one of Novak's":* Ibid., p. 180.

93   *"You're right":* Ibid.

93   *"Karl spoke to Novak?":* Ibid., p. 181.

94   *"No," Rove replied:* Ibid.

94   *He knew the press might come:* Isikoff and Corn, *Hubris,* Kindle location 5870–5871.

94   *"two top White House officials":* Ibid., p. 319.

94   *The source added that the leaks:* Rove, *Courage and Consequence,* pp. 347–48.

94   *"I couldn't accept the idea":* Ibid., p. 348.

95   *Before meeting with the press:* McClellan, *What Happened,* p. 182.

95   *"I know," Card said:* Ibid., p. 183.

95   *McClellan told reporters:* Rove, *Courage and Consequence,* p. 348.

95   *"I have spoken with Karl":* Isikoff and Corn, *Hubris,* p. 322.

96   *"What I'd said was not true":* McClellan, *What Happened,* p. 3.

96   *"to assure him that he would protect":* Murray Waas, "The Phone Call," *National Journal,* May 27, 2006.

96   *"You're not going to get burned":* Ibid.

96   *"I'm not going to let that happen":* Ibid.

96   *"Nobody in the Bush administration":* Ibid.

97   *"During a long conversation":* Rove, *Courage and Consequence,* p. 348.

97   *Here is where the difference:* Ibid.

97   *"I've heard that, too":* Isikoff and Corn, *Hubris,* p. 265.

97   *"That means something different":* Waas, "The Phone Call."

98   *"Novak treated my offhanded":* Rove, *Courage and Consequence,* p. 348.

98   *"And while it had sounded to me":* Ibid., pp. 348–49.

98   *"to help in any way I can":* Stewart, *Tangled Webs,* p. 163.

99   *"I told him everything about my call":* Rove, *Courage and Consequence,* p. 350.

99 *He added that the issue:* Stewart, *Tangled Webs,* p. 164.

99 *"I had told them the truth":* Rove, *Courage and Consequence,* p. 351.

99 *"I decided I needed":* Ibid.

99 *he "needed to give this":* Ibid.

99 *It was good advice:* Ibid.

99 *"I know when somebody's trying":* "Novak on Plame Leak: A Pattern of Contradictions," Media Matters, August 5, 2005, http://mediamatters.org/research/200508050005.

100 *"It's possible that prosecutors":* Waas, "The Phone Call."

100 *"you almost have to literally":* Ibid.

100 *Their relationship went back:* Goodman and Scahill, "The Ashcroft-Rove Connection—The Ties That Blind."

100 *Representative John Conyers (D-Mich.) called:* "Conyers Calls for Investigation into Ashcroft's Role in CIA Leak Case," Democracy Now!, August 18, 2005, www.democracynow.org/2005/8/18/conyers_calls_for_investigation_into_ashcrofts.

101 *"it was a belated but welcome":* Wilson, *Fair Game,* p. 174.

101 *But to Rove:* Rove, *Courage and Consequence,* p. 221.

101 *"determined not to let White House":* Rove, *Courage and Consequence,* p. 351.

101 *"Talk about a power grab!":* Ibid., p. 353.

101 *"Nearly three years later":* Ibid.

101 *The appointee, Patrick Fitzgerald:* Ibid.

102 *"Fitzgerald was not easily intimidated":* Wilson, *Fair Game,* pp. 175–76.

102 *"cold, calculating, and relentless":* Rove, *Courage and Consequence,* p. 353.

102 *"constituted a shock too severe":* Stewart, *Tangled Webs,* p. 182.

102 *The grand jury had assembled:* Rove, *Courage and Consequence,* p. 354.

103 *"[I]t was Rove v. Fitzgerald":* Ibid.

103 *"Fitzgerald asked whether I had had contact":* Ibid., p. 355.

103 *Rove's simple response:* Ibid.

103 *"Remembering any particular":* Ibid., p. 357.

Chapter 7: All Roads Lead to Rove

104 *The family's finances, photos:* Rove, *Courage and Consequence,* p. 356.

104 *He faced hundreds of thousands:* Ibid., p. 357.

104 *Even in the heat of the Plame:* Bill Barrow, "Riley's Ratings Are Low: Governor Would Trail Moore, Siegelman in 2006 Race," *Mobile Press-Register,* November 16, 2003, p. 6.

104 *In May 2004, Siegelman:* Scott Horton, "The Alice Martin Perjury Inquiry," *Harper's,* September 8, 2007, www.harpers.org/archive/2007/09/hbc-90001140.

105 *"They kept looking for a hook":* Author interview with Doug Jones.

105 *The judge even suggested:* Scott Horton, "Prosecution Continues to Disintegrate in Siegelman Case," *Harper's,* June 26, 2007, www.harpers.org/archive/2007/06/hbc-90000386.

105 *Alice Martin's case against him:* G. Douglas Jones, Testimony Before the Subcommittee on Crime, Terrorism & Homeland Security, "Allegations of Selec-

tive Prosecution: The Erosion of Public Confidence in Our Federal Judicial System," October 23, 2007.

105 *"One of the critical indications":* Author interview with Scott Horton.

106 *as Senator Sheldon Whitehouse (D-RI) later pointed out:* Amanda Terkel, "Number of White House Officials Allowed to Intervene in DOJ Cases Jumps by 10,325 Percent," Think Progress, April 20, 2007, http://thinkprogress.org/politics/2007/04/20/12119/whitehouse-gonzales/.

106 *But Republican contributors in Mississippi:* "Allegations of Selective Prosecutions: The Erosion of Public Confidence in Our Federal Justice System," House of Representatives, Committee on the Judiciary, October 23, 2007, p. 27.

106 *Paul Minor made an interesting target:* Ibid.

107 *To be more precise:* Donald C. Shields and John F. Cragan, "The Political Profiling of Elected Democratic Officials: When Rhetorical Vision Participation Runs Amok," ePluribus Media, February 18, 2007, www.epluribusmedia.org/columns/2007/20070212_political_profiling.html.

107 *The targets of these investigations:* Ibid.

107 *What was most striking about:* Ibid.

107 *"The real Pulitzer Prize–winning story":* Ibid.

108 *"We believe that this tremendous disparity":* Ibid.

108 *"There would be one person":* Rove, *Courage and Consequence,* pp. 361–62.

108 *And so, once a week, beginning February:* Ibid., p. 362.

109 *"[T]he notion of widespread":* Michael Waldman and Justin Levitt, "The Myth of Voter Fraud," *Washington Post,* March 29, 2007, www.washingtonpost.com/wp-dyn/content/article/2007/03/28/AR2007032801969_pf.html.

109 *"Karl Rove's obsession with voter fraud":* Jason Leopold, "Bush Operative Pushes Voter-ID Law," AlterNet, May 14, 2008, www.alternet.org/news/85419/bush_operative_pushes_voter-id_law/?page=entire.

109 *"After examining the evidence":* Ibid.

109 *between October 2002 and September 2005:* "In the Courts," *New York Times,* April 12, 2007, www.nytimes.com/imagepages/2007/04/12/washington/12fraud_graphic.html.

110 *another 80 million who voted:* "2002 General Election Turnout Rates," United States Elections Project, updated December 28, 2011, http://elections.gmu.edu/Turnout_2002G.html.

110 *"The Truth About Voter Fraud":* "Allegations of Voter Fraud," Brennan Center for Justice, www.brennancenter.org/content/section/category/allegations_of_voter_fraud.

110 *according to the Brennan Center report:* Keesha Gaskins, "Jim Crow Legacy Continues Today," Brennan Center for Justice, April 12, 2012, www.brennancenter.org/blog/archives/jim_crow_legacy_continues_today/.

110 *Not surprisingly, Democratic blogs:* LeoT, "Proof that 'Voter Fraud' Is Jim Crow 2.0," Daily Kos, March 15, 2012, www.dailykos.com/story/2012/03/15/1074779/-Proof-that-voter-fraud-is-the-new-Jim-Crow.

110 *"shirked its legal responsibility":* Joseph Rich, "Bush's Long History of Tilting Justice," *Los Angeles Times,* March 29, 2007, www.latimes.com/news/opinion/commentary/la-oe-rich29mar29,0,1507657.story.

111 *"Then Kerry gave us the line":* Rove, *Courage and Consequence,* p. 380.

111 *"I was dumbfounded":* Ibid., p. 381.

111 *Media Matters:* "Search Results for Swift Boat Veterans for Truth," http://mediamatters.org/search/tag/swift_boat_veterans_for_truth?page=4.

111 *Factcheck.org:* "Republican-Funded Group Attacks Kerry's War Record," Factcheck.org, August 6, 2004, updated August 22, 2004, www.factcheck.org/republican-funded_group_attacks_kerrys_war_record.html.

111 *nine major newspapers:* "Only One of 15 Newspaper Editorial Boards Found Merit in Swift Boat Veterans' Charges: An MMRA Survey," Media Matters, August 25, 2004, http://mediamatters.org/research/200408250006.

111 *"The Swifties did a damned good job":* Rove, *Courage and Consequence,* p. 390.

111 *"Of course, I was blamed":* Ibid.

112 *He neglected to say, however:* "Swift Vets & POWs for Truth: Top Contributors, 2004 Cycle," www.opensecrets.org/527s/527cmtedetail_contribs.php?ein=201041228&cycle=2004.

112 *Early in the summer:* "The Brutal Genius of Karl Rove," *Australian Financial Review,* October 29, 2004.

113 *Among the documents:* Joe Hagan, "Dan Rather Was Right About George W. Bush," *Texas Monthly,* April 16, 2012; Joe Hagan, "Truth or Consequences," *Texas Monthly,* May 2012, www.texasmonthly.com/2012-05-01/feature.php.

114 *"it blew up in [Rather's] face":* Hagan, "Truth or Consequences."

114 *"alarm and anger at the smear":* Rove, *Courage and Consequence,* p. 392.

114 *"every single one of these memos":* Paul Coletti, "Harry 'Buckhead' Mac-Dougald: The Interview," Coletti.co.uk, September 28, 2006, http://coletti.co.uk/?p=41.

114 *"who had been part of meetings":* Sidney Blumenthal, "Dan Rather Stands by His Story," Salon, September 27, 2007, www.salon.com/2007/09/27/dan_rather_suit/singleton/.

115 *"Rove was the guy":* Author interview with Mary Mapes.

115 *"The blogs were actually wrong":* Hagan, "Truth or Consequences."

115 *All of which meant:* Phoenix Woman, "Remember 'Rathergate'? A Key Instigator Admits the Killiam Memos Can't Be Debunked via the 'Fonts' Argument," My FDL, April 17, 2012, http://my.firedoglake.com/phoenix/2012/04/17/remember-rathergate-a-key-instigator-admits-the-killian-memos-cant-be-debunked-via-the-fonts-argument/.

115 *"I looked at them":* Hagan, "Truth or Consequences."

116 *"Based on what we now know":* Jim Rutenberg and Mark J. Prendergast, "CBS Asserts It Was Misled by Ex-Officer on Bush Documents," *New York Times,* September 20, 2004, www.nytimes.com/2004/09/20/politics/campaign/20CND-GUAR.html?pagewanted=print&position=.

117 *"buried the story so deeply":* Hagan, "Dan Rather Was Right About George W. Bush."

117 *"unavailable in typewriters":* Rove, *Courage and Consequence,* p. 391.

117 *"The revelation that a liberal journalist":* Ibid., p. 392.

117 *"Karl Rove was the mastermind":* Mary Mapes, *Truth and Duty: The Press, the President, and the Privilege of Power* (New York: St. Martin's Press, 2006), p. 316.

Chapter 8: Lady Luck

118 *As election day approached:* Author interview with sources with firsthand knowledge of the secretary of state's computer system in 2004.

119 *"We all had a firm belief":* Author interview with Bob Mangan.

119 *"We were pushing more than":* Dave Flessner, "Chattanooga Takes Center Stage in Connecting Voters for President," *Chattanooga Times Free Press,* March 19, 2004.

119 *microtargeting:* Rove, *Courage and Consequence,* p. 366.

120 *"as many as 225 pieces":* Ibid.

120 *"No one piece of information":* Ibid.

120 *Rove didn't name the computer database:* Author interview with Jeff Averbeck.

120 *"Hearne traveled to every battleground":* Jason Leopold, "Bush Operative Pushes Voter-ID Law," May 14, 2008, www.consortiumnews.com/ Print/2008/051308b.html.

120 *challenging voter registration drives:* Ibid.

120 *In October, Chad Staton:* "Ohio Election Activities and Observations," Report to the United States House of Representatives Committee on House Administration, Congressman Robert W. Ney, Chairman, submitted by the American Center for Voting Rights, March 21, 2005.

121 *"to engage in pre-election 'caging' tactics":* "Preserving Democracy: What Went Wrong in Ohio, Status Report of the House Judiciary Committee Democratic Staff," January 5, 2005.

121 *It occurred on October 15, 2004:* Rove, *Courage and Consequence,* p. 354.

122 *"By refusing to divulge the names":* McClellan, *What Happened,* p. 256.

122 *The story began early:* Jeralyn, "Viveca Novak Takes Leave of Absence From Time," Talk Left, December 11, 2005, www.talkleft.com/story/2005 /12/11/564/87543.

123 *"was genuinely surprised":* "What Viveca Novak Told Fitzgerald," *Time,* December 19, 2005, p. 1, www.time.com/time/magazine/article/0,9171,1139820,00 .html.

123 *"Karl doesn't have a Cooper problem":* Ibid.

123 *Luskin looked surprised:* Ibid.

123 *"I had been pushing back":* Ibid.

123 *"Thank you," he said:* Ibid.

123 *"So Luskin told me":* Rove, *Courage and Consequence,* p. 434.

124 *Rove did exactly that:* Ibid.

124 *Rove was now a "subject":* Stewart, *Tangled Webs,* p. 209.

124 *Luskin had already gone through:* Rove, *Courage and Consequence,* p. 358.

124 *"a holy shit moment":* Stewart, *Tangled Webs,* p. 209.

125 *"mentally beaten to a pulp":* Ibid., p. 208.

125 *But according to Rove, Luskin:* Rove, *Courage and Consequence,* p. 358.

125 *"While I still had no recollection":* Ibid.

125 *After examining the email:* Ibid., pp. 358–59.

125 *Fitzgerald was almost "quivering":* Ibid.

126 *"I did not understand":* Ibid., pp. 359–60.

126 *Not surprisingly:* Tim Grieve, "Bush's Brain Testifies," Salon, October 15, 2004, www.salon.com/2004/10/15/rove_31/singleton/.

126 *"Instead of hiding behind the lawyers":* Ibid.

Chapter 9: As Goes Ohio

127 *By not sending out absentee ballots:* "Preserving Democracy: What Went Wrong in Ohio, Status Report of the House Judiciary Committee Democratic Staff," January 5, 2005.

127 *Though African-American himself:* Thistime, "Ohio Rejects 1000s of Voter Registration Applications Due to Paper Weight," Daily Kos, September 27, 2004, www.dailykos.com/story/2004/09/27/53984/-Ohio-rejects-1000s-of -voter-registration-applications-due-to-paper-weight.

128 *As a result, local newspapers:* Kennedy, "Was the 2004 Election Stolen?"

128 *Blackwell decided to restrict the use:* "Preserving Democracy: What Went Wrong in Ohio, Status Report of the House Judiciary Committee Democratic Staff," January 5, 2005, p. 5.

128 *"likely disenfranchised thousands":* Ibid., p. 6.

128 *Figuring that supporters:* Ralph Z. Hallow, "Ohio Fears Race Will Hinge on Provisional Ballots," *Washington Times,* November 1, 2004, p. A03.

128 *"Particularly in Ohio":* Hannity & Colmes, Fox News, November 1, 2004.

128 *"I'm glad I'm not in Ken Blackwell's shoes":* Carl Weiser, "Ohio Is 'Ground Zero' on GOP Breakfast Circuit," Gannett News Service, August 30, 2004.

129 *Monday, November 1, was supposed:* Rove, *Courage and Consequence,* p. 394.

129 *"I wondered what was going on":* Ibid., pp. 394–95.

129 *"I decided we would add":* Ibid., p. 395.

129 *The president and first lady:* Ibid.

129 *"I took the numbers down":* Ibid., pp. 395–96.

130 *Rove didn't know:* Ibid., p. 396.

130 *"Everyone put on":* Ibid.

130 *voter turnout in Ohio was at:* Christine Jindra, "Ohio Voter Turnout No Record, Falls Short of Predictions," Cleveland.com, November 5, 2008, http://blog.cleveland.com/openers/2008/11/at_least_52_million_ohioans.html.

130 *Throughout the state: Uncounted,* a documentary film directed by David Earn-hardt.

130 *Voters waited:* Ibid.

130 *At liberal Kenyon College:* Kennedy, "Was the 2004 Election Stolen?"

130 *"caused by intentional":* Andy Kroll, "GOPer Behind Ohio's Botched 2004 Election Eyes Senate Run," *Mother Jones,* April 21, 2011, http://motherjones .com/mojo/2011/04/ken-blackwell-ohio-brown-senate.

130 *"We immediately went down":* Author interview with Bob Fitrakis.

131 *But because there were no clearly:* Kennedy, "Was the 2004 Election Stolen?"

131 *To further hamper Democratic voting:* Nick Mottern, "The Mighty Texas Strike Force," *Free Press,* February 28, 2005, http://freepress.org/departments/ display/19/2005/1177.

131 *Officially, the group was tasked with:* Lawsuit filed by Democratic National Committee, moritzlaw.osu.edu/electionlaw/ . . . /petitionforrehearingenbanc .pdf.

132 *By this point, members of the National Election Pool:* "Preserving Democracy: What Went Wrong in Ohio, Status Report of the House Judiciary Committee Democratic Staff," January 5, 2005, p. 74.

132 *Kerry taking Ohio:* Ibid.

132 *Television broadcasters began speculating:* Steven F. Freeman, "The Unexplained Exit Poll Discrepancy," December 29, 2004.

132 *"Either the exit polls":* "Notes from Campaign Trail," Fox News, November 2, 2004.

133 *"What I found shocked":* Rove, *Courage and Consequence,* pp. 396–97.

133 *"I had gone from being sick":* Ibid.

133 *This was Rove's own private war room:* Ibid.

133 *"My computer screen featured":* Ibid.

134 *"All I had to do":* Ibid.

134 *"Most of the election returns":* Author interview with Robert Destro.

134 *At nine, Bob Mangan:* Author interview with Bob Mangan.

135 *"Even in the big Democratic strongholds":* Rove, *Courage and Consequence,* p. 398.

135 *At 9:55, Democratic consultant Paul Begala:* "2004 US Presidential Election: Florida," The Command Post, November 2, 2004, www.command-post .org/2004/2_archives/cat_florida.html.

135 *"How on God's Earth":* Ibid.

135 *With 77 percent of the vote counted:* "America Votes 2004," CNN Live Event/ Special, November 2, 2004, http://transcripts.cnn.com/TRANSCRIPTS /0411/02/se.06.html.

135 *"And if the president carries":* Ibid.

136 *"Almost instantly, our load":* Author interview with technician.

Chapter 10: 11:14 P.M.

137 *Election day was over:* Email to author from Bob Fitrakis containing county-by-county election reports as submitted for *Moss v. Bush.*

137 *Three minutes later, Fox News:* Rove, *Courage and Consequence,* p. 401.

137 *"I've got a phone to my ear":* Ibid.

138 *The announcement could wait:* Ibid., p. 402.

138 *In 2005, the investigation:* "Preserving Democracy: What Went Wrong in Ohio, Status Report of the House Judiciary Committee Democratic Staff," January 5, 2005.

139 *"the tallied margin differs":* Freeman, "The Unexplained Exit Poll Discrepancy." *"geniuses in New Jersey":* Rove, *Courage and Consequence,* p. 397.

139 *"systematic fraud or mistabulation":* Freeman, "The Unexplained Exit Poll Discrepancies."

139 *In recent years, other polling experts:* Nate Silver, "Ten Reasons Why You Should Ignore Exit Polls," FiveThirtyEight: Politics Done Right, November 4,

2008, www.fivethirtyeight.com/2008/11/ten-reasons-why-you-should-ignore
-exit.html.

139 *Mark Blumenthal, polling editor:* Mark Blumenthal, "Mystery Pollster," November 17, 2004, www.mysterypollster.com/main/2004/11/the_freeman_ pap.html.

139 *argues that exit polls have a history:* Ibid.

140 *"I have never argued":* Ibid.

141 *"If you think about manipulating":* Author interview with Cliff Arnebeck.

141 *"They had to have formulas":* Ibid.

142 *"You are dealing with millions":* Ibid.

142 *"SmarTech was just a mirror site":* Author interview with Robert Destro.

143 *Connell testified that Ohio:* "Transcript of the Testimony of Michael L. Connell, taken on November 3, 2008, *King Lincoln Bronzeville Neighborhood Association et al. vs. Ohio Secretary of State Jennifer Brunne, et al.*

143 *"Anytime you are hauling traffic":* Author interview with Harry Hursti.

143 *"would be cause to launch":* "Declaration of Stephen Spoonamore," filed on September 17, 2008, for *King Lincoln Bronzeville v. Ohio Secretary of State Jennifer Brunner.*

143 *"This computer placement":* Ibid.

144 *"While he has not admitted":* Ibid.

145 *He is also the only person:* Richard Hayes Phillips, *Witness to a Crime* (Rome, NY: Canterbury Press, 2008).

145 *"All fourteen of the counties":* Author interview with Richard Hayes Phillips.

146 *In 2000, Al Gore got:* Phillips, *Witness to a Crime,* p. 26.

146 *"I can't believe it":* Juan Gonzalez, "Ohio Tally Fit for Ukraine," *New York Daily News,* November 30, 2004.

146 *But a malfunction:* "Preserving Democracy: What Went Wrong in Ohio, Status Report of the House Judiciary Committee Democratic Staff," January 5, 2005, p. 83.

146 *The answer, Ohio voters:* Phillips, *Witness to a Crime,* p. 113.

147 *This practice of "collocation":* James Q. Jacobs, "The 2004 Presidential Election: Cuyahoga County Analysis," April 4, 2008, http://jqjacobs.net/politics/ohio .html.

147 *"Voters were being told":* "Voting Errors Cited in Cleveland Area," Boston.com, December 11, 2004, http://articles.boston.com/2004-12-11/news/29203079_1_ voting-errors-wrong-precinct-voting-place.

147 *"their votes would be shifted":* Author interview with Richard Hayes Phillips.

148 *"I have no question":* Author interview with Brett Rapp.

148 *"It appears that hundreds":* "Preserving Democracy: What Went Wrong in Ohio, Status Report of the House Judiciary Committee Democratic Staff," January 5, 2005.

148 *"Those ballots were not altered":* Author interview with Richard Hayes Phillips.

149 *"to corrupt the election":* Author interview with Brett Rapp.

149 *"If you took exactly":* Ibid.

150 *"each precinct doesn't":* Ibid.

150 *"ballots cast for Kerry":* Author interview with Cliff Arnebeck.

150 *in heavily Republican Perry County:* "Preserving Democracy: What Went

Wrong in Ohio, Status Report of the House Judiciary Committee Democratic Staff," January 5, 2005.

151 *In one precinct, Gahanna Ward 1:* Ibid.

151 *touch screens had been programmed:* Email communication from Richard Hayes Phillips.

151 *"I saw what happened":* "Preserving Democracy: What Went Wrong in Ohio, Status Report of the House Judiciary Committee Democratic Staff," January 5, 2005.

151 *"The Secretary of State doesn't":* Author interview with Robert Destro.

152 *"have been unable to determine":* Greg Gordon, "Computer Expert Denies Knowledge of '04 Vote Rigging in Ohio," McClatchy Newspapers, November 3, 2008, www.mcclatchydc.com/2008/11/03/55233/computer-expert-denies-knowledge.html#storylink=cpy.

152 *"Kerry heard all the disquieting":* Robert Parry, "Kerry Suspects Election 2004 Was Stolen," Consortiumnews.com, November 6, 2005, www.consortium news.com/2005/110505.html.

153 *"Some of these boards did not":* Albert Salvato, "Ohio Recount Gives a Smaller Margin to Bush," *New York Times,* December 29, 2004, www.nytimes .com/2004/12/29/politics/29ohio.html.

Chapter 11: Drawing an Inside Straight

154 *In the immediate aftermath:* Mark Crispin Miller, "None Dare Call It Stolen: Ohio, the Election, and America's Servile Press," *Harper's,* August 2005, http://harpers.org/archive/2005/08/0080696.

154 *"Tons of people":* Author interview with Bob Fitrakis.

154 *"Blackwell made Katherine Harris":* Robert F. Kennedy Jr., "Was the 2004 Election Stolen?," Common Dreams, June 1, 2006, www.commondreams.org/views06/0601-34.htm.

155 *"unprecedented long lines":* "Preserving Democracy: What Went Wrong in Ohio, Status Report of the House Judiciary Committee Democratic Staff," January 5, 2005, p. 4.

155 *"Blackwell's decision to restrict":* Ibid., p. 5.

155 *"the Republican Party's pre-election 'caging' tactics":* Ibid., p. 6.

155 Triad *"essentially admitted":* Ibid., p. 7.

156 *Rove led the way:* Allegra Hartley, "Timeline: How the U.S. Attorneys Were Fired," *U.S. News & World Report,* March 21, 2007, www.usnews.com/usnews/news/articles/070321/21attorneys-timeline_3.htm.

157 *"The vast majority of U.S. Attorneys":* Email, Kyle Sampson to David Leitch, January 9, 2005, 7:34 p.m., Re: Question from Karl Rove, ibid.

157 *"That said, if Karl thinks":* Laurie Kellman, "GOP Support for Gonzales Erodes Further," *Washington Post,* March 15, 2007.

157 *"His first speech to us":* David Bowermaster, "Charges May Result from Firings, Say Two Former U.S. Attorneys," *Seattle Times,* May 9, 2007.

157 *Jill Simpson spoke to Rob Riley:* House interview of Dana Jill Simpson, pp. 49–51.

157 *As Simpson later testified:* Ibid.

158 *"Fuller would hang Don Siegelman":* Ibid., p. 56.

158 *according to Simpson's sworn testimony:* Greg Farrell, "Former HealthSouth CEO Scrushy Turns Televangelist," *USA Today,* October 25, 2004, www.usa today.com/money/industries/health/2004-10-25-scrushy-cover_x.htm.

158 *"They had come up with an idea":* House interview of Dana Jill Simpson, p. 85.

159 *"[T]he FBI and the feds":* Doug Jones testimony, p. 9.

159 *"For the first time it appeared":* Ibid.

159 *Finally, in October 2005:* "Allegations of Selective Prosecutions," p. 8.

159 *"It's a joke":* Adam Nossiter, "Ex-Governor Says Conviction Was Political": *New York Times,* June 27, 2007, www.nytimes.com/2007/06/27/us/27alabama .html?ref=us.

159 *No fewer than 146 contributors:* Scott Horton, "CBS: More Prosecutorial Misconduct in Siegelman Case," *Harper's,* February 2008, http://harpers.org/archive/2008/02/hbc-90002487.

160 *The scene is best recounted:* Alexander, *Machiavelli's Shadow,* p. 187.

160 *"[Vitter] could have been talking":* Ibid., pp. 187–88.

161 *"I could see where Rove was going":* Ibid., p. 189.

161 *But not that well:* Sidney Blumenthal, *How Bush Rules: Chronicles of a Radical Regime* (Princeton: Princeton University Press, 2006), p. 273.

161 *A year later:* Adam Nossiter, "Outlines Emerge for a Shaken New Orleans, *New York Times,* August 27, 2006, www.nytimes.com/2006/08/27/us/ nationalspecial/27orleans.html?_r=1.

161 *Six out of nine . . . Eighty-four percent:* John Esterbrook, "New Orleans: One Year Later," *60 Minutes,* January 11, 2009, www.cbsnews.com/stories /2006/08/25/60minutes/main1936523.shtml.

161 *All of which added up:* Sidney Blumenthal, "We'll Go No More a-Rove-ing," Salon, August 13, 2007, www.salon.com/2007/08/13/karl_rove/singleton/.

161 *"Karl Rove became interested":* Kate Sheppard, "'Heckuva Job Brownie' Speaks," *Mother Jones,* www.motherjones.com/environment/2011/06/heckuva -job-brownie-deadly-indifference.

162 *In addition to Katrina:* Rove, *Courage and Consequence,* p. 438.

162 *But this time testifying:* Ibid.

162 *"They didn't know what Luskin":* Ibid.

162 *"The decision not to charge Karl Rove":* Isikoff and Corn, *Hubris,* p. 400.

163 *"ultimately cooperated and told":* Murray Waas, "CIA Leak Case: Why Rove Testified for a Fifth Time," *National Journal,* April 28, 2006, http://murray waas.net/id85.html.

163 *"Will it make the difference":* "What Viveca Novak Told Fitzgerald."

163 *"I hadn't intended to tip":* Ibid., www.time.com/time/magazine/article/0 ,9171,1139820-2,00.html.

164 *"You've turned my world":* Stewart, *Tangled Webs,* pp. 228–29.

164 *"a piffle":* David Brooks, "A Guide for the Perplexed," *New York Times,* August 31, 2006, www.scooterlibby.org/news/Read.aspx?ID=152.

164 *"abuse of power":* Debra J. Saunders, "Plame Case Was Gossip, Not a Smear," *San Francisco Chronicle,* August 31, 2006, www.scooterlibby.org/news/Read .aspx?ID=165.

164 *"The disclosures about Armitage":* Christopher Hitchins, "Plame Out,"
Slate, August 29, 2006, www.slate.com/articles/news_and_politics/fighting_
words/2006/08/plame_out.html.

165 *"We have the final word":* "What You Aren't Hearing About Scooter Libby,"
www.scooterlibby.org/nothearing/.

Chapter 12: The Verdict

166 *"I'm not the slightest bit":* Rick Lyman, "In Race to Lead Alabama, It's Politics
as Usual," *New York Times,* March 22, 2006, www.nytimes.com/2006/03/22/
national/22alabama.html?scp=criti23&sq=Siegelman&st=nyt.

166 *As the* Birmingham News *reported:* Kim Chandler, "Siegelman, Scrushy Face
Corruption Charges Indicted Again," *Birmingham News,* p. 1A.

166 *"Every bank record":* Jones affidavit, p. 9.

167 *Even if one accepted the premise:* Ibid.

167 *"Bailey had said he walked":* Author interview with Jones.

167 *According to* 60 Minutes: Horton: "CBS: More Prosecutorial Misconduct in
Siegelman Case."

167 *But the defense team became:* Scott Horton, "An Interview with Legal Ethicist David Luban Regarding Judge Mark Fuller," *Harper's,* August 2007, www
.harpers.org/archive/2007/08/hbc-90000708.

168 *"rather fanciful theory":* Rove, *Courage and Consequence,* p. 506.

168 *But Doss was awarded a contract:* Horton, "Interview with David Luban."

168 *"To have deliberated":* Bob Johnson, "Siegelman Jury Continues Deliberations," *Decatur Daily,* June 22, 2006, http://archive.decaturdaily.com/decatur
daily/news/060622/jury.shtml.

169 *Two days later, however:* Mike Linn, "Siegelman Case Put in Limbo," *Montgomery Advertiser,* June 23, 2006.

169 *"Obviously, another trial":* Kim Chandler, "Jury Deadlocks After Six Days,"
Birmingham News, June 23, 2006, p. 1A.

169 *According to Cloud Miller:* Mike Linn, "Siegelman Trial Analyzed," *Montgomery Advertiser,* June 25, 2006, p. 1A.

169 *"no interest in continuing"* . . . *"last resort":* Kim Chandler, "Corruption Trial
Jury Still Deadlocked," *Birmingham News,* June 28, 2006, p. 1B.

169 *Fuller gave the jurors a second Allen charge:* Kim Chandler, "Siegelman Jury
Still Deliberating After 10 Days," *Birmingham News,* June 29, 2006, p. 2B.

169 *"It shocked me":* Author interview with Don Siegelman.

169 *"The judge said that he could keep us":* David Fiderer, "A Smoking Gun
Incriminates the Judge Who Ruled Against Don Siegelman," Huffington
Post, July 29, 2008, www.huffingtonpost.com/david-fiderer/a-smoking-gun
-incriminate_b_115720.html?page=2.

170 *"The amount of backstabbing":* Eric Lichtblau, "E-Mail Reveals Rove's Key
Role in '06 Dismissals," *New York Times,* August 11, 2009, www.nytimes
.com/2009/08/12/us/politics/12firings.html.

170 *a "very agitated" Karl Rove:* Ibid.

171 *indictment against Dr. Cyril Wecht:* Charlie Deitch, The Wecht Files," *Pitts-*

burgh City Paper, December 20, 2007, www.pittsburghcitypaper.ws/pittsburgh
/the-wecht-files/Content?oid=1339525.

171 *former attorney general Richard Thornburgh:* "Allegations of Selective Prosecutions," p. 25.

172 *"I was told by my probation officer":* Author interview with Don Siegelman.

174 *"One of the critical indications":* Author interview with Scott Horton.

Chapter 13: The Vanishing

175 *"More important than money":* Rove, *Courage and Consequence,* p. 494.

175 *"Don't you understand":* Ibid.

176 *"That was enough":* Ibid., p. 495.

176 *But Rove's ordeal:* Dan Froomkin, "The Rovian Theory," *Washington Post,*
March 23, 2007, www.washingtonpost.com/wp-dyn/content/blog/2007/03/23/
BL2007032301067.html

176 *"Now we are learning":* Paul Fidalgo, "Leahy Plays the Watergate Card, Has
Subpoenas in His Deck," ABC News, April 12, 2007, http://abcnews.go.com/
blogs/politics/2007/04/leahy_plays_the/.

177 *"Like the famous 18-minute gap":* Ibid.

177 *"about 50":* Michael Abramowitz, "Rove E-Mail Sought by Congress May
Be Missing," *Washington Post,* April 13, 2007, www.washingtonpost.com/wp
-dyn/content/article/2007/04/12/AR2007041202408.html.

177 *But when the House Committee:* "Investigation of Possible Presidential
Records Act Violations," U.S. House of Representatives, Committee on Oversight and Government Reform Majority Staff, June 2007.

177 *Rove's emails were missing:* Letter from Henry A. Waxman to Robert Gates,
April 12, 2007.

178 *"Mr. Kelner did not give any explanation":* Ibid.

178 *"revelations about the destruction":* Letter from Melanie Sloan to Patrick
Fitzgerald, April 13, 2007.

178 *In August 2006:* United States District Court for the Southern District of Ohio,
Eastern Division, *King Lincoln Bronzeville Neighborhood Association et al. v.
J. Kenneth Blackwell et al.,* Case 2:06-cv-00745-ALM-TPK .

178 *Brunner criticized Blackwell:* "Ohio's Elections Process Debated," *Mansfield
News Journal,* September 13, 2006, p. A3.

179 *"umpire who wore a jersey":* Ibid.

179 *New Media's clients included:* New Media's "Client Hall of Fame," http://web
.archive.org/web/20070321113057/http://www.technomania.com/clienthallof
fame.asp.

179 *Clients for GovTech Solutions:* Malia Rulon, "Ohio-Based Web Design Company Seeks to Give GOP Candidates the Edge," Associated Press, August 24,
2004.

180 *"fraudulent poseur":* http://markcrispinmiller.com/2012/02/new-details-on
-bushcheneys-stolen-re-election-and-what-looks-like-the-murder-of-mike
-connell/.

180 *"By the time I met Mike":* Author interview with Stephen Spoonamore.

181 *"I walked by one room"*: Author interview with Jennifer Brunner.

183 *Judge Marbley issued an order: King Lincoln Bronzeville Neighborhood Association et al. v. J. Kenneth Blackwell et al.*

183 *"Failure to preserve the unused ballots"*: Phillips, *Witness to a Crime*, p. 389.

183 *invalidate votes for John Kerry*: Jon Craig and Allison D'Aurora, "2004 Ballot Not Preserved," *Cincinnati Enquirer*, August 12, 2007.

183 *"the duty to preserve"*: Phillips, *Witness to a Crime*, p. 386.

183 *"a shred of evidence"*: Ibid., p. 387

183 *"received verbal instructions"*: Ibid., p. 388.

184 *"just plumb ran out"*: Craig and D'Aurora, "2004 Ballot Not Preserved."

184 *"The extent of the destruction"*: Steven Rosenfeld, "In Violation of Federal Law, Ohio's 2004 Presidential Election Records Are Destroyed or Missing," AlterNet, www.alternet.org/story/58328/.

184 *Brunner issued a report on the electronic*: Jet Gardner, "Two Years Later, Ohio Finally Admits to Security Problems with Voting Machines," Blogcritics, December 14, 2007, http://blogcritics.org/politics/article/two-years-later-ohio-finally-admits/.

184 *"On the one hand"*: Rosenfeld, "In Violation of Federal Law, Ohio's 2004 Presidential Election Records Are Destroyed or Missing."

185 *"Nothing like spending a few days"*: Rove, *Courage and Consequence*, p. 495.

185 *On his last day of work*: Ibid., p. 500.

186 *"It would be a mistake"*: David Broder, "Don't Expect Karl Rove to Just Fade into the Sunset," *Salt Lake Tribune*, August 23, 2007.

186 *"I actually took Mike's hand"*: Simon Worrall, *Cybergate: Was the White House Stolen by Cyberfraud?* (2012), Kindle location 440–46.

186 *"He said he got involved"*: Author interview with Stephen Spoonamore.

187 *"had the correct placement"*: Declaration of Stephen Spoonamore, September 17, 2008, *King Lincoln Bronzeville Neighborhood Association et al. v. J. Kenneth Blackwell et al.*

187 *"While he has not admitted to wrongdoing"*: Ibid.

187 *"Spoonamore made it his mission"*: Author interview with Bob Fitrakis.

188 *"He would never interfere"*: Simon Worrall, "The Mysterious Death of Bush's Cyber-Guru," *Maxim*, February 2010, www.newworldorderreport.com/News/tabid/266/ID/4988/The-Mysterious-Death-of-Bushs-Cyber-Guru.aspx.

188 *"I was amazed at how at peace"*: Author interview with Shannon Walton.

189 *"I know the game"*: Author interview with Cliff Arnebeck.

189 *"Connell will talk"*: Ibid.

190 *"a political prisoner"*: Anthony Day, "A Story That Should Not Have Been Told," *Los Angeles Times*, November 8, 1996, http://articles.latimes.com/1996-11-08/news/ls-62399_1_mark-singer.

190 *"the longest correction"*: Ibid.

190 *Ultimately, it turned out*: James Warren, "'Speedway Bomber' Sitting Pretty," *Chicago Tribune*, March 13, 1994, http://articles.chicagotribune.com/1994-03-13/features/9403130267_1_brett-kimberlin-prison-convicted.

190 *"Originally, I took the bait"*: James Warren, "A Reporter Confesses: He Was Conned by a Con," *Chicago Tribune*, October 4, 1996.

191 *"One possibility is"*: Author interview with Cliff Arnebeck.

192 *"I point-blank asked"*: Author interview with Heather Connell.

192 *"while he doesn't know whether"*: Rebecca Abrahams, "White House Emails: The Missing Link?" Huffington Post, October 21, 2008, www.huffingtonpost .com/rebecca-abrahams/white-house-emails-the-mi_b_136653.html.

193 *"in danger from Rove"*: Author interview with Cliff Arnebeck.

193 *"I told him of the high regard"*: Ibid.

193 *"a positive interaction"*: Ibid.

193 *"He really put me through the hoops"*: Ibid.

193 *"No," Connell replied*: Michael L. Connell testimony, November 3, 2008, *King Lincoln Bronzeville Neighborhood Association et al. v. Ohio Secretary of State Jennifer Brunner et al.*, 2:06 CV 745.

193 *"There had been a problem"*: Ibid.

194 *"I was not involved"*: Ibid.

194 *the Connell testimony was anticlimactic*: Gordon, "Computer Expert Denies Knowledge of '04 Vote Rigging in Ohio."

194 *Connell "denied any knowledge"*: Ibid.

195 *"That cross system communications protocol"*: Email from Cliff Arnebeck, May 16, 2012.

195 *"I interpreted it as him saying"*: Author interview with Bob Fitrakis.

195 *"I saw Connell as a dead man walking"*: Ibid.

196 *"Building a Coalition"*: David Frum, "Building a Coalition, Forgetting to Rule," *New York Times*, August 14, 2007.

197 *"Would you like a standard briefing"*: NTSB Identification: CEN09FA099, 14 CFR Part 91: General Aviation, Accident occurred Friday, December 19, 2008, in North Canton, OH, Probable Cause Approval Date: 01/28/2010, Aircraft: PIPER PA-32R, registration: N9299N. Injuries: 1 Fatal. www.ntsb.gov/ aviationquery/brief.aspx?ev_id=20081223X12815&key=.

197 *After about twenty minutes*: Worrall, "The Mysterious Death of Bush's Cyber-Guru."

197 *"moderate chop"*: Ibid.

198 *But according to a report*: NTSB Identification: CEN09FA099.

198 *"Uh, can we do a three sixty"*: Ibid.

198 *The plane was in a spiral dive*: "Republican IT Guru Dies in Plane Crash," CBS News, February 11, 2009, www.cbsnews.com/stories/2008/12/23/national/ main4684431.shtml#ixzz1QbiJR3Fm.

199 *"November nine nine"*: NTSB Identification: CEN09FA099.

199 *According to a report released by the National Transportation Safety Board*: Ibid.

199 *"a high likelihood"*: Ibid.

200 *"installed AMD"*: Anonymous document furnished to author by attorney Cliff Arnebeck.

200 *"revealed no anomalies"*: NTSB Identification: CEN09FA099.

200 *"an assassination"*: Author interview with Cliff Arnebeck.

200 *Spoonamore said Karl Rove had murdered*: Author interview with Stephen Spoonamore.

200 *Connell's sister, Shannon, believed*: Worrall, *Cybergate*, Kindle location 762.

200 *Project Censored called*: "Non Profit Calls for Federal Criminal Investiga-

tion into the Death of George Bush Technology Expert Michael Connell," www.prnewswire.com/news-releases/non-profit-calls-for-federal-criminal -investigation-into-the-death-of-george-bush-technology-expert-michael -connell-84465217.html.

200 *"more serious than Watergate":* Worrall, *Cybergate,* Kindle location 762.

Chapter 14: Back from the Dead

202 *He was depleted physically:* Rove, *Courage and Consequence,* p. 504.

202 *"Nobody who's come of age":* Horton, "Six Questions for Paul Alexander."

203 *"I enjoyed a new experience":* Rove, *Courage and Consequence,* pp. 511–12.

203 *"Karl is up to his eyeballs":* "Rove Developing Outside Groups to Help GOP in Fall," *National Journal,* April 18, 2008.

203 *"It's always sad to see":* Mike Allen, "Karl Rove Granted Divorce in Texas," Politico, December 29, 2009, www.politico.com/news/stories/1209/31036 .html.

204 *"is susceptible of no other interpretation":* Jeffrey Toobin, "Money Unlimited," *New Yorker,* May 21, 2012, www.newyorker.com/reporting/2012/05/21 /120521fa_fact_toobin?currentPage=all.

204 *one of "modest importance":* Ibid.

204 *changed the American electoral process:* Ibid.

204 *"an epic disaster":* Ibid.

205 *"Do you think the Constitution":* Ibid.

205 *regulate the contents of books:* Ibid.

205 *"Speech is an essential mechanism":* Ibid.

205 *"By taking the right to speak":* Ibid.

206 *The McCain-Feingold Act:* Elizabeth Drew, "Can We Have a Democratic Election?" *New York Review of Books,* February 23, 2012, www.nybooks.com/ articles/archives/2012/feb/23/can-we-have-democratic-election/?pagination =false&printpage=true.

206 *"He dislikes party elements":* Author interview with Roger Stone.

207 *"Clearly there was a tremendous amount":* Jim Kuhnhenn, "Midterm Elections 2010," Huffington Post, October 26, 2010, www.huffingtonpost.com /2010/10/27/midterm-elections-2010-an_n_774585.html.

207 *"We need to uptick our image":* Sara K. Smith, "Michael Steele to Reinvent GOP with Hip-Hop and Youthiness," Wonkette, February 19, 2009, http://wonkette .com/406404/michael-steele-to-reinvent-gop-with-hip-hop-and-youthiness.

208 *"I'm the chairman. Deal with it":* Philip Rucker and Chris Cillizza, "Steele's Book Release, Fiery Rhetoric Fuel Dissatisfaction with GOP," *Washington Post,* January 9, 2010.

208 *Donors were irate:* Jeanne Cummings, "Steele's Spending Spree Angers Donors," Politico, February 23, 2010.

208 *"Stuff it," he said:* Alex Koppelman, "Michael Steele Is a Hip Cat, You Dig" Salon, February 19, 2009.

208 *The coup de grâce came:* Jonathan Strong, "High Flyer: RNC Chairman Steele Suggested Buying Private Jet with GOP Funds," Daily Caller, March 29, 2010,

http://dailycaller.com/2010/03/29/high-flyer-rnc-chairman-steele-suggested
-buying-private-jet-with-gop-funds/#ixzz1vPWSGDxm.

209 *phone sex with a "nasty girl":* Ralph Z. Hallow, "Bondage Club, 'Nasty Girl'
Star in Steele's Horrible Week," *Washington Times,* April 2, 2010, p. A1.

209 *In early 2010:* Stone, "Bush's Brains, Rove + Gillespie Raise GOP Bucks."

209 *"I've hinted at this before":* "Conservative Leader: Don't Donate to RNC,"
UPI, April 1, 2010.

209 *"Michael Steele should resign":* Hallow, "Bondage Club, 'Nasty Girl' Star in
Steele's Horrible Week."

209 *"Sure it does," he said:* "Michael Steele Bondage-Gate Fallout," Huffington Post,
May 31, 2010, updated May 25, 2011, www.huffingtonpost.com/2010/03/31/
michael-steele-bondage-ga_n_520185.html#s77305&title=Rove_The_Incident.

209 *a Crossroads spokesman emailed:* Kenneth P. Vogel, "Karl Rove's Fight
Club," Politico, March 27, 2012, www.politico.com/news/stories/0312/74506
.html#ixzz1w7hx4Kx4.

210 *"The Republican Party's best-connected political operatives":* Allen and Vogel,
"Karl Rove, Republican Party Plot Vast Network to Reclaim Power."

210 *"When Karl didn't feel":* Author interview with Wayne Slater.

211 *"It is breathtaking in its scope":* Michael Waldman, "Bigger Than Bush v.
Gore," January 21, 2010, www.brennancenter.org/content/resource/bigger_
than_bush_v_gore/.

212 *"The right-wing base of the Republican party":* Steven Loeb, "Karl Rove:
Donald Trump Is Discrediting the Entire Party," Business Insider, March
31, 2011, www.businessinsider.com/donald-trump-oreilly-karl-rove-video
-2011-3#ixzz1wC1iNS63.

212 *No single force:* Jane Mayer, "Covert Operations," *New Yorker,* August 30,
2010, www.newyorker.com/reporting/2010/08/30/100830fa_fact_mayer#ixzz
1vzBZ8bUI.

212 *only eight thousand registered members:* Ibid.

213 *"What they don't say":* Ibid.

213 *David Koch took heart:* Ibid.

213 *First, Rove put together biweekly meetings:* Kenneth P. Vogel, "Karl Rove vs.
the Koch Brothers," Politico, October 10, 2011, www.politico.com/news/
stories/1011/65504.html#ixzz1vzcSXzGT.

213 *"It was very coordinated":* Ibid.

213 *Rove got American Crossroads to support:* Hagan, "Goddangit, Baby, We're
Making Good Time."

214 *By September, American Crossroads:* "Bush 'Architect' Karl Rove Behind Pro-
Angle Front Group," States News Service, September 7, 2010.

214 *"There were a lot of nutty things":* "Karl Rove Questions Christine O'Donnell's
'Serious Character Problems,'" *Hannity,* Fox News, September 14, 2010.

214 *"I just finished watching Karl Rove":* Evan McMorris-Santoro, "Conservatives Trash Karl Rove After He Insists O'Donnell Says 'Nutty Things,'"
Talking Points Memo, September 15, 2010, http://tpmdc.talkingpointsmemo
.com/2010/09/conservatives-trash-karl-rove-after-he-insists.php.

214 *"the hierarchy of the political machine":* Keach Hagey, "GOP's Struggles Play
out on Fox," Politico, September 17, 2010.

215 *"a quick woodshed moment"*: McMorris-Santoro, "Conservatives Trash Karl Rove After He Insists O'Donnell Says 'Nutty Things.'"

215 *Then, in one week in October alone:* Molly Ball, "Angle Rakes in $3.5M More," Politico, October 25, 2010.

215 *"Karl Rove is back"*: Kenneth P. Vogel, "Rove the Bogeyman Is Back," Politico, September 30, 2010.

215 *erased "any doubts"*: "Rove-Gillespie Group Has Spent $14 Million on Senate Races," Frontrunner, October 6, 2010.

215 *"It's a two-fer"*: Glenn Thrush and Kenneth P. Vogel, "W.H. 'Out of the Fetal Position,'" Politico, October 12, 2010.

215 *"This kind of money in 2010"*: "The $4 Billion Election," OpenSecrets.org, October 28, 2010, www.commondreams.org/headline/2010/10/28-4.

216 *gave $7 million:* Kenneth P. Vogel, "Secrecy Flip-Flop Fueled Crossroads," Politico, October 25, 2010.

216 *donated $2.3 million:* Kenneth P. Vogel, "GOP's Big Money Men Return," Politico, September 24, 2010.

216 *anonymous donations through Crossroads GPS:* Vogel, "Secrecy Flip-Flop Fueled Crossroads."

216 *"Rove's American Crossroads":* Jonathan D. Salant and Traci McMillan, "Rove-Backed Groups, U.S. Chamber Build Winning Record in Midterm Election," Bloomberg News, November 4, 2010.

Chapter 15: Last Man Standing

218 *"It's hard to imagine":* Tim Grieve, "Karl Rove to Resign," Salon, August 13, 2007, www.salon.com/2007/08/13/rove1/.

219 *"Now we're discovering":* Tim Dickinson, "How Roger Ailes Built the Fox News Fear Factory," *Rolling Stone,* May 25, 2011, www.rollingstone .com/politics/news/how-roger-ailes-built-the-fox-news-fear-factory -20110525#ixzz1w68NDo6v.

219 *"You can't run":* "The Elephant in the Green Room," *New York,* http://nymag .com/news/media/roger-ailes-fox-news-2011-5/index1.html.

220 *There was Levi Johnston:* Russell Goldman, "Levi Johnston to Name Baby Daughter After a Gun," ABC News, May 2, 2012, http://abcnews.go.com/ blogs/politics/2012/05/levi-johnston-to-name-baby-daughter-after-a-gun/.

220 *Because Fox's candidate-commentators:* Jonathan Martin and Keach Hagey, "Fox Primary: Complicated, Contractual," Politico, September 27, 2010, http://dyn.politico.com/printstory.cfm?uuid=506E9A42-0184-3BF7-6F2F8 D12EC95F5F3.

220 *Fox "indicated that once":* Ibid.

221 *Then, in March 2011:* Daniel Foster, "Fox News 'Suspends' Gingrich, Santorum," *National Review,* March 2, 2011, www.nationalreview.com/ corner/261117/fox-news-suspends-gingrich-santorum-daniel-foster#.

221 *Palin got a free ride:* Ben Dimiero, "The Sarah Palin/Fox News Debacle," Media Matters, October 6, 2011, http://mediamatters.org/blog/201110060008.

221 *"People are attracted to Fox News":* Martin and Hagey, "Fox Primary: Complicated, Contractual."

221 *"was an idiot":* "The Elephant in the Green Room."

221 *Enter Karl Rove:* Author interview with Roger Stone.

221 *"With all due candor":* Alex Spillius, "Karl Rove Questions Sarah Palin's Suitability for President," *Telegraph,* October 27, 2010, www.telegraph.co.uk/news/worldnews/us-politics/8090279/Karl-Rove-questions-Sarah-Palins-suitability-for-president.html.

222 *"Did you see that?":* "Is Palin's Series a Reality Show?" Politico, November 1, 2010, www.politico.com/blogs/onmedia/1110/Is_Palins_series_a_reality_show.html.

222 *"Karl has planted":* "What Rove Knows," *News & Observer,* September 8, 2011.

222 *"He's a joke candidate":* "Rove: Trump a 'Joke Candidate,' Part of the 'Nutty Right,'" Fox News, April 16, 2011, http://nation.foxnews.com/donald-trump/2011/04/16/rove-trump-joke-candidate-part-nutty-right.

223 *"He's off there":* Ibid.

223 *"It's not just your own":* http://dailycaller.com/2011/05/23/rove-on-herman-talk-radio-guy-in-atlanta-wont-be-next-huckabee/#ixzz1wC9h2inq.

223 *"strong executive experience":* Jonathan Stein, "Mitt Romney Would Be Karl Rove's Handpicked VP," *Mother Jones,* August 28, 2008, www.motherjones.com/mojo/2008/08/mitt-romney-would-be-karl-roves-handpicked-vp.

224 *"Rick Perry Looks to Leave":* David Paul, "Rick Perry Looks to Leave Mitt Romney and Karl Rove in the Dust," Huffington Post, August 18, 2011, www.huffingtonpost.com/david-paul/rick-perry-looks-to-leave_b_929984.html.

224 *On August 16, Rove entered:* "Rove: Perry 'Not Presidential,'" Daily Beast, August 16, 2011, www.thedailybeast.com/cheats/2011/08/16/rove-perry-not-presidential.html.

224 *Two former Bush aides:* Matt Latimer, "Perry's War with the Business," Daily Beast, August 17, 2011, www.thedailybeast.com/articles/2011/08/17/rick-perry-s-war-with-the-bushies-why-karl-rove-is-fighting-his-2012-bid.html.

224 *"Karl Rove problem":* Chris Cillizza and Aaron Blake, "Does Rick Perry Have a Karl Rove Problem?" *Washington Post,* August 17, 2011, www.washingtonpost.com/blogs/the-fix/post/does-rick-perry-have-a-karl-rove-problem/2011/08/16/gIQACSXGKJ_blog.html.

224 *"I'm not much of a gambler":* Fox News Sunday with Chris Wallace, Fox News, August 21, 2011.

224 *"Three years ago DC pundits":* Elspeth Reeve, "Karl Rove's and Sarah Palin's Fox News Feud," *Atlantic Wire,* August 23, 2011, www.theatlanticwire.com/politics/2011/08/karl-roves-and-sarah-palins-fox-news-feud/41601/#.

225 *"It is a sign of enormous":* "Rove Levels Palin Accusation," CNN, August 25, 2011, http://politicalticker.blogs.cnn.com/2011/08/25/rove-levels-palin-accusation/.

225 *On September 12:* "2012 Republican Presidential Nomination," Real Clear Politics, www.realclearpolitics.com/epolls/2012/president/us/republican_presidential_nomination-1452.html#polls.

225 *"The Bush people don't fool"*: Daniel Strauss, "Dean: Bush Camp Will 'Take Perry Out,'" *The Hill*, August 17, 2011, http://thehill.com/blogs/blog-briefing -room/news/177229-howard-dean-bush-camp-will-take-perry-out.

225 *"At Rick Perry's Texas Hunting Spot"*: Stephanie McCrummen, "At Rick Perry's Hunting Spot, Camp's Racially Charged Name Lingered," *Washington Post*, October 1, 2011, www.washingtonpost.com/national/rick-perry -familys-hunting-camp-still-known-to-many-by-old-racially-charged-name /2011/10/01/gIQAOhY5DL_story.html.

225 *"In the early years of his political career"*: Ibid.

226 *"offensive name that has no place"*: Ibid.

226 *If she were to run*: Lindsey Boerma, "Palin Won't Run for President," *National Journal*, October 5, 2011.

227 *"What has Karl Rove done?"*: Jon Bershad, "Herman Cain Accuses Karl Rove of 'Deliberate Attempt to Damage' Him," Mediaite, October 24, 2011, www .mediaite.com/online/herman-cain-accuses-karl-rove-of-deliberate-attempt -to-damage-him/.

227 *"It is suspicious"*: Rick Manning, "The Despicable Data Dump," *The Hill*, October 31, 2011, http://thehill.com/blogs/pundits-blog/presidential -campaign/190709-the-despicable-data-dump.

227 *Three days later*: "2012 Republican Presidential Nomination."

227 *"Nobody breaks out of the pack"*: Christian Heinze, "Rove: Romney's Doing Just Fine," *The Hill*, November 7, 2011, http://gop12.thehill.com/2011/11/ rove-romneys-doing-just-fine.html.

228 *"embarrassing to be so poorly organized"*: Juli Weiner, "Karl Rove on Newt Gingrich: 'It's Embarrassing to Be So Poorly Organized," *Vanity Fair*, December 8, 2011, www.vanityfair.com/online/daily/2011/12/Karl-Rove-on-Newt -Gingrich-Its-Embarrassing-to-Be-So-Poorly-Organized.

228 *"The master, obviously"*: Karoli, "Romney Will Win Because He Has Those Super-PACs and Karl Rove's Support," Crooks and Liars, January 4, 2012, http://crooksandliars.com/karoli/romney-will-win-because-he-has-super -pacs-a.

228 *As attack ads hit*: Paul Blumenthal, "The $200 Million Man," Huffington Post, January 12, 2012, www.huffingtonpost.com/2012/01/12/huffpost-fundrace -the-2_n_1203063.html.

228 *Fox News anchor Chris Wallace*: Fox News, January 4, 2012.

229 *Not long ago few thought*: Karl Rove, "A Big Win for Romney in Iowa," *Wall Street Journal*, January 5, 2012, http://online.wsj.com/article/SB100014240529 7020347100457714078348818 3486.html.

229 *In other words, Rick Santorum*: John Avlon, "Did Rick Santorum Win the Iowa Caucuses, Not Mitt Romney?" Daily Beast, January 18, 2012, www .thedailybeast.com/articles/2012/01/18/did-rick-santorum-win-the-iowa -caucuses-not-mitt-romney.html.

230 *"the figure most intricately"*: Alexander Burns, "American Crossroads Brass Defend Carl Forti's Role," Politico, June 24, 2011, www.politico.com/news/ stories/0611/57705.html#ixzz1wMLgYIv0.

230 *"Carl is a contract employee"*: Ibid.

230 *"The work that Carl does"*: Ibid.

231 *"Newt Gingrich released":* Peter Hambly, "Gingrich Hit by Another Suspicious Email in South Carolina," CNN, January 20, 2012, http://politicalticker.blogs.cnn.com/2012/01/20/gingrich-hit-by-another-suspicious-email-in-south-carolina/.

231 *Similarly, thousands of bogus:* "Newt Gingrich Responds to Abortion Allegations," http://fitsnews.com/wp-content/uploads/2012/01/gingrich-abortion-response.jpg.

232 *"It gives him the upper hand":* "Interview with Karl Rove," *Sean Hannity Show,* CNN, February 12, 2012.

233 *"The biggest thing he ever":* "Here's Romney's Plan to Take Out Santorum," BuzzFeed, February 14, 2012, www.buzzfeed.com/buzzfeedpolitics/heres-romneys-plan-to-take-out-santorum.

233 *"Never" asserted that:* "Mitt Romney Ad: Never," Feburary 24, 2012, https://electad.com/video/mitt-romney-ad-never/.

233 *The money poured in:* "Restore Our Future Independent Expenditures," Open Secrets, www.opensecrets.org/pacs/indexpend.php?cycle=2012&cmte=C00490045.

233 *On February 28:* Nate, "Romney Wins Michigan and Arizona, Santorum Holds 2nd," 2012 Election Central, www.2012presidentialelectionnews.com/2012/02/romney-wins-michigan-and-arizona-santorum-holds-2nd/.

234 *"Mr. Santorum is focused":* Maggie Haberman and Jonathan Martin, "Super Tuesday: GOP Looks for an Ohio Finale," Politico, March 4, 2012, www.politico.com/news/stories/0312/73578.html.

Chapter 16: Mitt Romney's Last Buyout

237 *"without portfolio to the likely GOP":* Jonathan Martin, "Ed Gillespie Joins Team Romney," Politico, April 5, 2012, www.politico.com/news/stories/0412/794857.html.

237 *"I am pleased that Ed is joining":* Ibid.

238 *"The only way Romney can get back":* Doug Schoen, "A Critical Juncture for Mitt Romney," *Forbes,* April 9, 2012, www.forbes.com/sites/dougschoen/2012/04/09/a-critical-juncture-for-mitt-romney/.

238 *"SuperPACs have to be entirely separate":* www.cbsnews.com/8301-503544_162-57345598-503544/mitt-romney-super-pacs-are-a-disaster/.

238 *"I can't tell you," Colbert explained:* "Late Night: Stewart and Colbert Push Limits of 'Not Coordinating,'" *Los Angeles Times,* January 18, 2012, http://latimesblogs.latimes.com/showtracker/2012/01/late-night-stewart-and-colbert-push-limits-of-not-coordinating.html.

239 *"We were great friends":* Matt Viser, "Longtime Romney Aide to Lead VP Search," *Boston Globe,* April 17, 2012, http://articles.boston.com/2012-04-17/nation/31347901_1_romney-aide-campaign-staff-presidential-campaign/2.

239 *"She and Karl still remain friends":* Samuel P. Jacobs, "Rove Rides Again, as a Force Behind Romney," Reuters, April 19, 2012, www.reuters.com/article/2012/04/19/us-usa-campaign-rove-idUSBRE83I1K120120419.

239 *"Having played a role"*: Karl Rove, "I Was Wrong About Dick Cheney," *Wall Street Journal,* April 26, 2012, http://rove.com/articles/381.

240 *"Alexander the Great"*: Kenneth P. Vogel and Ben Smith, "Karl Rove's Karl Rove," Politico, October 18, 2010, www.politico.com/news/stories/1010/43731.html.

240 *Haley Barbour, a longtime friend:* "Barbour Won't Formally Endorse Romney, but Offers Advice," CNN Politics, April 12, 2012, http://politicalticker.blogs.cnn.com/2012/04/12/barbour-wont-formally-endorse-romney-but-offers-advice/.

240 *"He is without peer":* Jim VandeHei, Andy Barr, and Kenneth P. Vogel, "The Most Powerful Republican in Politics," Politico, August 20, 2010, www.politico.com/news/stories/0810/41236.html#ixzz1wTrPE3tq.

240 *On April 10, Foster Friess:* Kenneth P. Vogel and Dave Levinthal, "Foster Friess Swings to Romney," Politico, April 10, 2012.

240 *"I'm not sure if I have already":* Ibid.

240 *had already given $21.5 million:* Jon Ralston, "Adelson Going Underground with Political Money—I Smell a Rove—and Adamantly Against Web Poker," *Las Vegas Sun,* April 27, 2012, www.lasvegassun.com/blogs/ralstons-flash/2012/apr/27/adelson-going-underground-political-money-i-smell-/.

241 *"He's not the bold decision-maker":* Jay Firestone, "Sheldon Adelson on Newt: 'He's at the End of His Line,'" JewishJournal.com, March 28, 2012, www.jewishjournal.com/nation/article/sheldon_adelson_on_newt_hes_at_the_end_of_his_line_20120328/.

241 *a positive sign for Romney:* Robin Bravender, "Newt's Billionaire, Sheldon Adelson, Gives $5M to Establishment," Politico, April 15, 2012.

241 *"gushing admiration for Karl Rove":* Ralston, "Adelson Going Underground with Political Money."

241 *"[Adelson] is very focused":* Kevin Bohn, "Will Adelson Place a Big Bet on Romney?" CNN, May 30, 2012.

241 *On June 6:* Sabrina Siddiqui, "Sheldon Adelson to Donate $1 Million to Romney-Allied Super PAC," Huffington Post, June 7, 2012, www.huffingtonpost.com/2012/06/07/sheldon-adelson-mitt-romney-super-pac_n_1577137.html.

241 *A week later, the casino billionaire:* Paul Blumenthal, "Sheldon Adelson Gives to Mitt Romney Super PAC," Huffington Post, June 13, 2012, www.huffingtonpost.com/2012/06/13/sheldon-adelson-mitt-romney-super-pac-10-million_n_1593369.html?utm_hp_ref=politics.

241 *Adelson himself had said:* Steven Bertoni, "Adelson's Pro-Romney Donations Will Be 'Limitless,' Could Top $100M," *Forbes,* June 13, 2012, www.forbes.com/sites/stevenbertoni/2012/06/13/exclusive-adelsons-pro-romney-donations-will-be-limitless-could-top-100m/.

242 *gave $1 million:* Richard W. Stevenson, "Tea Party Movement Takes the Long View," *New York Times* Blogs (The Caucus), March 9, 2012.

242 *slammed Obama's policies:* Kenneth P. Vogel, "Kochs Linked to Anti-Obama Gas Ad," Politico, March 29, 2012.

242 *"funding yet another shadowy outside group":* Ibid.

242 *putting aside their reservations:* Vogel, "Karl Rove's Fight Club."

242 *At times, the Koch brothers:* Vogel, "Kochs Linked to Anti-Obama Gas Ad."

242 *a report by Peter Stone:* Peter H. Stone, "Koch Brothers Plan to Funnel Tens of Millions to Conservative Allies to Influence 2012 Elections," Huffington Post, June 1, 2012, www.huffingtonpost.com/2012/06/01/koch-brothers -network_n_1560596.html?1338564191.

242 *"Think the $$ political system":* Tim Dickinson, "The Billion-Dollar Mitt Machine," *Rolling Stone,* May 30, 2012, www.rollingstone.com/politics/blogs/ national-affairs/the-billion-dollar-mitt-machine-20120530.

243 *"the Kochs can exploit":* Stone, "Koch Brothers Plan to Funnel Tens of Millions to Conservative Allies to Influence 2012 Elections."

244 *the RNC's "'greatest asset'":* Stuart Rothenberg, "GOP Struggles to Figure Out Voter File Future," *Roll Call,* March 29, 2012.

244 *"running from his tax-raising":* Josh Lederman, "Ohio Dems Accuse Chamber of Doctoring Photo in Ad Against Sen. Sherrod Brown," *The Hill,* Ballot Box, December 1, 2011, http://thehill.com/blogs/ballot-box/senate-races/196575 -ohio-dems-accuse-chamber-of-doctoring-photo-in-brown-ad.

244 *outspent by more than three to one*: Heidi Przybyla, "Senate Democrats Outspent 3 to 1 on Ads by Super-Pacs," *Bloomberg BusinessWeek,* May 29, 2012, www.businessweek.com/news/2012-05-29/senate-democrats-outspent-3-to -1-on-ads-by-super-pacs#p1.

245 *In June:* "American Crossroads Says Tim Kaine Urged $500 Billion in Medicare Cuts," PolitiFact, www.politifact.com/virginia/statements/2012/jun/20/ american-crossroads/american-crossroads-says-tim-kaine-urged-500-billi/.

245 *under the influence of cocaine:* Ibid.

245 *"Mack's claim is pretty bananas":* "Connie Mack Says Bill Nelson Voted to Study Monkeys on Cocaine," PolitiFact, April 13, 2012, www.politifact.com/ florida/statements/2012/apr/13/connie-mack/connie-mack-says-bill-nelson -voted-study-monkeys-c/.

245 *And, thanks to Rove's friends at Fox News:* Ben Dimiero and Eric Hananoki, "24 Hours of Fox News' Karl Rove Problem," http://mediamatters.org/ blog/201204270004.

246 *"The president and Democrats":* Brent Budowsky, "Karl Rove's Grand Slam," *The Hill,* May 31, 2012, http://thehill.com/opinion/columnists/brent -budowsky/230239-karl-roves-grand-slam.

246 *had not reupped:* Ben Smith and Rebecca Elliott, "Obama's 2008 Donors Don't Give in 2012," BuzzFeed, www.bussfeed.com/bensmith/obamas-2008-donors -don't-give-in-2012.

246 *Bill Maher and . . . James H. Simon:* Kenneth P. Vogel and Robin Bravender, "Dem Super PACs Still Trail GOP," Politico, April 13, 2012.

247 *Rove posted an Electoral College map:* Brett LoGiurato, "Karl Rove's Early Electoral Map: Obama Wins," Business Insider, April 26, 2012 www.business insider.com/karl-rove-electoral-map-obama-wins-2012-4?nr_email_referer=1.

247 *tougher voter identification requirements:* Michael D. Shear, "Obama Campaign Grapples with New Voter ID Laws," *New York Times,* April 29, 2012, www.nytimes.com/2012/04/30/us/politics/obama-campaign-confronts-voter -id-laws.html.

247 *"We have to assume":* Ibid.

247 *more than $11 million:* T. W. Farnam, "Mystery Donor Gives $10 Million to Crossroads GPS Group to Run Anti-Obama Ads," *Washington Post,* April 13, 2012, www.washingtonpost.com/politics/mystery-donor-gives-10-million -to-crossroads-gps-group-to-run-anti-obama-ads/2012/04/13/gIQAzdtdFT_ story.html?hpid=z2.

247 *"It's not what we do well":* Paul Blumenthal, "HUFFPOST FUNDRACE— Soros, Dem Donors Jump Into Super PAC Game," Huffington Post, May 8, 2012.

248 *"Mr. Obama long ago lost":* Karl Rove, "Romney's Roads to the White House," *Wall Street Journal,* May 24, 2012, www.rove.com/articles/389.

248 *"When asked 'Which candidate'":* Karl Rove, "Why 2012 Is Not 2004," *Wall Street Journal,* May 31, 2012, www.rove.com/articles/390.

248 *the GOP-leaning Rasmussen tracking poll:* "General Election: Romney vs. Obama," Real Clear Politics, www.realclearpolitics.com/epolls/2012/president /us/general_election_romney_vs_obama-1171.html.

249 *Bauer also wrote Rove:* Michael D. Shear, "Obama's Lawyer Demands Information on Group's Donors," *New York Times,* June 19, 2012, http://thecaucus .blogs.nytimes.com/2012/06/19/obamas-lawyer-demands-information-on -groups-donors/.

249 *"This is, frankly":* "Rove: Obama Campaign Trying to Intimidate My Crossroads GPS Group with 'Thuggish Behavior,'" *On the Record with Greta Van Susteren,* June 20, 2012, www.foxnews.com/on-air/on-the-record/2012/06/21/ rove-obama-campaign-trying-intimidate-my-crossroads-gps-group-thuggish -behavior.

250 *wealthy bankers "behaved":* Connor Simpson, "Karl Rove Was the Funniest Person at Romney's Big Park City Retreat," *Atlantic Wired,* June 24, 2012, www.theatlanticwire.com/politics/2012/06/karl-rove-was-funniest-person -romneys-big-park-city-retreat/53863/.

250 *In addition to rubbing elbows:* Ibid.

250 *"That's the price of admission":* Michael Barbaro, "For Wealthy Romney Donors, Up Close and Personal Access," *New York Times,* June 23, 2012, www.nytimes.com/2012/06/24/us/politics/for-wealthy-romney-donors-up -close-and-personal-access.html?pagewanted=all.

252 *"No one else":* Author interview with Roger Stone.

BIBLIOGRAPHY

Abrahams, Rebecca. "White House Emails: The Missing Link?" Huffington Post, October 21, 2008.

Abramowitz, Michael. "Rove E-Mail Sought by Congress May Be Missing." *Washington Post,* April 13, 2007.

Agiesta, Jennifer. "Behind the Numbers." *Washington Post,* July 24, 2007.

Aikman, David. *A Man of Faith: The Spiritual Journey of George W. Bush.* Nashville: Thomas Nelson, 2005.

Alexander, Paul. *Machiavelli's Shadow.* New York: Rodale Press, 2008.

Allen, Mike. "Karl Rove Granted Divorce in Texas." Politico, December 29, 2009.

Allen, Mike, and Dana Priest. "Bush Administration Is Focus of Inquiry." *Washington Post,* September 28, 2003.

Allen, Mike, and Kenneth P. Vogel. "Karl Rove, Republican Party Plot Vast Network to Reclaim Power." Politico, May 6, 2010.

Avlon, John. "Did Rick Santorum Win the Iowa Caucuses, Not Mitt Romney?" Daily Beast, January 18, 2012.

Ball, Molly. "Angle Rakes in $3.5M More." Politico, October 25, 2010.

Barbaro, Michael. "For Wealthy Romney Donors, Up Close and Personal Access." *New York Times,* June 23, 2012.

Barrow, Bill. "Riley's Ratings Are Low: Governor Would Trail Moore, Siegelman in 2006 Race." *Mobile Press-Register,* November 16, 2003.

Bershad, Jon. "Herman Cain Accuses Karl Rove of 'Deliberate Attempt to Damage' Him." Mediaite, October 24, 2011.

Blumenthal, Paul. "The $200 Million Man." Huffington Post, January 12, 2012.

———. "Huffpost Fundrace—Soros, Dem Donors Jump into Super PAC Game." Huffington Post, May 8, 2012.

———. "Sheldon Adelson Gives to Mitt Romney Super PAC." Huffington Post, June 13, 2012.

Blumenthal, Sidney. *Pledging Allegiance.* New York: Harper, 1991.

———. *The Clinton Wars.* New York: Farrar, Straus & Giroux, 2003. Kindle edition.

———. *How Bush Rules: Chronicles of a Radical Regime.* Princeton: Princeton University Press, 2006.

———. "Upending the Mayberry Machiavellis." Salon, April 12, 2007.

———. "We'll Go No More a-Rove-ing." Salon, August 13, 2007.

———. "Dan Rather Stands by His Story," Salon, September 27, 2007.

Boerma, Lindsay. "Palin Won't Run for President." *National Journal*, October 5, 2011.

Bowermaster, David. "Charges May Result from Firings, Say Two Former U.S. Attorneys." *Seattle Times*, May 9, 2007.

Bravender, Robin. "Newt's Billionaire, Sheldon Adelson, Gives $5M to Establishment." Politico, April 15, 2012.

Broder, David. "Karl Rove's Trajectory: The Presidential Adviser, Famously Smart, Is Getting Too Much Attention." *Pittsburgh Post-Gazette*, May 15, 2003.

———. "Don't Expect Karl Rove to Just Fade into the Sunset." *Salt Lake Tribune*, August 23, 2007.

Brooks, David. "A Guide for the Perplexed." *New York Times*, August 31, 2006.

Budowsky, Brent. "Karl Rove's Grand Slam." *The Hill*, May 31, 2012.

Burns, Alexander. "American Crossroads Brass Defend Carl Forti's Role." Politico, June 24, 2011.

Bush, George W. *Decision Points.* New York: Random House, 2010. Kindle edition.

Chandler, Kim. "Siegelman, Scrushy Face Corruption Charges Indicted Again." *Birmingham News*.

———. "Jury Deadlocks After Six Days." *Birmingham News*, June 23, 2006.

———. "Corruption Trial Jury Still Deadlocked," *Birmingham News*, June 28, 2006.

———. "Siegelman Jury Still Deliberating After 10 Days." *Birmingham News*, June 29, 2006.

Cillizza, Chris, and Aaron Blake. "Does Rick Perry Have a Karl Rove Problem?" *Washington Post*, August 17, 2011.

Conason, Joe. "Rove Waves Flag for G.O.P. Candidates." *New York Observer*, January 28, 2002.

Cooper, Matthew. "What I Told the Grand Jury." *Time*, July 17, 2005.

Courter, Barry. "Lights, Camera, Chattanooga Sitcom: Pilot Links Local Talent, First, Restaurant." *Chattanooga Times Free Press*, April 8, 2001.

Craig, Jon, and Allison D'Aurora. "2004 Ballot Not Preserved." *Cincinnati Enquirer*, August 12, 2007.

Cummings, Jeanne. "Steele's Spending Spree Angers Donors." Politico, February 23, 2010.

Day, Anthony. "A Story That Should Not Have Been Told." *Los Angeles Times*, November 8, 1996.

Deitch, Charlie. "The Wecht Files." *Pittsburgh City Paper*, December 20, 2007.

DePaulo, Lisa. "Karl Rove Likes What He Sees." *GQ*, April 2, 2008.

Dickinson, Tim. "How Roger Ailes Built the Fox News Fear Factory." *Rolling Stone*, May 25, 2011.

———. "The Billion-Dollar Mitt Machine." *Rolling Stone*, May 30, 2012.

Dimiero, Ben. "The Sarah Palin/Fox News Debacle." Media Matters, October 6, 2011.

Drew, Elizabeth. "Can We Have a Democratic Election?" *New York Review of Books*, February 23, 2012.

Edsall, Thomas B., and Dana Milbank. "White House's Roving Eye for Politics." *Washington Post*, March 10, 2003.

Eskenazi, Stuart. "Rogue Elephant." *Houston Press*, September 3, 1998.

Esterbrook, John. "New Orleans: One Year Later." *60 Minutes*, January 11, 2009.

Farnam, T. W. "Mystery Donor Gives $10 Million to Crossroads GPS Group to Run Anti-Obama Ads." *Washington Post,* April 13, 2012.

Farrell, Greg. "Former HealthSouth CEO Scrushy Turns Televangelist." *USA Today,* October 25, 2004.

Fidalgo, Paul. "Leahy Plays the Watergate Card, Has Subpoenas in His Deck." ABC News, April 12, 2007.

Fiderer, David. "A Smoking Gun Incriminates the Judge Who Ruled Against Don Siegelman." Huffington Post, July 29, 2008.

Firestone, Jay. "Sheldon Adelson on Newt: 'He's at the End of His Line.'" Jewish Journal.com, March 28, 2012.

Fitrakis, Bob. "Behind the Firewall: Bush Loyalist Mike Connell Controls Congressional Secrets as His Email Sites Serve Karl Rove." *Free Press,* July 29, 2008.

Flessner, Dave. "Chattanooga Takes Center Stage in Connecting Voters for President." *Chattanooga Times Free Press,* March 19, 2004.

Foster, Daniel. "Fox News 'Suspends' Gingrich, Santorum." *National Review,* March 2, 2011.

Freeman, Steve, and Joel Bleifuss. *Was the 2004 Presidential Election Stolen? Exit Polls, Election Fraud, and the Official Count.* New York: Seven Stories Press, 2006. Kindle edition.

Froomkin, Dan. "The Rovian Theory." *Washington Post,* March 23, 2007.

Frum, David. "Building a Coalition, Forgetting to Rule." *New York Times,* August 14, 2007.

Gerstein, Josh. "Avalanche of Cash Is Set to Descend on Election Battle." *New York Sun,* October 12, 2006.

Gigot, Paul. "The Mark of Rove." *Wall Street Journal,* August 13, 2007.

Goldberg, Jonah. "Baghdad Delenda Est, Part Two." *National Review,* April 23, 2002.

Goldman, Russell. "Levi Johnston to Name Baby Daughter After a Gun." ABC News, May 2, 2012.

Gonzalez, Juan. "Ohio Tally Fit for Ukraine." *New York Daily News,* November 30, 2004.

Gordon, Greg. "Computer Expert Denies Knowledge of '04 Vote Rigging in Ohio." McClatchy Newspapers, November 3, 2008.

Grant, Alison. "Diebold Defends Vote Machines: Company Says Critic Used Wrong Software, Faulty Testing Procedures." *Cleveland Plain Dealer,* July 26, 2003.

Green, Joshua. "The Rove Presidency." *Atlantic,* September 2000.

———. "The Brutal Genius of Karl Rove." *Australian Financial Review,* October 29, 2004.

———. "Karl Rove in a Corner." *Atlantic,* November 2004.

Grieve, Tim. "Bush's Brain Testifies." Salon, October 15, 2004.

———. "Karl Rove to Resign." Salon, August 13, 2007.

Gundlach, James H. "A Statistical Analysis of Possible Electronic Ballot Box Stuffing." Paper presented at the Annual Meeting of the Alabama Political Science Association, April 11, 2003.

Haberman, Maggie, and Jonathan Martin. "Super Tuesday: GOP Looks for an Ohio Finale." Politico, March 4, 2012.

Hagan, Joe. "Goddangit, Baby, We're Making Good Time." *New York,* February 27, 2011.

———. "Dan Rather Was Right About George W. Bush." *Texas Monthly,* April 16, 2012.

———. "Truth or Consequences." *Texas Monthly,* May 2012.

Hagey, Keach. "GOP's Struggles Play Out on Fox." Politico, September 17, 2010.

Hallow, Ralph Z. "Ohio Fears Race Will Hinge on Provisional Ballots." *Washington Times,* November 1, 2004.

———. "Bondage Club, 'Nasty Girl' Star in Steele's Horrible Week." *Washington Times,* April 2, 2010.

Hamburger, Tom, and Peter Wallsten. *One Party Country: The Republican Plan for Dominance in the 21st Century.* Hoboken, NJ: Wiley, 2006. Kindle edition.

Hartley, Allegra. "Timeline: How the U.S. Attorneys Were Fired." *U.S. News & World Report,* March 21, 2007.

Havighurst, Craig. "Online Feature Films Just Got Better," *Tennessean,* November 22, 2000.

Heinze, Christian. "Rove: Romney's Doing Just Fine." *The Hill,* November 7, 2011.

Hitchins, Christopher. "Plame Out." Slate, August 29, 2006.

Hook, Janet. "GOP Seeks Lasting Majority." *Los Angeles Times,* July 21, 2003.

Horner, William. *Ohio's Kingmaker: Mark Hanna, Man and Myth.* Athens: Ohio University Press, 2010.

Horrock, Nicholas M. "Shades of Watergate?" United Press International, July 14, 2003.

Horton, Scott. "Prosecution Continues to Disintegrate in Siegelman Case." *Harper's,* June 26, 2007.

———. "An Interview with Legal Ethicist David Luban Regarding Judge Mark Fuller." *Harper's,* August 2007.

———. "The Alice Martin Perjury Inquiry." *Harper's,* September 8, 2007.

———. "The Remarkable 'Recusal' of Leura Canary." *Harper's,* September 14, 2007.

———. "CBS: More Prosecutorial Misconduct in Siegelman Case." *Harper's,* February 2008.

———. "Six Questions for Paul Alexander, Author of *Machiavelli's Shadow."* *Harper's,* July 2008.

Isikoff, Michael, and David Corn. *Hubris: The Inside Story of Spin, Scandal, and the Selling of the Iraq War.* New York: Crown, 2006.

Jacobs, Samuel P. "Rove Rides Again, as a Force Behind Romney." Reuters, April 19, 2012.

Jehl, Douglas. "After the War Weapons Intelligence: Iraq Arms Critic Reacts to Report on Wife." *New York Times,* August 8, 2003.

Johnson, Bob. "Siegelman Jury Continues Deliberations." *Decatur Daily,* June 22, 2006.

Kamen, Al. "There's a PAC for That." *Washington Post,* March 22, 2012.

Kaplan, Lawrence F., and William Kristol. *The War Over Iraq.* New York: Encounter Books, 2003.

"Karl Rove Likes What He Sees," *GQ,* April 2, 2008.

Kellman, Laurie. "GOP Support for Gonzales Erodes Further." *Washington Post,* March 15, 2007.

Kirkpatrick, David D. "Does Corporate Money Lead to Political Corruption?" *New York Times,* January 23, 2010.

Koppelman, Alex. "Michael Steele Is a Hip Cat, You Dig." Salon, February 19, 2009.

Kranish, Michael, and Scott Helman. *The Real Romney.* New York: HarperCollins, 2012. Kindle edition.

Kristof, Nicholas. "Missing in Action: Truth." *New York Times,* May 6, 2003.

Kroll, Andy. "GOPer Behind Ohio's Botched 2004 Election Eyes Senate Run." *Mother Jones,* April 21, 2011.

Kuhnhenn, Jim. "Midterm Elections 2010." Huffington Post, October 26, 2010.

Lamis, Alexander P. *The Two-Party South.* New York: Oxford University Press, 1990.

Lardner, George, Jr., and Lois Romano. "Bush Name Helps Fuel Oil Dealings." *Washington Post,* July 30, 1999.

Latimer, Matt. "Perry's War with the Business." Daily Beast, August 17, 2011.

Lederman, Josh. "Ohio Dems Accuse Chamber of Doctoring Photo in Ad Against Sen. Sherrod Brown." *The Hill,* December 1, 2011.

Lemann, Nicholas. "The Controller: Karl Rove Is Working to Get George Bush Reelected." *New Yorker,* May 12, 2003.

Lichtblau, Eric. "E-Mail Reveals Rove's Key Role in '06 Dismissals." *New York Times,* August 11, 2009.

Linn, Mike. "Siegelman Case Put in Limbo." *Montgomery Advertiser,* June 23, 2006.

———. "Siegelman Trial Analyzed." *Montgomery Advertiser,* June 25, 2006.

Lizza, Ryan. "The Most Powerful Bushie You've Never Heard Of." *New Republic,* July 30, 2001.

Lyman, Rick. "In Race to Lead Alabama, It's Politics as Usual." *New York Times,* March 22, 2006.

Manning, Rick. "The Despicable Data Dump." *The Hill,* October 31, 2011.

Mapes, Mary. *Truth and Duty: The Press, the President, and the Privilege of Power.* New York: St. Martin's Press, 2006.

Martin, Jonathan. "Ed Gillespie Joins Team Romney." Politico, April 5, 2012.

Martin, Jonathan, and Keach Hagey. "Fox Primary: Complicated, Contractual." Politico, September 27, 2010.

Mayer, Jane. "Covert Operations." *New Yorker,* August 30, 2010.

———. "Attack Dog." *New Yorker,* January 13, 2012.

McClellan, Scott. *What Happened: Inside the Bush White House and Washington's Culture of Deception.* New York: Public Affairs, 2008.

McCrummen, Stephanie. "At Rick Perry's Hunting Spot, Camp's Racially Charged Name Lingered." *Washington Post,* October 1, 2011.

McMorris-Santoro, Evan. "Conservatives Trash Karl Rove After He Insists O'Donnell Says 'Nutty Things.'" Talking Points Memo, September 15, 2010.

"Michael Steele Bondage-Gate Fallout." Huffington Post, May 31, 2010.

Miller, Laura. "Powers Behind the Throne." Center for Media and Democracy's PR Watch, 2004.

Moore, James, and Wayne Slater. *Bush's Brain.* Hoboken, NJ: Wiley, 2003.

———. *The Architect.* New York: Three Rivers Press, 2007.

Mottern, Nick. "The Mighty Texas Strike Force." *Free Press,* February 28, 2005.

Naymik, Mark, and Julie Carr Smyth. "State to Buy Voting Machines." *Cleveland Plain Dealer,* February 26, 2003.

Nossiter, Adam. "Outlines Emerge for a Shaken New Orleans. *New York Times,* August 27, 2006.

———. "Ex-Governor Says Conviction Was Political." *New York Times,* June 27, 2007.

Novak, Robert D. *The Prince of Darkness: 50 Years Reporting in Washington.* New York: Crown, 2007.

"Ohio's Elections Process Debated." *Mansfield News Journal,* September 13, 2006.

Paul, David. "Rick Perry Looks to Leave Mitt Romney and Karl Rove in the Dust." Huffington Post, August 18, 2011.

Peale, Cliff. "Friends of Bush Drawn Into Spotlight." *Cincinnati Enquirer,* January 18, 2001.

Phelps, Timothy M., and Knut Royce. "Columnist Blows CIA Agent's Cover." *Newsday,* July 22, 2003.

Phillips, Richard Hayes. *Witness to a Crime.* Rome, NY: Canterbury Press, 2008.

"Political Bug Leads to the Web." *Crain's Cleveland Business,* November 3, 2001.

Przybyla, Heidi. "Senate Democrats Outspent 3 to 1 on Ads by Super-Pacs." *Bloomberg BusinessWeek,* May 29, 2012.

Ralston, Jon. "Adelson Going Underground with Political Money—I Smell a Rove—and Adamantly Against Web Poker." *Las Vegas Sun,* April 27, 2012.

Reeve, Elspeth. "Karl Rove's and Sarah Palin's Fox News Feud." *Atlantic,* August 23, 2011.

Rich, Joseph. "Bush's Long History of Tilting Justice." *Los Angeles Times,* March 29, 2007.

Riskind, Jonathan. "GOP Expects Presidential Race to Be Tight in Ohio." *Columbus Dispatch,* February 26, 2003.

Rollins, Ed. *Bare Knuckles and Back Rooms.* New York: Broadway Books, 1996.

Rothenberg, Stuart. "GOP Struggles to Figure Out Voter File Future." *Roll Call,* March 29, 2012.

"Rove Developing Outside Groups to Help GOP in Fall." *National Journal,* April 18, 2008.

Rove, Karl. *Courage and Consequence.* New York: Simon & Schuster, 2010.

———. "A Big Win for Romney in Iowa." *Wall Street Journal,* January 5, 2012.

———. "I Was Wrong About Dick Cheney." *Wall Street Journal,* April 26, 2012.

———. "Romney's Roads to the White House." *Wall Street Journal,* May 24, 2012.

———. "Why 2012 Is Not 2004." *Wall Street Journal,* May 31, 2012.

Rucker, Philip, and Chris Cillizza. "Steele's Book Release, Fiery Rhetoric Fuel Dissatisfaction with GOP." *Washington Post,* January 9, 2010.

Rulon, Malia. "Ohio-Based Web Design Company Seeks to Give GOP Candidates the Edge." Associated Press, August 24, 2004.

Rutenberg, Jim. "Rove Returns, with Team, Planning G.O.P. Push." *New York Times,* September 25, 2010.

Rutenberg, Jim, and Mark J. Prendergast. "CBS Asserts It Was Misled by Ex-Officer on Bush Documents." *New York Times,* September 20, 2004.

Salant, Jonathan D., and Traci McMillan. "Rove-Backed Groups, U.S. Chamber Build Winning Record in Midterm Election." Bloomberg News, November 4, 2010.

Salvato, Albert. "Ohio Recount Gives a Smaller Margin to Bush." *New York Times,* December 29, 2004.

Sarles, Judy. "Firm Ramps Up for IPO." *Nashville Business Journal,* April 2, 2000.

Saunders, Debra J. "Plame Case Was Gossip, Not a Smear." *San Francisco Chronicle,* August 31, 2006.

Schoen, Doug. "A Critical Juncture for Mitt Romney." *Forbes,* April 9, 2012.

Shear, Michael D. "Obama Campaign Grapples with New Voter ID Laws." *New York Times,* April 29, 2012.

———. "Obama's Lawyer Demands Information on Group's Donors." *New York Times,* June 19, 2012.

Sheppard, Kate. "'Heckuva Job Brownie' Speaks." *Mother Jones,* June 2011.

Sherman, Jake. "Boehner's Own Karl Rove." Politico, July 30, 2010.

Siddiqui, Sabrina. "Sheldon Adelson to Donate $1 Million to Romney-Allied Super PAC." Huffington Post, June 7, 2012.

Simpson, Connor. "Karl Rove Was the Funniest Person at Romney's Big Park City Retreat." *Atlantic Wired,* June 24, 2012.

Slater, Wayne. "Karl Rove: How to Build a Multi-Million Money Machine." *Dallas News,* February 12, 2012.

Smith, Erika D. "Ohio Counties Choose Diebold: 40 of 71 Select Green Company to Supply Voting Machines." *Beacon Journal,* January 16, 2004.

Smyth, Julie Carr. "Voting Machine Controversy." *Cleveland Plain Dealer,* August 28, 2003.

Spillius, Alex. "Karl Rove Questions Sarah Palin's Suitability for President." *Telegraph,* October 27, 2010.

Stein, Jonathan. "Mitt Romney Would Be Karl Rove's Handpicked VP." *Mother Jones,* August 28, 2008.

Stevenson, Richard W. "Tea Party Movement Takes the Long View." *New York Times* Blogs (The Caucus), March 9, 2012.

Stewart, James B. *Tangled Webs: How False Statements Are Undermining America: From Martha Stewart to Bernie Madoff.* New York: Penguin Press, 2011.

Stone, Peter. "Campaign Cash: The Independent Fundraising Gold Rush Since 'Citizens United' Ruling." iWatch News, Center for Public Integrity, October 4, 2010.

Stone, Peter H. "Bush's Brains, Rove + Gillespie Raise GOP Bucks." *National Journal,* March 31, 2010.

———. "Inside the Shadow GO." *National Review,* October 27, 2010.

———. "Koch Brothers Plan to Funnel Tens of Millions to Conservative Allies to Influence 2012 Elections." Huffington Post, June 1, 2012.

Strauss, Daniel. "Dean: Bush Camp Will 'Take Perry Out.'" *The Hill,* August 17, 2011.

"st3 Technology Firm Goes Bankrupt and Closes Doors." *Chattanoogan,* January 9, 2002.

Suskind, Ron. "Why Are These Men Laughing?" *Esquire,* January 2003.

———. "Faith, Certainty and the Presidency of George W. Bush." *New York Times Magazine,* October 17, 2004.

———. *The Price of Loyalty.* New York: Simon & Schuster, 2004.

Thorpe, Helen. "Hail the Conquering Hero." *New York,* September 1999.

Thrush, Glenn, and Kenneth P. Vogel. "W.H. 'Out of the Fetal Position.'" Politico, October 12, 2010.

Toobin, Jeffrey. *Too Close to Call: The Thirty-Six-Day Battle to Decide the 2000 Election.* New York: Random House, 2001. Kindle edition.

————. "Money Unlimited." *New Yorker,* May 21, 2012.

Unger, Craig. *House of Bush, House of Saud: The Secret Relationship Between the World's Two Most Powerful Dynasties.* New York: Scribner, 2004.

————. *The Fall of the House of Bush.* New York: Scribner, 2007.

VandeHei, Jim, Andy Barr, and Kenneth P. Vogel. "The Most Powerful Republican in Politics." Politico, August 20, 2010.

Viser, Matt. "Longtime Romney Aide to Lead VP Search." *Boston Globe,* April 17, 2012.

Vogel, Kenneth P. "Rove the Bogeyman Is Back." Politico, September 30, 2010.

————. "Secrecy Flip-Flop Fueled Crossroads." Politico, October 25, 2010.

————. "Karl Rove vs. the Koch Brothers." Politico, October 10, 2011.

————. "Karl Rove's Fight Club." Politico, March 27, 2012.

————. "Kochs Linked to Anti-Obama Gas Ad." Politico, March 29, 2012.

Vogel, Kenneth P., and Robin Bravender. "Dem Super PACs Still Trail GOP." Politico, April 13, 2012.

Vogel, Kenneth P., and Dave Levinthal. "Foster Friess Swings to Romney." Politico, April 10, 2012.

Vogel, Kenneth P., and Ben Smith. "Karl Rove's Karl Rove." Politico, October 18, 2010.

Waas, Murray. "CIA Leak Case: Why Rove Testified for a Fifth Time." *National Journal,* April 28, 2006.

————. "The Phone Call." *National Journal,* May 27, 2006.

Waldman, Michael, and Justin Levitt. "The Myth of Voter Fraud." *Washington Post,* March 29, 2007.

Wallace-Wells, Benjamin. "Getting Ahead in the GOP." *Washington Monthly,* October/November 2005.

Warren, James. "'Speedway Bomber' Sitting Pretty." *Chicago Tribune,* March 13, 1994.

————. "A Reporter Confesses: He Was Conned by a Con." *Chicago Tribune,* October 4, 1996.

Weiner, Juli. "Karl Rove on Newt Gingrich: 'It's Embarrassing to Be So Poorly Organized.'" *Vanity Fair,* December 8, 2011.

Weiser, Carl. "Ohio Is 'Ground Zero' on GOP Breakfast Circuit." Gannett News Service, August 30, 2004.

"What Viveca Novak Told Fitzgerald." *Time,* December 19, 2005.

Wilson, Joseph. *The Politics of Truth.* New York: Carroll & Graf, 2004.

Wilson, Joseph C., IV. "What I Didn't Find in Africa." *New York Times,* July 6, 2003.

Wilson, Valerie Plame. *Fair Game.* New York: Simon & Schuster, 2007.

Woodward, Bob. *Bush at War.* New York: Simon & Schuster, 2002.

————. *State of Denial: Bush at War, Part III.* New York: Simon & Schuster, 2006.

————. *Plan of Attack.* New York: Simon & Schuster, 2004.

Worrall, Simon. *Cybergate: Was the White House Stolen by Cyberfraud?* (2012).

————. "The Mysterious Death of Bush's Cyber-Guru." *Maxim,* February 2010.

INDEX

ABOUT THE AUTHOR

Craig Unger is the author of the *New York Times* bestseller *House of Bush, House of Saud* and *The Fall of the House of Bush*. He is a contributing editor of *Vanity Fair* and has appeared frequently as an analyst on CNN, the ABC Radio Network, and many other broadcast outlets. The former deputy editor of the *New York Observer* and editor in chief of *Boston* magazine, he has written about George H.W. Bush and George W. Bush for *The New Yorker, Esquire,* and *Vanity Fair*. He lives in New York City.